IMPERIAL FOOTPRINTS

SUMITA MUKHERJEE

Imperial Footprints
A History of South Asian Child Migrants in Britain

HURST & COMPANY, LONDON

First published in the United Kingdom in 2026 by
C. Hurst & Co. (Publishers) Ltd.,
New Wing, Somerset House, Strand, London, WC2R 1LA
© Sumita Mukherjee, 2026
All rights reserved.

The right of Sumita Mukherjee to be identified
as the author of this publication is asserted by her in accordance
with the Copyright, Designs and Patents Act, 1988.

A Cataloguing-in-Publication data record for this book
is available from the British Library.

ISBN: 9781805265283

EU GPSR Authorised Representative
Easy Access System Europe Oü, 16879218
Address: Mustamäe tee 50, 10621, Tallinn, Estonia
Contact Details: gpsr.requests@easproject.com, +358 40 500 3575

www.hurstpublishers.com

CONTENTS

List of Illustrations   vii

Introduction   1
1. The White Indians   15
2. The Victorian Curiosities   29
3. The Young Brown Englishmen   47
4. The Nationalists   65
5. The Sporting Stars   85
6. The Suffragists   105
7. The Casualties of War   121
8. The Lascars' Children   139
9. The Leftists   157
10. Partition   173
Epilogue: Where are you from?   189

Acknowledgements   197
Notes   199
Bibliography   225
Index   239

LIST OF ILLUSTRATION

1. Author's mother, uncle and grandparents in Staples Corner, London, c. 1955, © Sumita Mukherjee.

2. Dolly Parnell and Betty Naldera Ali Khan, 1918. © National Portrait Gallery, London.

3. N. C. Bakhle, Form Classical Remove, Dulwich College, 1919. With kind permission of the Governors of Dulwich College.

4. A.B. Habibullah (Sonny), Watson's House Fives team, Clifton College, 1927. Courtesy of Clifton College Archives.

5. Rajkumari Amrit Kaur, Aldhelmsted Senior Floor, Sherborne Girls' School, 1905. Courtesy of Sherborne Girls' Archive.

6. 'Why not make your own dug-out?', *The Graphic*, 29 September 1917. Mary Evans Picture Library.

7. Kamal Chunchie and children, c. 1930s. Courtesy of Eastside Community Heritage.

8. M. K. Sahebzada, Fancy Dress Dance 1926, Sherborne School. Courtesy of Sherborne School Archives.

INTRODUCTION

The seeds of this book are rooted in a black and red hardback notebook I obtained on a visit to Sydney in early 2019. The pages remind me of a significant time in my own history; soon after my return, I became pregnant, and then, the following year, life was affected by the COVID-19 pandemic. In it I had been making notes about this book—about South Asian child migrants through history—to remind myself of thoughts, arguments, individuals and books to read. Secure within its pages, I have kept a black and white photograph of a young family: a man, a woman and two young children.[1] It is there to remind me why I have been writing this book. The father is dressed in a suit and tie, the mother in a sari with her hair in a bun. The son has a white Punjabi shirt and dhoti on; the young girl, who is maybe about five years old, is wearing a tucked-in sari with a clip in her hair. They are standing in front of a brick wall and a shed. This photo is from 1950s Britain and the people in it are my family. The young girl is my mother and the couple are my grandparents. They moved to London in 1953 when my mother was four years old. This photo was taken just one or two years later next to the house that my mother grew up in. It was an end terrace, probably built in the 1930s. The children are dressed up for the photo but the fact that my very young mother is wearing a sari in Britain was not unusual. Though brought up in Britain, she would often wear saris—rather than Western clothing—as a young girl and, having now lived in the

UK most of her life, in adulthood she has only worn saris, just like her mother before her.

I have another black and white photo that sits next to my computer, at home in Bristol. In it, two young children stand in front of the same brick wall and shed but this time they are clad in school blazers, my mother in a skirt and school cap and my uncle in shorts. They look, to me, like quintessential English school children of the post-war era despite the colour of their skin. When I was growing up, I always thought my mother had a very posh British accent. Unlike other South Asians in Britain who migrated when older, like my father, she has no trace of an 'Indian' accent. My mother likes to recall that when she would open the door to strangers as a child they would often ask her if she understood English and she would reply in her posh North London accent. I used to like the way she would surprise people with her voice when they had already formed their first impressions of her because of her clothing and skin colour. People were so often taken aback when she started to speak—and still are. When I was a child, I used to wish to emphasise to people that my mother was not just a new immigrant to Britain but had spent her childhood here and was therefore more British than they thought. Based on appearances alone, it was not obvious to them that she had grown up alongside British children and so people made assumptions about her identity and upbringing which were ignorant of a broader connected history.

I think of my mother's childhood often and what it must have been like growing up in 1950s and 1960s Britain as a child and then a teenager. Her saris, in particular, are a thread that keeps coming back to me. I recall a story she once told me about applying for work at the BBC when she was nineteen. A blind recruiting agent in Oxford Street interviewed her and was keen to offer her the job to start the following Monday. When she returned home, the agent rang her. 'My secretary told me that you were wearing a sari,' he said. That was going to be a problem. She would not be allowed to wear a sari to this job. Faced with this, my mother had to wear her old school uniform to work instead.

My mother was born in Calcutta, now Kolkata, India in 1949. Her parents were both born in what is now Bangladesh. The family had moved to West Bengal before the partition of the subcontinent in 1947. Both my grandfather and grandmother came from wealthy landowning families. Their families lost their properties in East Bengal during partition but they had properties in Calcutta too. They were secure enough to survive largely unscathed, with relatively little pain. Despite their wealth, the family had not been well educated. My grandfather was an exception. My grandmother had married my grandfather when she was about 14 years old, a common feature of family life in India in the 1930s. She had little choice in the matter and little education. As a child her life was upended but that was part and parcel of life for young girls in the subcontinent at that time.

In 2017, a British television producer got in touch with me as they were looking into stories of South Asian migration to Britain. They primarily got in touch because of my historical expertise but then we started talking about my own family history. The programme would centre stories around a group of passengers on the same ship, looking at the diverse stories and events of the year. They decided not to include my grandparents' story because they did not do anything 'radical' enough in their lives in Britain, according to the producer. My grandfather moved to London by himself and left his wife and young son in India while he joined Gray's Inn in November 1948. He was officially called to the Bar in 1953 but did not practise as a barrister. Afflicted with anxiety, he could not face the public act of speaking in courts. He also had a strong aversion to wealth because of his family experiences. He took up a job in the local council and his favourite pastime was reading books from the local library.

While the producer did not include my family story, they did send me a copy of the shipping record that brought my mother to Britain. The ship was the SS *Carthage* which had voyaged from Hong Kong, via Colombo and Bombay, to London. It arrived in London on 6 May 1953, just in time for the coronation of Queen Elizabeth II on 2 June. My grandfather had returned to Calcutta in October 1952, aged 29, in order to bring his family over to Britain. By then my mother had been born and the four of them took the train to Bombay before embarking on their long journey. Family lore goes that my grandfather informed my grandmother that he merely wanted to take the family to London to see the coronation as it would be a historic spectacle. He did not tell her that he had no intention of allowing his family to return to live in India, wanting to get away from his overbearing father and his extended family and start a new life in London. When, in 2017, my mother asked my grandmother more about the journey she had made aged twenty-three, my grandmother was in the late stages of her life and could remember little. She did recollect that her husband left her to her own devices for the journey—a not unusual occurrence—and that she spent most of her time with a family from Madras who played bridge. My uncle, aged eight at the time, went to play with other children on the ship. My mother was four and clung onto her mother.

My grandmother was an expert in Bengali cuisine, having been taught by her mother and sisters-in-law in Calcutta before and during her early marriage. When she came to London, she soon learned how to cook English food. Her neighbour on the terraced street in Staples Corner taught her how to make sponge cakes and roasts. Every year, she would make the Christmas pudding in October ready for December. She knew all the bus routes in North and Central London and the best grocery shops for Indian vegetables. She knew very little English on her arrival though and my grandfather's younger brother, who was a student at the time and lived with them in London, taught my grandmother English.

In the winter of 2021, I helped my mother clear out the house that my grandmother and mother first arrived to in 1953. My grandparents had lived in that same house until their deaths. I was keen to find more records and photos from my mother's childhood. My mother found some school photos from her primary school in Dollis Hill. She also found the menu card from the SS *Carthage*. My grandmother had collected 'autographs' from some of her fellow passengers. There is an entertainment programme for the ship among the papers. Activities include children's sports, a cinema showing of *The Pickwick Papers* and a children's fancy dress party.

My grandparents were not the most affectionate of people. Nor were they the most communicative or generous. I often feel that my mother led a secretive childhood. It was certainly a fairly silent childhood that involved little communication with her parents, although she did learn to adapt to Bengali and English customs. She would help my grandmother in the kitchen, folding over samosa pastries and rolling out *luchis*. She relied on her mother's old saris to wear as she was rarely bought anything new. She would play with the children on her street but they rarely entered each other's lives. When she was a teenager, sometimes she would spend the day at friends' houses but she did not go out much. At sixteen and seventeen, in the summers, she worked at a little shop called Indiacraft on Oxford Street. She was allowed to wear her saris then. By 1965, Indiacraft was becoming a popular store for British people interested in Indian culture—including hippies. My mother said that she did not feel out of place there. George Harrison remembers visiting the store sometime between August–October 1965 to buy his first sitar.[2] Might my mother have been working in the store at that time?

My mother was not particularly interested in rock 'n' roll. She liked literature and later studied child psychology at university. In many ways she had a traditional upbringing at home but she was not fully immersed into Indian (or Bengali) culture either. She had very few Indian friends as a child and her father was a committed atheist. Bengali families and friends would visit her father regularly at home—as an early settled migrant he was known widely among the Hindu Bengali community in North London, even if he mocked some of the Hindu rituals they followed. For lunch they would often eat sausages and mash, pie or fish fingers. The mash usually had chilli in it. Her father taught her to read and write Bengali but she never felt that she was as fluent as people brought up in India, like her cousins. In her early twenties, when looking for love, she would have dilemmas about bridging the gap between the two cultures.

My mother attended North London Collegiate School in Edgware, North London, from 1960. It was then what was known as a direct grant grammar school. One quarter of the places in these schools were directly funded by central government, while the remainder attracted fees, some paid by the local government and some by the parents of pupils; the amounts were set according to ability to pay. On average, the schools received just over half of their income from the state, which was how my mother's fees were paid. Despite their wealthy upbringing in Bengal, my grandparents kept little money and my grandmother did not work. My mother's school was over five miles away from her home and she would take the trolley bus or sometimes walk if her parents failed to give her the fare. She was the only Indian girl at school but she was not the first Indian admitted there. The first Indian girl had been admitted in 1897, over 60 years earlier. She was Manoramabai Medhavi, the daughter of an Indian social reformer, women's rights activist and single (widowed) mother Pandita Ramabai. In September 1919, the same school admitted Padmini Satthianadhan, the 14-year-old daughter of an Indian writer and women's rights activist Kamala Satthianadhan (also widowed). In 1972, a contemporary of Satthianadhan gave an interview for the school and remembered three Egyptian girls who attended the school at the same time as Padmini in the 1920s: 'But you see now everybody takes coloured people for granted. They don't take any notice but then it seemed really peculiar to have 3 or 4 coloured girls in the school.'[3] In 1942, the school admitted sisters Maya Ray and Chaya Ray who were both involved in legal and political careers in India.

My mother was a child migrant to Britain. She was one of the early ones, as more South Asian children came over or were born in Britain from the 1950s onwards. But I am particularly interested in the children who were born before my mother, before the Second World War, before the partition of the Indian subcontinent and before the end of formal British rule in that part of the world. I am interested in how they, too, navigated multiple cultures and the tensions between family and community. I am interested in how they understood their identity and connection to the Indian subcontinent, especially at a time when the nations of India (and Pakistan/Bangladesh) were not fully realised themselves. I am interested in how they dealt with being separated from home and their extended families and how they interacted with different colonial systems and states around the world. At a time when the British Empire was at its height, Indian children were moving around that very empire and interacting with the colonial state away from the subcontinent—having to grapple with being colonial subjects and also what it meant to be both Indian and part of the new spaces that they lived in—all while being very young and impressionable, and with limited independence. Empire was not an abstract system of railways and elephants—as it may have been reduced to in some popular imaginations—but an everyday imposition on young people's lives and an institution that wished to control and constrain their liberties and their futures.

My mother's journey from India to Britain was a direct one. Before 1947, South Asians were involved in migratory journeys to other parts of the world such as the Caribbean, East and South Africa, Southeast Asia and the Pacific; some migrated onwards to Britain later but not all of them. Living in Britain myself, a product of the British education system like my mother, and identifying as a British South Asian, I have become increasingly wary and concerned about the narrative of British exceptionalism that even British South Asians imbibe. We live in a global world now but that world was global for centuries. Indians could be citizens of nowhere and everywhere in the nineteenth century too. The world was not only shaped by adult men. Children could be historical agents and lead historical change. Even more recently, children of South Asian heritage have been influencing world affairs, such as Malala Yousafzai or Mya-Rose Craig (aka 'Birdgirl'): one an internationally recognised campaigner for girls' education who was a forced child migrant from Pakistan to Britain after being shot by the Taliban; the other a leading environmentalist campaigner from childhood, born in Britain and of Bangladeshi heritage. But beyond well-known figures, it is important to remember that children were important parts of society in historical times too. They were crucial for the growth of family settlement and community groups; schools and centres were built around them and educational practices were developed that were important for nation-building and mythmaking. They would use their childhood experiences and ideas about the world to influence their actions as adults. How can we truly understand the effects of empire without discussing the role of, and effects on, children? How can we understand the global effects of migration without thinking about the families and young children who moved around the world and were subject to harsh journeys and erratic immigration controls while navigating new colonial systems in the nineteenth and early twentieth centuries before international travel became cheaper and quicker (for some)? In gaining better understanding of these historical contexts, we can better understand how children from migrant backgrounds in Britain and around the world are grappling with similar issues and explore questions about home, belonging, education, family and identity.

* * *

Between 1857 and 1947, during what has been labelled the 'British Raj' era, over 28 million Indians left the subcontinent to work, study and live in other parts of the world, their movements entwined in the operations of empire. At the time of writing, India has the largest diaspora in the world; there are approximately 18 million Indians living overseas, and many more of South Asian heritage from what are now the states of Pakistan and Bangladesh, with some estimates of up to 50 million people of South Asian heritage living outside the subcontinent. Their links with the subcontinent continue to shape global politics and identity formations to this day. For the purposes of this book, to discuss events pre-1947, I will be using the terms 'India' and 'Indian' as they were historically used, to refer to the geographical areas that now encompass the states of India, Pakistan and Bangladesh and the people and products of them. While the parameters of 'South Asia' as a term have not been fixed historically and politically—and it has encompassed, at different times, Afghanistan, Bangladesh, Bhutan, India, the Maldives, Nepal, Pakistan and Sri Lanka—I use 'South Asian' primarily to denote those I discuss within the scope of this book with Indian, Pakistani, Bangladeshi and Sri Lankan heritage. I will also use 'British South Asian' where appropriate for those with South Asian heritage who also identify with a British nationality. From earlier migrations in smaller numbers to the height of post-World War II migration, British South Asians have had a significant impact on British society, culture, the economy and, increasingly, political decision-making; the UK's first British South Asian prime minister, Rishi Sunak, appointed in 2022, is a product of imperial migration, his mother migrating to Leicester as a child from Tanganyika in the 1960s. The time is, then, right to readjust the historical record by challenging mainstream histories and highlighting the role of children of colour in shaping

INTRODUCTION

the largest empire in human history and helping to build the world's largest democracy.

Involved in multiple migrations, children were crucial players in founding new Indian communities abroad but their experiences of empire have hardly been considered. For this reason, *Imperial Footprints* focuses on the imperial era, up until the partition of India and Pakistan in 1947. The ten chapters in this book follow a chronological and thematic approach to showcase the diverse backgrounds and experiences of children from South Asia, encompassing the white children born in British India, elite South Asian public-school boys, working-class children of dual heritage and those affected by partition. During the nineteenth and early twentieth century, ideas of Britishness were in flux, shaped by the world dominance and then decline of the British Empire. The British Sri Lankan theorist Ambalavaner Sivanandan's 'We are here because you were there' is oft-quoted to explain the post-Windrush generation of migrants from the former Empire to Britain but this book also foregrounds how imperial migrants were engaged and lived in Britain well before the Second World War. To better understand and engage with contemporary conversations about migrant identities and the longstanding effects of empire on the present day, we need to better understand the historical context for migration to Britain, why South Asians continue to settle across the UK and how children in the past were affected by the imperial project. Many of these children became politically radicalised by their migratory journeys and engagement with the Empire, fundamentally shaping ideas of nationalism, suffrage, anticolonialism and socialism; so, to truly understand the full reach and effect of the British Empire, we must engage with their stories and how they were told.

Two of the most famous Indians in Britain before the twentieth century were the Maharajah Duleep Singh and Sake Dean Mahomed. Sake Dean Mahomed was first brought to the attention of a wider public by pioneering historian Rozina Visram whose work detailed the long history of South Asians in Britain dating back 400 years; he is also mentioned in Sathnam Sanghera's more recent *Empireland*.[4] Sake Dean Mahomed was the first known Indian to publish a book in English (in 1794). In January 2019, he was honoured with a Google

Doodle on the occasion of his 260th birthday and the children's television programme *Horrible Histories* featured his life in an episode, with the comic actor Sanjeev Bhaskar playing his part. Sake Dean Mahomed is known for his varied exploits in Britain and connections with British politics and society. He first moved to Ireland from India in 1784 and then moved to London in 1807 where he set up the Hindoostane Coffee House, credited as the first Indian restaurant in Britain. Following this, in 1814 he moved to Brighton where he set up a bathhouse and became 'shampooing surgeon' to George IV and William IV; he is credited with introducing the Turkish practice of shampooing to Britain.[5]

Mahomed's legacies extended to his children and grandchildren who were born in Britain. He had five children with his Irish wife, Jane: Arthur, Frederick, James, Henry and Adeline. Arthur took over the bathhouse. Frederick, born in Brighton in 1818, started out a career as a dancer in Liverpool but returned to Brighton by the time he was 20, where he ran a boxing, fencing, gymnastics and callisthenics academy in Hove. His son, Frederick Henry Horatio Akbar Mahomed was born on 11 April 1849 in Brighton to Frederick's second wife, Sarah Hodgkinson. Frederick Akbar Mahomed, as he was known, was educated in Brighton prior to attending medical school. He became a British physician and was well known for his key work in understanding hypertension.[6]

Frederick Akbar Mahomed's main contribution to medicine was his study of high blood pressure when he was only 23 years old and still a medical student and junior doctor at Guy's Hospital in London. He was the first to attempt clinical measurement of blood pressure and was a pivotal figure in the recognition of the effects of high blood pressure on health, being the first to recognise that high blood pressure was in itself a primary health condition while accurately describing how high blood pressure could progress in people. He explained that healthy people could develop the illness in old age and that environmental factors such as alcohol, stress, exercise and work could all have an effect. Despite his highly influential contributions to medicine, this British South Asian man has hardly been recognised in either the medical fields or the history books. I am interested in thinking more about people like Frederick, who grew up as children

INTRODUCTION

in Britain and were intimately involved in the creation of British society while facing racial hierarchies and prejudices at the height of the British Empire. I think we are ignorant and forgetful on two counts—about the presence of children in history generally but also in realising that there were relatively large numbers of people, including children, of South Asian descent living, working and contributing to British life during the time of empire.

As a child, Frederick Akbar was, in his own words, 'rampageous, irritable and passionate'. He was 'always restless and excitable' and an average school student with a leaning towards mathematics and building mechanical toys. He liked to be known as Akbar and was first admitted as a medical student at Sussex County Hospital when he turned 18, before studying at Guy's Hospital, where his brother Arthur also trained. His colleagues remembered him as tall, commanding and intelligent. However, some of his students said his methods were 'as foreign as his name' and a history of Guy's Hospital published in 1892 described his 'Oriental strain'. I would like to discuss these kinds of childhood traits and experiences for other children of empire in this book. Frederick Akbar died tragically at the age of only 35 from typhoid fever and was buried at Highgate Cemetery.[7] He had six siblings and five children of his own: Archie and Ellen, born to his first wife Ellen Chalk in the 1870s; Dorothy, Janet and Humphrey, all born in Southwark, London, in the 1880s, to Ada Chalk, the sister of Ellen. All of his children dissociated themselves from the family and the Mahomed name, largely because of the rise of racism at the turn of the century. Frederick Akbar's two sons both changed their surnames to 'Deane' in a nod to their great grandfather's name.

The Maharajah Duleep Singh, meanwhile, was the exiled prince of the Punjab—a Sikh Empire in northwestern India—who was born in 1838. In 1849, aged only 10, Duleep Singh was removed from the Punjab, and his mother, by the British who took away his title and devolved his power. The Koh-i-noor diamond was 'surrendered' to the East India Company and later presented to Queen Victoria. Duleep Singh became the ward of Sir John Spencer Login, a Scottish surgeon, and his wife Lena Campbell Login and they brought him to England in 1854 after he had converted to Christianity.[8] In England, still a teenager, Duleep Singh became a 'favourite' of Queen Victoria. As a former prince (and thus of 'royal blood'), he was presented in the Queen's Court and became close to her family. In 1855, Login rented Castle Menzies in Perthshire, Scotland, a large sporting estate, and Duleep Singh moved there with an annual pension. Known to dress in kilts and Highland costume, he became 'something of a local', with a keen interest in hunting and shooting.[9]

In 1864, Duleep Singh married Bamba Müller (of German and Ethiopian descent) in Cairo. On 4 August 1865, Duleep Singh and Müller's first son had been born in Scotland but tragically the baby only lived for 24 hours. The baby was not named but was born a Christian and buried in Kenmore Parish Church. The inscription on the grave reads: 'To the memory of the infant son of the Maharajah Duleep Singh, late ruler of the Sikh Nation, Punjab, India and the Maharanee, his wife. Born 4th August 1865. Died 5th August 1865.'[10] Duleep and Bamba then moved and established their family at Elveden Hall in Suffolk. In Elveden, Duleep Singh continued to be known for his so-called extravagant lifestyle and his love for the countryside and game-shooting. He also rebuilt the church, cottages and school in Elveden. Duleep and Bamba had six children together (who survived infancy) and Queen Victoria was godmother to their children. I will discuss some of those children later in this book. Despite his upbringing and the attempts by Login and the British state to monitor his 'Indianness', in 1886 Duleep Singh decided to fight to reclaim his land and title in Punjab, returning to India and re-converting to Sikhism. He was unsuccessful and then moved to Paris where he had two more children with Ada Wetherill, his mistress, and died in 1893. His body was buried in Elveden.[11]

Duleep Singh had a privileged life but he was someone who was divested of his power as a very young child. He was seen as someone who could be moulded and 'saved' by British imperial power and Christianity. The imperial state robbed an 'innocent' of his heritage, even if he was then able to live in large estates in Perthshire or Suffolk. The author and journalist Christy Campbell has suggested taking a psychoanalytical perspective—that when he tried to reclaim his kingdom, this could have been because he 'wanted his childhood back'.[12] There are parallels in the ways in which this individual child was treated and the ways in which imperial thought depicted India as a childlike country which was primitive and innocent and needed to be 'guided' by the 'adult' British power. Meanwhile, Indian civilisation and the Sikh Empire were seen as dead, backwards and no longer relevant to the modern age. In removing Duleep Singh from his home and his mother, it was easy to wrest power from the Punjab ruler and, as he was a child, it was easy to make him a favourite at Queen Victoria's court. In his later life, Duleep Singh's imperial guardians could not prevent the political awakening and realisation of injustice that came with adulthood. The removal of Duleep Singh to Britain as a child had huge repercussions for Sikh identity and politics, both in Britain and in the subcontinent. As we'll touch on later, it enabled the downfall of the Sikh Empire and the British annexation of the Punjab. Subsequent generations have dealt with the legacies and domino effects of these actions, including the later partition of the Punjab in 1947, presided over by its then-rulers, the British.

* * *

Sake Dean Mahomed is often cited now in history books and popular websites as an example of an early Indian pioneer to Britain. One of the 'firsts': first book, first restaurant, first shampoos. Meanwhile, Duleep Singh is lauded as the first British Sikh and that is why I mention both examples at this start. But I am not merely interested in firsts. Or greats. The ways in which we write history needs to reflect our understanding of how society ran in the past and runs today. If we focus solely on the leaders, the pioneers, the successes, we forget the multitudes and the masses who constitute society, who shape politics and economics, who are our forebears. In the 1970s, women historians strived tirelessly to bring the stories and perspectives of women to the forefront of history, to show that women were present, involved, important and historical agents of change. Equally, in more recent decades, historians have been drawing attention to other marginalised groups of society who are instrumental in historical change—whether marginalised because of their class, caste, sexuality, gender, religion or race. These include children. While children are fundamental objects for politics, society and economics in the twenty-first century—the focus of education policy, citizenship, migration, housing, social security, demographics and family change—they were also crucial subjects in history too, especially within and about the British Empire. Their presence, numbers, actions, influences, activities and impacts have often been overlooked—children who are seen but not heard, mentioned in passing but not recognised. I want to challenge these assumptions about the historical voices that we foreground and the historical importance that we place on certain stories. I want to tell a story, a history—of the British Empire, of Britain, of the Indian subcontinent—through the story of migration, race, gender, class and nationality, through the perspectives of young Indians who lived, studied, worked and played in Britain in the nineteenth and early twentieth century. I want to show that these children of empire shaped the imperial trajectory as much as the 'great men' did and that, in order to understand how multicultural, postcolonial Britain has been shaped, we need to acknowledge the presence, activities and influence that a young generation had at the height of the Empire. This book is called *Imperial Footprints*. For me, this refers to the footprints laid by these children in their migratory journeys between Britain and the subcontinent and the marks they made on Britain, India and the Empire. As I will show, these footprints were multidirectional as they influenced British history but also the histories of Indian nationalism, socialism, suffrage and involvement in world wars. Throughout the course of this book, we will trace the 'imperial footprints' of these children and the mark they made on the British Empire and the world that followed.

1

THE WHITE INDIANS

In a 2018 episode of BBC's *Who Do You Think You Are?*, the celebrated actress Olivia Colman discovered that her three times great-grandmother, Harriot Slessor, had been born in India in Kishanganj around 1807. Her father, William Slessor, was a captain in the East India Company but he died when Harriot was three or four years old. During the television programme, there was speculation that Harriot's mother might have had Indian heritage but, after the show aired, this was disproved. Either an orphan, or at least separated from her mother, Harriot's paternal grandmother, Elizabeth Slessor, paid for her to be sent to England in December 1811. She first had to travel from Kishinganj to Calcutta to board an East India Company ship. Harriot was seven years old and undertook the six-month journey alone but on board her ship were at least twelve other children with ages ranging from 1 to 9. The passage cost thousands of pounds. On 20 May 1812, she disembarked at Longreach, Kent, and was enrolled at a boarding school in Bristol, living under the care of Miss Mills in Park Street.[1]

In 1832, Harriot returned to India and married William Garrett but he died a year later. She then married Charles Bazett in 1838, who was in the Indian Army, and they had four children: two sons and two daughters. One of their sons subsequently served in the

Royal Artillery in India. Whether Harriot's mother was indeed of Indian heritage or not, Colman's family had a strong connection with lives lived and loved in India. The journey to Bristol of the young girl born in India was not unusual for the time. Many children born in India, whatever their ethnic heritage, travelled to Britain across the nineteenth century. In addition, many British people who consider themselves white Britons have strong connections to the land and migratory histories of India.

To take another example, Jane Cumming Gordon, the first known Anglo-Indian (someone of mixed British and Indian heritage) pupil in a Scottish school, was born to an Indian mother and white British father. Rather like Harriot Slessor, after the death of her father, George Cummings Gordon, Jane was brought to a school in Edinburgh by her grandmother, Lady Helen Cumming Gordon. The reason we know a little about Jane's experiences is because, in 1810, Jane and Lady Helen were involved in a legal case against the two female owners of the boarding school, Marianne Woods and Jane Pirrie. In 1809, the fourteen-year-old had chanced upon Woods and Pirrie engaging in sexual relations with each other. Her grandmother withdrew her from the school and filed a case of 'improper and criminal conduct'. In 1811, Woods and Pirrie countersued for libel but were unsuccessful. In 1812, on appeal, they were able to overturn the original case and Lady Helen had to pay damages to the boarding school. Doubt was cast over the truthfulness of Jane's account with attention drawn to her mixed heritage.[2] Children, then, were at the heart of debates about the language and identity of race in Britain and, as we will see, also at the very heart of the ongoing longevity of the British imperial mission in India.

According to the 1901 Census of India, there were 154,691 British subjects living in India of whom nearly 22,000 were under the age of 12.[3] British power in the Indian subcontinent had developed through the East India Company who conquered much (but not all) of India between 1757 and 1818 and whose military endeavours were supplemented by an expansive tax regime and a lucrative trade business. The presence of white British families in India, therefore, was crucial to the ongoing reach of imperial power and they ranged from people serving in the military, to merchants, bureaucrats and politicians, Christian missionaries and labourers. Before the nineteenth century, British families in India had often embraced the 'oriental' side of their Indian lives, wearing Indian fashions. British colonial officials engaged in sexual relationships with Indian women with relative freedom, often bringing up children with mixed heritage. However, at the beginning of the nineteenth century, a more deliberate policy of racial separation hardened in British India. Sexual relationships with Indian people were prohibited, although this did not mean that they stopped.[4] A stronger Victorian emphasis on the family and separation of the feminine domestic sphere led to more attention on how children were raised and looked after in Britain. More focus was placed on education and leisure, child labour laws were introduced to limit the working hours of children and ideas of class within childhood became more entrenched.

In May 1857, a 'revolt' and uprising, first of Indian 'sepoys' over a rumour about cartridges greased with cow and pig fat, spread primarily across North India with an attempt to restore the last Mughal Emperor Bahadur Shah II to the throne in Delhi. At the same time, various local battles led to bloodshed and attacks on families, both Indian and white British. The events of 1857 led to heightened tensions around the safety of British women and children in India. Estimates vary but many Indian children and over 60 white British children died during the Lucknow siege, which was one of the main sites of conflict.[5] Following events in 1857, the British Crown took over formal control of India from the East India Company. The Indian Civil Service, its administrative arm, grew its ranks and required more (male) British civil servants to migrate to India, often taking wives or settling down with families in India. Meanwhile, missionary numbers increased in the late nineteenth century and their children were increasingly born in the colonies. As more white British children were born in India, Victorian racial ideas deepened into concerns about the health and wellbeing of children who were brought up in India for too long. Families were concerned that the climate would turn children 'Indian' and also affect their health in other ways. Infant mortality rates were higher in India than in Britain but families also became concerned about language as children might develop accents or 'native ways' or not understand and maintain racial hierarchies if they became too 'Indian'.[6] British families started to look at ways to prevent this and maintain the imperial racial order.

Across the nineteenth century, racialised ideas about childhood innocence became popular in the Western world. While previous to this, 'childhood' was not even really a concept, by the late eighteenth century the prevalent Western idea of children as asexual and oblivious to worldly concerns took hold. As Robin Bernstein has explained, these ideas of innocence, though, were rooted in racial ideas: children of colour were not afforded this distinction.[7] Across the nineteenth century, the industrial economy of Britain continued to develop, while British public schools were at their zenith. Radhika Mohanram has pointed out that in 1857, at the same time as bloody events in India were happening, the popular novel *Tom Brown's School Days*—written by Thomas Hughes about public school life at Rugby—was published.[8] The adventures of Tom Brown were part of a growing literary market for adventure stories, many of which like Robert Ballantyne's *Coral Island* (also published in 1857) or H. Rider Haggard's *King Solomon's Mines* (1885) were set in colonial contexts and had imperial 'adventure' at their heart. These kinds of novels were part of a growing ideal of British masculine imperial adventurers, and these ideologies were being imparted to young British boys through their reading, through their schools and through extra-curricular activities like the Boy Scouts. Bound up with this was an ideology of whiteness, linked to ideologies of Christianity, imperialism and gender, that was bred through youth and soon became part of a universalising discourse that 'othered' non-whites to the extent that whiteness became invisible.[9] But for children in this period, especially those born in India and moving through different colonial and imperial spaces, navigating relationships with different adults and children, understanding and living through changing imperial policies and politics, this whiteness was not always an easy identity to take on. Their specific navigations of race, empire and identity were crucial for shaping the imperial project as well as ideas of Britishness from the Victorian era right through to the end of empire.

British colonial families, though, were central to the preservation of the Empire in India. They populated the large port cities of

Calcutta, Bombay and Madras, were found in military cantonments around inland urban centres and often decamped to the cooler hill stations in the summer heat. Many of the political and racial tensions, directives and impetus around the running of empire in India emerged out of the interactions, activities and drive of the families living in India and many of their domestic concerns were shaped by their children and concerns about their children. As Ellen Filor has argued, the white children born in India, even if they were sent back to Britain, were 'bred in and for Empire' and were agents of empire themselves. Their own understanding of their race, identity and language, and their difference from white British-born children, shaped ideas of race that underpinned the imperial project across the nineteenth and twentieth century.[10]

As Niamh Dillon has argued, white British children born in India during the Raj almost universally viewed Britain as 'home', even if they had never visited there. The sense that Britain was home was encouraged through 'British' spaces in India such as churches or the Club—an exclusive social space for elite British people in India.[11] As members of the imperial workforce, families understood that Britain was the home of the Empire and that British Christian culture was one of the ideological underpinnings of the mission of empire. A collective memory of Britain was fostered through the white British community in India; their children breathed in and imbibed that memory. When white children who were born in India were sent to Britain, they were expected to feel at home in Britain at once. Many of these children were torn from all that was familiar and this transition was unlikely to be straightforward. As we progress further through this book, and look at brown Indian children making the same journey as white British children, it will be interesting to consider to what extent these expectations and emotions were mirrored.

White British children were sent back to Britain for their education as a matter of course by the time they reached school age. Although there were 'British' schools in India, particularly in the hill stations such as Darjeeling, Simla and Ooctamund, middle- and upper-class imperial families were keen to send their children back 'home'. The most well-known public schools such as Eton, Harrow and Rugby were always popular choices for the colonial elite but there were also other schools that had strong imperial connections. These included Haileybury in Hertfordshire, United Services College in Devon, Marlborough College in Wiltshire and Wellington College in Berkshire, as well as day schools in Bedford. Some of these schools, like United Services College in Westward Ho!, which catered to sons of military officers, were known as 'nurseries of empire' because of their important function in educating colonial children.[12] Between 1824 and 1833, the Edinburgh academy admitted at least 72 boys who had been born in India and so the numbers were sizeable.[13]

The economy of British boarding schools, especially in the first part of the nineteenth century, was kept afloat by children who journeyed from India, largely white but many of whom were of mixed heritage and had been subsumed into the families of their white fathers, like Olivia Colman's ancestor. The civil servant, Alexander Pringle, for example, was disparaging of Scottish boarding schools in 1816 because they 'teem with East & West India bastards of various shades of colour ... disguised with fine clothes'.[14] Edinburgh High School was described as having, between 1810 and 1820, 'the variety of nations: for in our class under Mr Pillans there were boys from Russia, Germany, Switzerland, the United States, Barbadoes, St. Vincent, Demerara, the East Indies, besides England and Ireland'.[15] Children who were designed to be brought up white and British, even with mixed heritage, were trained to regard Britain as home, rather than the India of their birth (and sometime heritage). However, many of them returned to India in service of the Empire. Careers in the military or civil service were popular, especially for families who had childhood connections to the colonies and thus a circular economy around empire and boarding schools emerged, where imperial and racial ideas, informed by migration and childhood experiences, developed and solidified. The 'white' Indian children were at the heart of this imperial endeavour.

* * *

The long journey to Britain from India was often considered too arduous for young children, especially in the age of ship travel.

However, once children reached around the age of six, British parents in India were keen to either accompany or find travellers willing to take their children to Britain for their schooling and subsequent upbringing. Ayahs were Indian nursemaids who looked after the children of white British families in the Indian subcontinent. On the journey to Britain, then, many families used these ayahs to accompany those children on the long ship journeys.[16] On board the ships, and indeed in the homes, the ayahs had multiple duties associated with the care of young children. These tasks often included cleaning, laundry and preparation of meals alongside the usual care of the children. The migration of Indian ayahs alongside their wards to Britain dates to at least the eighteenth century. There is a record in St Marylebone, on 15 April 1787, of Mary Ann Flora, 'a native of the East Indies, aged 19' and the record of the burial of Flora, 'an East Indian', in Woolwich on 26 May 1769. By the 1870s, it was estimated that there were roughly 100 ayahs in Britain.[17]

Tragically, many ayahs were discarded in Britain because the families no longer needed or wanted Indian domestic servants in the British home but also refused to help them return to India. There are so many cases of ayahs who were abandoned that an Ayahs' Home was built in East London in 1891 by the London City Mission to house them and help them find return passage. It was moved to larger premises in Hackney in 1921 and had about thirty rooms to accommodate around 100 women. The ayahs often knew very little English and were put in a very vulnerable status, having once been prized domestic servants. We know of many of their stories because of the letters that were sent from the Ayahs' Home to the India Office regarding reimbursement for passages home.[18]

In Frances Hodgson Burnett's classic children's novel, *The Secret Garden* (1911), the story opens by telling us that an ayah had cared for the heroine Mary Lennox in her early years in India. Indeed, Mary's mother had not wanted a girl and so 'when Mary was born she handed her over to the care of an Ayah, who was made to understand that if she wished to please the Memsahib she must keep the child out of sight as much as possible'.[19] Cholera spread through the Lennox household, first affecting the ayah and then Mary's parents. It is the death of the ayah which leads to Mary feeling more abandoned, than that of her parents, although—and this is part of Mary's initial character—she does not feel sad at her nurse's demise, thinking only of herself. It is also the death of the ayah that sets in train the events that lead to Mary being sent to Yorkshire, eventually befriending Colin Craven and discovering the secret garden.

The figure of the ayah is important for understanding children's lives but also how the language of childhood was evoked in imperial rhetoric. Ayahs were often infantilised by their employers. Household guides for British women in India explained that 'the Indian servant is a child in everything save age, and should be treated as a child', and that 'their brains are not properly developed and they cannot always see things in the same light as we do'.[20] Ayahs were described as speaking 'chi-chi' (broken) English and were seen as needing constant supervision while they supervised children. They were only required to look after infants and, of course, once children were old enough, they were sent to school in Britain away from the pernicious influences of India and the ayahs. Reading some accounts, one might wonder why British families consented to employing ayahs as they treated them with disdain and yet they performed such an essential role in the household. Even in the Ayahs' Home in Hackney, these ayahs were often treated like children and they were often described as child-like in contemporary literature.[21]

Ayahs abandoned in cities other than London could not always find the Ayahs' Home in Hackney. In 1895, an ayah called Angelica McBarnett was found at a Manchester workhouse. The guardians of the Manchester Poor Law unions had to pay for her return passage as part of their poor relief. However, it is important to note that Indian families also brought ayahs over to Britain. In 1910, Mr A. Chaudhuri, a Bengali barrister from Calcutta, travelled to England with his wife, son and two servants. One of the servants was Mary, an ayah. However, in August 1910, the India Office received a complaint letter from the Ayahs' Home stating that Mary had been overworked by the Chaudhuris, who owed her 25 rupees for her passage and 25 rupees per month for five months of work in England. In defence of the Chaudhuri family, their governess, Edith Anthony, told the India Office 'ayah had for a long time been very troublesome, always trying to make mischief with the English servants' and that 'the whole affair originated with ayah who really had so little work that she occupied herself in causing continual trouble.' The India Office decided not to intervene, despite the destitution of the ayah.[22]

For many very young British children then, even before they joined school, empire was an integral part of their upbringing. Their nursemaids and nannies were important figures who could be 'of empire' or 'for empire'. In the 1964 film *Mary Poppins*, which is set in 1910, Mr Banks sings about the importance of the nanny for his children, Jane and Michael: 'A British nanny must be a general! / The future empire lies within her hands'. With the longevity of the British Empire in mind, imperial ideologies firmly placed children at the heart of the future strength of British overseas power.

* * *

The imperial project was shored up by people who had not all been born in India but the history of Britain and the British Empire cannot be told without acknowledging the role of these Indian-born cohorts in sustaining the generational hold on empire. Frederick Lugard was born in Madras in 1858 to missionary parents. His mother, Mary Jane, decided to take her three children and two stepdaughters to England in 1863 on the *Trafalgar*. Frederick was five years old. Journeying in a cramped cabin, via the Cape of Good Hope, for four months, they arrived in England in July 1863 and proceeded to York. There, Mary Jane soon found a small house for the family, a seventeen-year-old governess, a servant and a twelve-year-old nursemaid and arranged for the children to be educated at home. As an evangelical Christian, Mary Jane ensured that religious instruction was at the forefront of the children's education and the children wrote weekly letters to their father who remained in India. In 1864, their father returned to England and moved the family to Worcester and a year later, when Frederick was only seven years old, his mother Mary died.[23] Frederick then moved from school to school with the ambition to become a rector like his father, or perhaps join the Indian Civil Service, but his school performance indicated that this might be an ambition too far. Eventually, inspired by his uncle Sir Edward Lugard, who had served in the British Army in

India during the events of 1857 and then taken up a political career, Frederick took up a military career. He then became well known for his role in the Imperial British East Africa Company—where he was influential in the setting up of the Uganda Protectorate in 1894, which brought Buganda and neighbouring states under direct British rule—followed by a role as High Commissioner for Northern Nigeria. Lugard was a highly influential figure in the expansion and maintenance of empire, following the line of his missionary parents and military uncle in their service of empire. It is worth noting his birth in India and early childhood followed by an itinerant childhood in Britain; these influences cannot be divorced from his later adult life nor from the trajectory of the British Empire project.

Like Frederick Lugard, Clement Benthall was born in India. Born in 1841, his missionary parents decided to send Clement and his younger brother and sister to England in 1847, travelling with acquaintances called Mr and Mrs Fisher. They were sent to live with their uncle, the Revd John Benthall, and two aunts. These new guardians were paid to look after the Benthall children and tried to set up a business fostering other children born in India. Clement went on to join the Army and was sent to India in 1859. He died in Allahabad in 1873 at the age of thirty-two, having been a lonely child and adult but one who had pursued the ambition of imperial service.[24]

A lucrative business in providing lodgings and guardianship in Britain for children migrating from India grew across the nineteenth century. Adverts in newspapers specified the availability of such provisions, specifically for children coming from India. For example, in September 1886, a Mrs Burrill at Chilcombe Lodge had an advert in the *Hampshire Chronicle* noting that she had special arrangements to look after Indian children who were planning to attend Winchester High School.[25] Similarly, in 1900, a Mrs Huybers had an advert in *The Morning Post* that discussed arrangements for 'Indian children' in Brussels. In both cases, we can take 'Indian children' to mean primarily white British children born in India. Mrs Huybers was English and specifically catered for young girls whom she looked after and introduced to society while they attended day school.[26] In the same year, an advert in *The Scotsman* offered board for 'colonial or Indian children' attending school in Edinburgh, but these are just the tip of the iceberg as adverts would have been placed in Indian publications and through word of mouth and recommendation.[27]

Vyvyen Brendon has researched the lives of white British children born in India and found that many young children who were sent to Britain were very unhappy. Children like Theophilus Metcalfe (the son of Sir Thomas Metcalfe, the Resident in Delhi), Alick and Harry Lawrence (the sons of Brigadier-General Sir Henry Lawrence), spent 'miserable childhoods' in lodging houses and boarding schools, separated from their parents, with strict and reserved guardians and in the cold, unfriendly British climate.[28] These are all echoed and evoked in the life and writings of the famous writer Rudyard Kipling. Rudyard Kipling's short story 'Baa Baa Black Sheep' (1888) is an insight into his own experiences as a young child, born in India in 1865, who had to move to England in 1871, aged six.[29]

In 'Baa Baa Black Sheep', 5-year-old Punch and 3-year-old Judy have travelled to England with their parents. Separated from their ayah, who remains in India, young Judy soon forgets her, while their mother weeps throughout the journey. They are taken to meet their aunt and uncle but the children do not understand who they are or what their relation is. When their parents leave to return to India, Punch and Judy are distraught. They run away, hoping to find their ship, but to no avail. Slowly, Punch learns to read and is taught more about the Bible but is also subject to the discipline of his aunt who describes him as the black sheep of the family because she does not like the stories he wants to read. Punch is then sent to school where he meets boys from a range of class and ethnic backgrounds, whom he does not approve of on grounds of their difference from the elite class of people his family socialised with in India. This leads to more discipline from his aunt and bullying from his classmates, forming a very unhappy childhood. While the story is not entirely autobiographical as Rudyard Kipling and his sister Trix were put in the care of a captain and Mrs Holloway of Southsea, who had advertised in *The Times of India* for child boarders, it is clear that Kipling was able to draw upon the sentiments of a child who is separated from their parents at such a young age. Mrs Holloway had favoured his sister Trix and beaten him, calling him a 'black sheep'.[30]

When Kipling turned sixteen he returned to India and his parents and took up a job as a journalist. His later stories and novels which often concentrated on childhoods in India, such as *The Jungle Book* (1894) or *Kim* (1901), reveal how resonant his own childhood was for his later career.

These feelings and experiences of white British children continued well into the twentieth century. Iris Butler, later best known for being a journalist and the grandmother of Justin Welby (latterly Archbishop of Canterbury), was born in Simla in 1905 to Sir Montagu Butler, then an Indian civil servant, and Ann Butler. She described her school in Britain as a refuge for 'orphans of the Empire'. There, she said, they were not encouraged to be homesick or blame their parents for leaving them behind, but rather to be 'very proud of our parents' share in the Empire and to feel that we were doing our bit by being left behind'.[31] She always felt that India was 'home', missing the atmosphere there, and did not like school in particular. However, she remembered that many children at her boarding school were in a similar situation; they would compare notes and all want to go back but never felt any resentment towards their parents as they had always known and accepted that they would have to go to school in England.[32] On the other hand, Wallace Burnet-Smith, who was born in Calcutta in 1922, was sent to Brighton College at the age of eight. His father was in the military and his parents remained in Calcutta. Burnet-Smith was extremely homesick but also felt very much 'at home' in England.[33] John Christie was sent to England in 1913 at the age of seven to join St Cyprian's boarding school in Eastbourne as a boarder. While John had been keen to attend school with other boys who had an Indian connection, he soon found that although many boys had been born in India they were not encouraged to discuss their Indian childhoods nor allowed to speak in Hindi or other Indian vernaculars.[34]

According to the historian David Gilmour, most white British children were bewildered and then depressed when they arrived 'home' in Britain. It was colder, darker and noisier than their colonial homesteads and then things would get worse when these children had to go to school in scratchy school uniforms, eat bland school dinners and get chilblains on their toes. They yearned for India, for their parents and all that was familiar. They found it difficult to make friends with other children who did not understand their Indian experiences or all the references to the things they missed.[35]

Wilfred Bion, who was sent to England in 1905, explains how the description of 'homesickness' was not apt though as he had no 'home' to miss in India, or indeed anywhere else. Many of these children lived nomadic lives in India, following their parents in imperial service, and their homes in India were never allowed to feel like permanent domestic roots. Bion said he missed people and things but perhaps as is the lot for many boarding school children, there was an uprootedness that was fundamental to their upbringings.[36] There was also a separation from family that often felt like a betrayal. For while Iris Butler suggested that she did not blame her parents for sending her to Britain and understood the broader imperial project, Leila Brown, the daughter of missionaries, said that even at the age of ninety-two, she never got over the parting with her parents, who only visited her once during her whole time at school.[37]

* * *

The story of white Indian-born children sets the scene for *Imperial Footprints*. These children were the ones who would shore up the Empire and were indoctrinated into imperial mentalities. They were groomed to shed their Indian upbringings while retaining loyalty to the mission of empire and with continued interest in the affairs of the subcontinent. These children were integral to the shoring up of empire in its heyday and we need to remember the role of the young and often ignored members of society in perpetuating this vast institutional endeavour. These children were racialised as white and taught to feel at home in Britain but they were migrants too. As we shall see, the experiences of brown Indian children who took similar journeys to Britain at a young age were initially not so different.

2

THE VICTORIAN CURIOSITIES

In 2018, the British South Asian actor Dev Patel was cast in the title role of the film adaptation of Charles Dickens' novel *David Copperfield* in an example of 'colour-blind casting'. Patel first came to fame for British audiences when he was just sixteen and cast as Anwar Kharral, a British Pakistani Muslim teenager, in the popular teen drama *Skins*, which followed a group of British teenagers in Bristol in the early 2000s. *The Personal History of David Copperfield* is set primarily in the 1840s and follows the journey of David Copperfield from child to novelist. In the film, we follow the young brown David (played by Ranveer Jaiswal) through the streets of Victorian England and boarding school, before observing his various enterprises with family, romance, work and adventure as he grows up and is played by Patel.

Dickens' literary portrayals of Victorian life, especially the working class, have dominated the public imagination of what life in nineteenth-century urban Britain looked like. To cast an actor of South Asian heritage in the role of David Copperfield may have just been a commercial and artistic decision, however it is not without some historical merit to consider the life and adventures of a brown boy—of Indian origin—in England in that period. The 'ragamuffin' child of Dickens' London may be a stereotype but there are similarities here with contemporary stereotypes of the Indian child. Indian children were exoticised and objectified heavily in this period. Influenced by what is known as 'Orientalism', a way of thinking that characterised people from the 'East' as religious, traditional, backward and unable to change, in contrast to the industrialising, modernising, secular and rational 'West', the Victorian stereotype of the Indian child was perpetuated through exhibitions, art and literature which included the depiction and the physical presence of Indian children in Victorian Britain who were used to reinforce these stereotypes.[1]

While it is much easier to write about the more elite Indians who lived and worked in Britain during this period, less attention has been given to working-class Indians in Britain and those living in poverty, precisely because it is much harder to find out about them and hear from them. British popular imagination and interest in the literature and history of the Victorian poor, often focuses on urban streets and Charles Dickens. While historians such as Lydia Murdoch have explained how ideas of empire were passed on to British children and discussed the training of poor British children into 'citizens of empire', what is rarely recognised is that South Asian children were key constituents of this class; they populated urban areas such as the East End of London in the nineteenth century, were visible begging on streets around the country and were integral parts of Victorian life in Britain.[2]

In 1861, Henry Mayhew, an English journalist and playwright, wrote a book on *London Labour and the London Poor*. He conducted numerous interviews across the 1850s with street-sellers, stall-keepers and sweepers, to draw together his account. These vignettes were initially reproduced in the London newspaper the *Morning Chronicle*, a newspaper that Charles Dickens had begun reporting for from 1834. Mayhew's accounts were a huge influence on his literary contemporaries and those interested in poverty and social welfare. Looking through the pages reveal a range of Indian presences which highlight the racial diversity of Victorian London. For example, Mayhew's book includes an interesting picture of a young Indian child in a dress and flat cap—almost like a sailor's costume—alongside an Indian man selling 'Hindoo religious tracts'. According to Mayhew, some sellers used the tracts as a pretext for begging and the particular man in question could not speak a word of English. Mayhew suggested that there were at least twenty-five foreign tract sellers in London at the time.[3] What is more interesting, for my purposes, though is the young child who accompanies the seller and who receives little attention. Poverty and invisibility affected young and old alike but the child is even less visible than the adult. How many other young Indians were there living around British urban centres in this period who have had no voice and have been unremarked upon in official historical and literary accounts of this period? Could David Copperfield have conceivably had dark skin like the boy in Mayhew's illustration?

Mayhew also described a Muslim tom-tom player from Bengal who was accompanied by his young son. The musician's wife was an Englishwoman and he had initially come to Britain as a servant to a now deceased military officer. The musician had then made his way to London. Living in poverty, with very little earnings and dependent on food for bread, as his former master had died without giving him a reference, the tom-tom player was desperate to return to Calcutta where things were cheaper. He had resorted to playing and begging to make a living. The six-year-old son, a poor pitiless boy with dark skin, danced to accompany his father who played the drum and sang.[4] While we hear the tom-tom player's life story, we know very little about the child from Mayhew's account. Who knows what happened to that young child afterwards?

One relatively well-known Indian child, to historians, who lived in poverty and begged on the streets in the East End of London was Albert Mahomet. Albert Mahomet was born in April 1858 in Limehouse in East London. His father, John Essau Mahomet, was an Indian pedlar and former ships' cook from Calcutta, who would go from place to place selling jewellery, watches, knives and scissors. John had left his wife and six children when they were young and later died in a workhouse in London in 1879 (although Albert believed that his father had returned and died in Calcutta). Albert's mother was an English woman, Audrey Ann Jenkerson (known as Ann), and she lived from hand to mouth with her young children.[5]

Living a hungry childhood, Albert would walk barefoot to the Ragged School in the snow, with bleeding chilblains, and depend upon scraps of food. The siblings shared a straw bed in the corner of a room in their slum house. By the age of seven he was selling newspapers and being reprimanded by the police. He soon became the leader of a gang of children who, like the Artful Dodger and the pickpocketing children in Dickens' *Oliver Twist*, would earn money through begging, stealing, singing, gymnastics or pretending to be lost. He needed the money for his food and would share it with his mother, who unfortunately often spent her time and money on drink. He would paint his face and got more money if his clothes were ragged and in turn described himself as a 'Street Arab'.[6]

Albert wrote some memoirs about his childhood, as he later became a pastor and was keen to stress the long way he had come from slum beggar to evangelist. Apart from describing his father's origins and describing himself as a 'Street Arab', he makes little mention either of his own appearance or racial identity or that of any of the people he encountered as a child (the police, people who gave him money, neighbours, etc.). It is possible that he may have been too weak and dirty to have attracted attention to his skin tone. In the later parts of his memoir, once he had become a Sunday School teacher, he recalls that people often asked him questions about his origins and whether his father was a 'black man'. He recoiled from such questions. 'The inquiries used to unsettle my mind and make me uncomfortable, for my pride wished to draw the curtain and hide all my past life'.[7] He was known by the name Mahomet in various institutions as a child and clearly there was some recognition of his racial and religious background but in practice he shunned identification based on his father's race.

In 1866, Albert's older brother Eli was sent to a reformatory in Feltham for stealing from a little girl. A year later, their mother Ann was arrested for a street brawl and the four remaining children, including Albert, who was 11, were sent to Limehouse workhouse. At the workhouse, Albert's brother Sake Husson died of consumption. Albert vividly remembered the harsh conditions in the workhouse, living like orphans with little sympathy or kindness. They were moved to Thursford workhouse, to be closer to their mother's place of birth, and Albert was separated from his two sisters. He lived with about twenty-five other boys and followed a very regimented schedule but was permitted to meet with his sisters once a fortnight. Two years later, his uncle, William Jenkerson, a labourer, was able to remove Albert from the workhouse; he took him to Wells and then got him a job as a servant. Albert would have been 14 years old by then and worked for several families including a teacher, doctor and lawyer. When he turned 18, he moved to Lincoln and took up a job as an apprentice to a blacksmith and started to get more involved with the Church. He began to work as a lay preacher and Sunday School teacher, converting to Methodism, and continued to work as an evangelist throughout his adulthood. He also became a photographer and was probably the first British-born Indian photographer.[8] He had twelve children of his own and died in 1933. His rags to riches story is indicative of the very presence and involvement of children of empire in Victorian London and the main institutions for the poor at the time.

By the end of the nineteenth century, there were roughly 70,000 Indians in Britain within a total population of around 35 million people living in England, Scotland and Wales. The Indian population included servants and nannies, seamen—also known as lascars—who were left destitute by British shipowners, teachers, medical professionals and entertainers. One notorious entertainer was Ramo Samee, a juggler who lived in Britain from 1819 until his death in 1850. His act included swallowing a flaming sword and swallowing a handful of beads and hair which he then was able to pull out of his mouth with the beads strung on the hair. He performed at notable London theatres and was feted in the press and by writers like William Thackeray. One of his student disciples included a young Indian boy who started juggling in London when he was about 14 years old. The boy had run away from home at an early age in London and had started earning money by 'tumbling' (i.e. gymnastics) in the street and at fairs, before seeing Samee perform and take up juggling.[9] There were other Indian children who roamed the streets performing for pay and who were very much part of the English poor. At the same time, they fulfilled stereotypes of Indian spectacle—exotic, alien and also very much subservient.

Joseph Salter was a missionary who worked with the Strangers' Home for Asiatics, Africans and South Sea Islanders in London.

This was a Home founded in 1857, with some financial help from the Maharajah Duleep Singh, to cater for the overseas seamen who largely worked on British ships on imperial trading routes who were otherwise usually uncared for when they arrived in Britain. In Salter's account of his work with Asian sailors in London from 1873, he described the many different lascars and lascar families he met who were faced with destitution. Around 2,000 Asian lascars visited Britain each year at this time, with many embarking at shore and trying to find a life for themselves in Britain, staying in Britain temporarily if they were unable to find ship work that would offer them passage back to the subcontinent. Many lived and worked in prisons or workhouses. Salter's account includes a description of an Indian in Staines who lived with a woman and child. The child was not theirs but they had adopted it from the poorhouse having been abandoned by other 'Asiatic parents'. Sadly, this Indian man also soon abandoned the woman and child to move to Manchester.[10] Another Indian, a Hindu called Ringa Swamee, who grew up in Benares, had been brought over to England by a 'sahib' (white man) in the 1850s. His master had died and Ringa Swamee had become helpless, resorting to begging in the streets and life in and out of prison. He had an English wife and they had a daughter.[11] Children were being born and raised by former Indian sailors across Britain—in England and Scotland—across the nineteenth century. Many lived in poor conditions and it may be that if there were subsequent generations their links to Asian heritage has been lost. We will encounter more of these children in Chapter 8.

* * *

The poverty and subservience of South Asian children in Victorian Britain needs further attention, from the street sellers and sailors' children described, to those who worked in domestic servitude. Young Indian boys were often used as domestic servants in Britain and had been brought over from at least the seventeenth century. We know about some of these boys as they came to Britain with prominent, wealthy families who discussed them in their diaries. We also know about them through notices in newspapers looking for runaway servants. For example, in 1688 the *London Gazette* contained a notice of reward of one guinea for a 'black boy, an Indian, about 13 years old' who had run away from Lady Broomfield in Putney. In February 1795, there was a notice, with a promise of handsome reward, in the *Morning Chronicle*, about a young servant boy from Bengal called Hyder who had fled the premises and employ of Mrs Ramus of Baker Street. He had taken his livery and other clothing, which Mrs Ramus wanted the return of (along with the boy): 'The said Hyder is about 14 years of age, is about 5 ft or 5ft 6ins high, thin made, and upright, talks broken English and is pretty fluent in the Moorish language.' What did Moorish language mean in this context? Arabic or just an uninformed knowledge of Hyder's vernacular? A few months later, the *Morning Chronicle* contained another notice about a 16-year-old East Indian with a lame right foot who his owners were looking for.[12] More adverts described runaways as 'Indian Blacks', such as the advert in the *Flying Post; or, The Post Master* in July 1702, detailing the 15-year-old 'Indian black Boy with long hair', called Morat, who was wearing a brown Fustian frock, blue waistcoat and scarlet breeches, when he left his master's house in Drury Lane, Central London, and who had been spotted since in Tottenham Court Road, Hampstead and Highgate.[13] Across the nineteenth and twentieth century, 'Black' was often used as a description for all people of colour in Britain, whether they were of African descent or not, including people of South Asian descent. While the unity of 'political blackness' was helpful for antiracist campaigners in the twentieth century, in the nineteenth century this broad label epitomised the subjection of colonised people as different and 'other' without attention to specific ethnic and cultural identities and practices. It also means it is often difficult to trace children who specifically came from the Indian subcontinent as they were often categorised in institutional, colonial and public records in unclear language.

There are more. The 12-year-old East Indian called George Ganges who ran away from his master in Smithfield, London, in 1774.[14] An East Indian boy called Campbell who had run off in Edinburgh in 1775.[15] Runaway slaves and runaway servants were often reported in daily newspapers in the UK like this.[16] Where did they run away to? How many were of South Asian descent? How many were children? They would have been very conspicuous in seventeenth- or eighteenth-century Britain and there were often handsome rewards for their return. They were not just boys either. In December 1773, Lucy Strange, from the 'East Indies', came to the Foundling Hospital in London with her baby. She had been sent to England by her master to care for his child but had become pregnant on the voyage and had to return to India to her master and so left the child, Christopher Rowland, in the care of the children's home. Christopher died on 21 March 1774.[17] There were also notices when servants were found and not just in England. In 1776, a notice in Dublin reported on a runaway: an 11-year-old East Indian boy, going by the name of Thomas, who said he had lived with Captain Skinner in the Irish town of Portarlington. He was found in Great George Street in Dublin wearing a turban and coat but no shoes or stockings and the notice stated that if any gentleman could prove he was their property and pay the necessary expenses then the boy would be returned to them.[18] There were further notices for the sale of Indian servants. In 1766, an auctioneer Peter Thomson in Edinburgh was responsible for selling some mathematical instruments including a telescope and barometer. At the same time 'to be sold' was a 'handsome East Indian Black Boy' who was fifteen years old and could wait at tables.[19]

Indian child servants did not necessarily all run away but little is known of what happened after they left domestic service, if they were ever indeed able to. Did they stay in Britain or did they return to India or another country? Warren Hastings, the Governor General of India from 1775 to 1785, brought over two Indian boys, aged around thirteen or fourteen, in the 1780s. These boys were described as having 'longish faces, beautiful black eyes, fine eyebrows, sleek black hair, thin lips, fine teeth, a brownish complexion and kindly intelligent faces'. They did not speak English. William Hickey, a lawyer who had served in Calcutta, also brought back a young boy in 1779. He was called Nabob and was a 'little pet boy'. He was not much use as domestic help but had become an object of fascination for the family, who liked to 'pet' him.[20] Nabob returned to India in 1783 but following retirement Hickey brought the 13-year-old Munnoo to England in 1808 as a servant and ward. Hickey had smuggled both Nabob and Munnoo over on ships as neither were recorded on shipping logs. Munnoo converted to the Church of England in 1809 and became known as William Munnew. He married a woman called Anne in around 1813 and they had two children (Anne and William).[21] As later generations integrated into British society, marrying into white society, their racial roots became less obvious visually or through their names, like the family of Sake Dean Mahomed set out in the Introduction who adopted the surname 'Deane'. What we can take from this, though, is that young working-class and poor Indians were integral parts of Victorian urban life and their legacy may be forgotten but their roots can be found in the historical record if we care to look deeply enough.

* * *

India and Indians were exoticised throughout the Victorian era. In 1858, after the uprising of 1857, the British Crown took over formal direct rule of India from the East India Company. In 1877, the Conservative Prime Minister Benjamin Disraeli passed the Royal Titles Act, which made Queen Victoria Empress of India. The 'spectacle' of empire and its 'jewel in the crown', India, was brought home to British people through the celebrations of Queen Victoria's jubilees in 1887 and 1897 and the coronation of Edward VII in 1902. Indian princes were brought over to attend these events and expected to attend in their full regalia. The pomp of these ceremonies displayed the ways in which the Empire had made Indians subservient, as well as the huge wealth it had appropriated—evident to all in the centrepiece of the Koh-i-noor diamond in the crown jewels: a diamond that had been taken from the child prince Maharajah Duleep Singh when the British annexed the Punjab in 1850 and that was proudly presented as part of the 1851 Great Exhibition in London.

Queen Victoria formed her own collection of Indian children whom she took special interest in, from the Maharajah Duleep Singh to Princess Gouramma, when their families were deposed from Indian princely rule by the British. Princess Gouramma was the daughter of the Raja of Coorg, Chikka Veerarajendra, who had been deposed in 1834. In 1852, he arranged for eleven-year-old Gouramma to be taken to England, wishing for her to live under Queen Victoria's guardianship. In June, Gouramma was christened at Buckingham Palace and given the name Victoria. Miles Taylor has described these young Indians as Victoria and Albert's 'Indian exhibits'.[22] The Queen also took interest in the young Sarah Forbes Bonetta from Nigeria, who she met for the first time in 1850 when Sarah was seven and Albert Victor Pomare from New Zealand, who was born in 1863 and to whom Queen Victoria was godmother.

At the same time, several exhibitions were held which were put on to display and emphasise the wealth and trade of the British Empire. At these exhibitions, alongside goods, wares, paintings and displays, Indian people, including Indian children, were brought over specifically to be used as exhibits. The children were put on display, often performing some kind of artisanal task associated with Indian industries, for audiences to observe, watch, gawk at and feel superior to. The most prominent of these was the 1886 Colonial and Indian Exhibition which was held in South Kensington in London and had a large focus on India. The exhibition was opened by Queen Victoria in May 1886, lasting for five months and attracting roughly 5.5 million visitors. The Indian Court was adorned with large gateways, such as the Jaipur Gate, paid for by the Maharaja of Jaipur. Within the exhibition, goods like silks were displayed but alongside them were thirty-four Indian men and boys who had been brought over to London as 'artisans'. The artisans were actually recruited from Central Jail in Agra where they were inmates. They were put to work as artisans as part of a living anthropological display for visitors to observe 'natives' at work. The two youngest, Ramphal and Ramlal, were only nine years old. They were carpet weavers.[23]

In early July 1886, Queen Victoria invited the Indian artisans to Windsor Castle for lunch with the other people on display at the exhibition from Australia, Ceylon, British Guiana, Hong Kong and the Cape of Good Hope. They were accompanied by Dr John William Tyler, the superintendent of the Agra Central Jail, who read out a statement from the group to Queen Victoria. It began: 'We are thy children, O mother!'[24] I draw attention to this because Indians were so often in this period depicted as childlike, even if they were adults. This was partly related to the idea that they were backward and needed educating in British values. India was invariably depicted as a childlike region, the colony that the motherland (or fatherland), usually depicted by mother Britannia, had to look after, civilise, educate and nurture into becoming an adult, civilised, modern nation. This is worth reflecting upon as the adult Indians were depicted as childlike so that the actual 'children' almost did not register as novel or worthy of care. Indian children in these stereotypes were immaterial and not equated with ideas about British children or childrearing. Indian children were not expected to engage in play with dolls or toys in the same way that British children were. Their difference was marked by their race and ethnicity, and their childlike status was intimately entwined with Orientalist ideas of India.

Rudolf Swodoba, an Austrian painter, was commissioned to paint five portraits of the Indians from the exhibition for the Queen. They included one of young Ramlal in his turban. That portrait remains in the royal collections and is indicative of how images of children were manipulated. Ramlal is painted wearing a turban and looking down in sadness. He is presented as a type—a model of an Indian skilled labourer.[25] There is no acknowledgement of his origins, his young age or the way in which he was brought to Britain without any say merely to be put on display like a performing zoo animal. What is important here is that Indian children were being deliberately used and brought to Britain to extend and entrench imperial stereotypes. They were young spectacles who could be gawped at, pitied, patronised and studied in person on British soil and not merely as distant ideas. Bringing these colonised children to Britain could make British people feel superior about their empire but very little individual care was afforded to these young colonial subjects.

The Hungarian dancer, choreographer and producer Imre Kiralfy was the architect of the Empire of India Exhibition that opened the Earl's Court Exhibition Grounds in London in 1895. One of the highlights was 'India: A Grand Historical Spectacle', written and directed by Kiralfy and performed in the Empress Theatre. The spectacle opened in July and presented the history of India, from 1024 to the then-present day, in dance, mime and songs. The spectacle ran again in 1896 when Kiralfy revised the exhibition as the 'India and Ceylon Exhibition'. It was expanded to now include Ceylon (Sri Lanka), Burma and Borneo, and brought over craftsmen, 'native villagers' and a team of Burmese football players.[26]

On 17 September 1896, a baby was born to one of the artisan performers in the exhibition—a lacemaker. The father of the baby was not in Britain. Some press reports described him as Indian, others as Ceylonese. The mother, Caroline Hami, was from Galle in present day South-West Sri Lanka. The baby was described in press reports and advertisements as 'Cingalese', i.e. Sinhalese Sri Lankan. The girl was named London, after her birthplace. Following her birth, London Hami was incorporated into the exhibition as an exhibit in her own right. A Buddhist 'baptism' ceremony for the baby was arranged with tickets sold to spectators for sixpence a head.

A curiosity and spectacle and only a new-born baby. Thousands of people attended the Buddhist christening. *The Illustrated Police News* described the public Buddhist naming ceremony in detail, describing it as a 'strange ceremony' and also described London as a 'little mahogany-coloured infant'. A square of 'Oriental carpet' adorned an altar. A Buddhist priest recited Sanskrit invocations described as 'weird chants' and flowers were scattered over mother and child, followed by songs and dancing.[27] The *Lloyds' Weekly Newspaper* described her as 'dusky' and the dances as both 'grotesque and clever'.[28]

The *Morning Post* newspaper pointed out an important and relevant coincidence—on the same day as the naming ceremony, members of the Church Missionary Society gathered in Exeter Hall in London to say farewell to their missionaries who were departing for India and Ceylon.[29] This was the crux of empire. These South Asians were spectacles, oddities, curiosities and exhibits. They were performers of the alien and the Orient. The strange and otherworldly but also the traditional and backward, the subjects of an empire that missionaries and politicians were keen to 'civilise' and draw under Christian and British control. The Indian, Burmese and Ceylonese artisans and performers at the exhibition were taken to Windsor Castle to meet Queen Victoria on Tuesday 21 July 1896. The baby was presented to the Queen and press reports claimed that the baby 'salaamed' at the Queen. 'What a dear little thing!', the Queen said in response.[30]

There were other exhibitions and other opportunities to objectify Asian babies. The Ideal Home Exhibition held in Olympia in West London in 1910 was not just about furnishings and decor, although it did include exhibits on how to decorate a nursery, but also included a baby exhibition with real-life babies on display all day and throughout the exhibition. A creche and 'Oriental' nursery was set up to include babies from Britain and all over the world— including two babies from India and babies from Jamaica, China and Zanzibar as well as Europe. Cared for by Indian and Chinese ayahs and amahs as well as British nannies, the babies were all dressed in national costume and their ages ranged from two months to three years.[31] The baby exhibition was sponsored by Virol, a malt extract and bone marrow supplement, that was designed as a nutritional supplement for infants by Bovril as a competitor to Horlicks. The company wished to demonstrate the worldwide use of Virol and in doing so were willing to use babies as living adverts rather than just two-dimensional images.[32] It was also seen as a unique opportunity for the British mothers attending the exhibition to see how babies around the world were being brought up.[33]

The Babyland exhibition was repeated at Olympia in 1912. Once again sponsored by Virol, for three weeks 100 children were exhibited and made to come in turn for a couple of hours to play with toys while visitors gawped at them. The international babies were put up in three houses in Olympia, and came from India again, as well as Egypt, China, Japan and across Europe. Dressed in 'native' costumes, they were expected to conform to racial stereotypes. The *Pall Mall Gazette* described them as 'dark kiddies from the tropics, all with strongly marked racial types'.[34] The language demonstrates how they were objectified and racialised. The practice of displaying young Indians may have happened elsewhere. The Festival of Empire in Crystal Palace in London in 1911 appeared to have an Indian woman and child on display according to postcard photos.[35]

* * *

When considering these Victorian stereotypes of South Asian children, it is also worth drawing attention to the stereotype of the mystical East. Spiritualism was extremely popular in Victorian Britain, from the use of mediums to the attraction to Buddhist and Hindu philosophies. The stereotype of the mystical Indian was seen in novels such as Wilkie Collins' *The Moonstone* (1868) and the public's fascination with figures and 'gurus' such as Swami Vivekananda, who toured Britain from 1895 to 1896, and extended to the projection of mystical abilities onto Indian children. This was seen primarily through the Theosophical Society. Founded in 1875 by the Russian Madam Blavatsky, theosophy combined several philosophical traditions, including elements of Buddhism and Hinduism, and was based on an idea of brotherhood but also the search for hidden 'Mahatmas'. It offered an alternative to mainstream prescriptive religious traditions and seemed accessible to Western audiences because of its international reach, character and leadership. At its peak in the late 1920s, the Theosophical Society had a membership of 45,000.[36]

A prominent member of the Theosophical Society in the 1890s was Charles Webster Leadbeater, who lived in Ceylon from 1886 to 1889 looking for the reincarnation of his murdered younger brother, Gerald. He found a thirteen-year-old, Curuppumullage Jinarajadasa, whom he took to England in November 1889. In 1895, they moved in with the socialist and women's rights campaigner (and Theosophist) Annie Besant in London, and Jinarajadasa enrolled at Cambridge University. Jinarajadasa later became a president of the Theosophical Society.[37] In 1913, Leadbeater discovered another young Indian, Rajagopal Desikacharya, from South India, who was also brought to England and went to Cambridge, and later became another prominent Theosophist. Yet, the most important person Leadbeater met and sponsored was Jiddu Krishnamurti, whom he met in Adyar in April 1909. By this time, the Theosophical Society had been shaken by scandal. Leadbeater had admitted to encouraging young boys under his care to masturbate regularly (and often under Leadbeater's supervision) arguing that this ensured celibacy and spiritual growth. Although he resigned in 1906 from the Society, Besant readmitted him in 1908 and, in 1909, Leadbeater introduced

Besant to the fourteen-year-old in Madras. Leadbeater, who investigated past lives, argued that Krishnamurti had experienced numerous lives and that he was the avatar of Lord Maitreya, the World Teacher. Besant took over guardianship of Jiddu Krishnamurti and his younger brother Nitya and in 1911, when their biological father started to contest this custody, she took the young boys to London.[38]

Emily Lutyens, the wife of architect Edwin Lutyens and daughter of Edward Robert Bulwer-Lytton who served as Viceroy of India from 1876 to 1880, was part of a crowd of Theosophists who welcomed the arrival of the boys at Charing Cross Station in May 1911.[39] Emily Lutyens soon became very close to Jiddu Krishnamurti and took an increasingly prominent role in the organisation of the Society. Both brothers addressed Annie Besant as 'mother' and described themselves as her 'son[s]' in their frequent correspondence; Jiddu Krishnamurti also soon addressed Lutyens as 'dearest Mother' and 'Mummy' too.[40] Mary Lutyens, daughter of Emily and Edwin, recalls that as a child she had known that Krishnamurti was destined to become this 'World Teacher'.[41] But Krishanmurti was also brought up as an 'Englishman' with interests in activities such as motorcycles and golf. Krishnamurti had long hair, his teeth were straightened by a London dentist and he was given expensive clothing from Savile Row and Jermyn Street, shoes from Lobb, suits from Meyer & Mortimer, shirts from Beale & Inman and ties from Liberty.[42] At first, Lutyens saw them very much as 'boys', and as Besant's children, and allowed them to spend a lot of time with her five children.[43] A custody battle with their father raged on until 1914, when Besant was ultimately awarded full guardianship. Besant attempted, but failed, to get the brothers admitted into Oxford University. Instead Krishnamurti considered enlisting for the War in 1914 but Besant dissuaded him from doing so, arguing that he would be forced to eat meat.[44] Krishnamurti volunteered in a British military hospital in 1914 but was asked to leave within a month, partly, he believed, because he was Indian.[45] Despite Krishnamurti's interest in leisurely pursuits such as the theatre, cinema and motor cars, Theosophists such as Lutyens increasingly recognised a spiritual side to him and regarded him as a 'guru'.[46]

Although Krishnamurti was declared to be a World Teacher and to espouse universal brotherhood, the accounts from the Lutyens family members on his life all indicate that a clique of Theosophists, all friends of Annie Besant, surrounded and pampered him as a teenager and young adult. They 'mothered' him and indulged him. They also let him be a 'boy', one that was British, while grooming him for spiritual leadership. Unlike the Indian children brought over for exhibitions or the street sellers, he was afforded the opportunity to engage in child's play and be 'young'. But he was also objectified and exoticised. His childhood was based on a stereotype, nonetheless.

* * *

South Asian children were objectified in Victorian Britain and used to perpetuate British Orientalist ideas of the 'exotic' subcontinent in these varied ways. These children were used as imperial tools. Many were unable and unwilling to subvert these stereotypes and their colonial identities were tied into their objectification. They were exhibits of curiosity, whether put on formal display or not, but also, and importantly, most of these children were boys and coded male even if sometimes depicted as effeminate. Young South Asian girls were hardly registered in Victorian Britain unless they were princesses or babies, as they remained rooted in stereotypes that fixed them in marriage and domestic situations. While other parts of the Empire in Africa and the Caribbean were objectified in different ways, conservative and stereotypical ideas of India that included exoticisation of Indian religions, clothing and appearance, and that underpinned the imperial mission, were apparent in the ways in which Indian children were treated in this period.

Indian children were key figures in Victorian culture, though, even if they were often hidden in the historical record, from Queen Victoria's favourites and the exhibitions to the runaway servants and poor beggar children in London's urban slums. The imperial stereotypes of infantile Indians that had encouraged British men and women to colonise the subcontinent were brought home to the streets of Britain through these (mainly male) child migrants, in an earlier period than many may have imagined. They were entertainers, in all senses of the word, and an integral part of the Victorian poor and British society, especially in London. The casting of Dev Patel as Charles Dickens' David Copperfield was not an anomaly but representative of the hidden presences of Indian children in Victorian Britain and the ways in which they have left their imperial footprints on British history.

3

THE YOUNG BROWN ENGLISHMEN

The term 'coconut' is a slang term that has come in use from post-war Britain and elsewhere to describe someone who is 'brown on the outside and white on the inside'. For example, someone who might look South Asian because of their skin colour but who socialised, acted like and had the sensibilities of a 'white' person. In my own childhood—in London in the 1990s—it was a common term that was perhaps used with the (misguided) intention of being affectionate but sometimes with more intent to harm. In November 2023, a teacher of South Asian heritage, who marched in solidarity with the Palestine cause in London, was targeted for her placard which depicted the then-Prime Minister Rishi Sunak and Home Minister Suella Braverman as coconuts. She was acquitted in September 2024 of a racially aggravated public offence order at Westminster Magistrates Court following a discussion about whether 'coconut' was a racially abusive term. During the court case, and in British media discourses around the trial, commentators and academics including Gus John, Gargi Bhattacharyya and Kehinde Andrews, explained that the term was not a racial slur but derived from the experiences of colonialism, a term that emerged as a way of critiquing those who 'collaborated with our oppressors', as Nels Abbey put it.[1] If we look back to colonial history, including the history I am recounting here of South Asian child migrants to Britain, we can see the roots of the term 'coconut', although different expressions were historically used, such as 'collaborator', 'mimic', and more recently 'Bounty' (after the chocolate bar). The British Empire had relied on people of colour believing and behaving as though they were socially equal to the white colonisers—as Indians were needed to work in the colonial administration and uphold the day to day running of empire on the ground—even though the ideology of racial hierarchies and pseudo-scientific ideas about the innate difference of 'races' were pivotal to underpinning the mission of empire.

On 2 February 1835, Thomas Babington Macaulay, the law member for the governing Supreme Council of India, wrote a 'Minute on Education' for Lord William Bentinck, the first Governor-General of British India. It called for and required that all higher education in India should be taught through the medium of the English language. In following his recommendations, the government set up a system that would formalise English medium schooling in India. This 'Minute' has had ongoing legacies for the use of the English language in India, as it remains one of the official languages of modern-day India. Macaulay's minute has become infamous among historians too because he explained that he wanted to create 'a class of persons Indian in blood and colour, but English in tastes, in opinions, in morals and in intellect'.[2] This was interpreted as a desire to create a class of 'Brown Englishmen', a phrase used since to gloss Macauley's argument.[3] The proliferation of English education in India in the nineteenth century meant that educated Indians became well versed in British history, geography and English literature as they were taught these subjects in schools instead of Indian history or geography. They became very familiar with British ideas and felt 'British', even if they did not visit Britain. Many elite Indians soon decided that they should send their children to Britain for schooling—like the white British children who were being sent 'home'—for the best type of English education. Their deliberate intention was to mould their children into 'Brown Englishmen' in order to succeed within the imperial structures in India and they had very little desire to overthrow the institutions that would allow them to socially climb. An elite class of Anglophile Indians known as 'collaborators' to the Empire were moulded through their childhoods in Britain. Some may describe them as 'coconuts'; their education and cultural influences in Britain certainly made them willing allies to the British imperial state throughout their life.

In the nineteenth century, there was a rise in young, privileged Indian children attending British boarding schools in attempts to ingratiate themselves within British society. Many of their journeys and trajectories followed similar lines to the 'white Indians' I discussed in the first chapter, although others had more ignominious lives. Among these, of course, were the two Duleep Singh brothers, the surviving sons of the Maharajah Duleep Singh. The eldest, Victor Duleep Singh, who was born in 1866, was a keen member of the boat club and the musical society at Eton College in Windsor.[4] His younger brother, Frederick, born in 1868, was also admitted to Eton. The boys were notorious at Eton College because of their princely background and royal connections. Apparently one of the brothers even introduced betting to the school, although it was not a pastime that was necessarily welcomed by all.[5] In March 1882, the pupils at Eton College visited Windsor Castle and Queen Victoria to present an address; the Queen specifically asked for the Duleep Singh brothers to be presented to her, well known to her and 'favourites' of hers as they were.[6] The brothers went on to live highly anglicised lives in Britain and were particularly engaged in high society and shooting. Victor married Lady Anne Coventry, although he died in 1918 following bankruptcy. Frederick became an amateur archaeologist and historian; he was immensely loyal to the royal family and never visited India. They were remembered fondly at Eton and a small memorial garden was planted in memory of Victor and Frederick Duleep Singh. A plaque listing the subscribers to the memorial had at least fifty-eight names. And so, they made their mark on the most elite elements of British society and were fully 'Brown Englishmen'.

Other Indian children in Britain in this period came from princely and aristocratic backgrounds like Raj Rajendra, known as Rajey, the son of Nripendra (the prince of Cooch Behar) and Sunity Devi. He was born on 11 April 1882 and in 1894 was sent to Mr Carter's Prep School in Farnborough with the hope he would be brought up as an 'ordinary boy' and not an Indian prince; he spent his holidays, however, with Prince Arthur of Connaught and other members of the British royal family. In 1897, he was admitted to Eton College like the Duleep Singh brothers. Contemporaries of Rajey at Eton included Nawab Wali ud Deen, who was the Nawab Mir Ekhram Hussain of Hyderabad and Kumar Shri Jareja, the Yuvraj of Gondal, Kathiawar, who all wore their 'gorgeous native dress' at the College celebrations for the Queen's Jubilee in 1897, which Queen Victoria herself attended. Rajey was a popular pupil at Eton and matriculated at Oxford in 1900. Despite the privileges he enjoyed in Britain, Rajey did not have the opportunity to learn other Indian languages that could help his princely reign and suffered with alcoholism, dying in 1913.[7]

Prince Wasif Ali Mirza (b. 7 January 1875) and Prince Nasir Ali Mirza (b. 15 March 1876) were the sons of Nawab Sir Sayyid Hassan Ali Mirza Khan Bahadur of Murshidabad, Bengal and Amir Dulhan Kulsum un-Nisa Begum Sahiba. On 30 June 1887, for the purpose of their being educated in England, the two princes were made wards of the Reverend John Jefferies Bartlett Coles (1848–1935), Principal of Doveton College, Calcutta. A contract had been signed to this effect by the Nawab that stipulated that Coles should find a furnished house in Sherborne and arrange their tutoring and school admissions with the ultimate aim that the eldest should attend Oxford. The boys would be allowed to play sports without any liability faced by Coles for injuries and he should ensure that any meat served was halal. Coles was to provide monthly reports and yearly photographs. In July 1887, the two princes travelled with Coles from Bombay to England on the Peninsular & Oriental steamer *Nizam*.[8] They attended Sherborne Preparatory School in Dorset as day boys from 22 September 1887 to 1890, then under the Headmaster William Heitland Blake. In April 1890, Prince Wasif Ali Mirza came second in the Prep School Flat Race 100 yards and the school magazine noted that the 'presence of the two Indian Nawabs excited more than usual interest'.[9]

On 29 September 1887, Coles moved into a leased house in Sherborne as planned. It is probable that the Coles originally intended that the princes would later move up to Sherborne School but, in November 1889, a libel case (Malan v. Young), in which the Rev.

Coles was cited, was brought against the headmaster, the Rev. E.M. Young, by one of his masters. As a consequence, the princes attended Rugby School instead from 1890 to 1892. In 1891, the princes (aged 15 and 16) were living with Mr and Mrs Coles at Crescent House, Horton Crescent, Rugby. They subsequently studied at Trinity College, Oxford and on 27 October 1895, they both returned to Murshidabad. Prince Wasif represented Bengal at the coronation of King Edward VII and Queen Alexandra at Westminster Abbey on 9 August 1902, the 1903 Delhi Durbar and also the coronation of King George V and Queen Mary in 1911. On the death of their father on 25 December 1906, Prince Wasif Ali Mirza succeeded Hassan Ali Mirza as Amir ul-Omrah, His Highness the Nawab Bahadur of Murshidabad (1906–1959).[10] While the East India Company had, often violently, annexed and taken over the rule of princely states in India and incorporated them into British India, including infamously the Punjab, after 1858 the British Crown formalised its rule and stopped annexing any further princely states. Instead, the Crown demanded loyalty of Indian princes and cooperation through new administrative arrangements while Indian royal families were able to enjoy the privileges of their titles and a degree of autonomy. The strong loyalty of Indian princely families to the Empire was strengthened in this period through the travel and education of their children in Britain.

* * *

Other non-royal children excelled and developed as part of British cultural life without aristocratic ties. Manmohan Ghose was born in 1869 in Bengal and became good friends with Laurence Binyon at St Paul's School in London, which he began attending in 1884. At school, Binyon had been enchanted with the exoticism of Ghose as well as his recitations of Shakespeare. Binyon would later become a poet and dramatist who worked at the British Museum in London. The pair were childhood friends, bonding over their mutual interest in the Classics and poetry—with Binyon remembering that Ghose was better read than him and perhaps attracted to literatures that were different from his 'traditions'.[11] But Ghose's interest in the

Classics came from his earlier education at Manchester Grammar School and his early childhood in the home of Reverend William H. Drewett in Manchester. Manmohan and his brothers, Benoybhusan and Aravinda—the latter best-known for becoming a spiritual leader famously known as Sri Aurobindo—had been brought to England in 1879 by their father, a medical doctor, Krishna Dhan Ghose. In the 1881 Census, we find that Benoy, Manmohan and Aravinda were boarders at the house of Drewett in Chorlton-upon-Medlock, taking up residence alongside Drewett's wife, mother and sister-in-law (who was an English teacher). Benoy was 13, Manmohan 12 and Aravinda 8. It is worth noting that they had a younger sister, Sarojini, who was four years younger than Aravinda and not educated in England. She was brought over in 1879 as part of the family visit but then returned to India with her parents. William Drewett, the minister of Stockport Road Congregational Church in Ardwick, was a friend of their father and he tutored the boys in Classics and English literature. Krishna had given Drewett strict instructions that the boys should not eat Indian food or have any Indian influences while in England and they were encouraged to become English in taste and manners.[12]

In 1881, Manmohan and Benoy were both admitted to Manchester Grammar School, likely the first Indian pupils at the school, whilst seven-year-old Aurobindo was tutored by the Drewetts. Manmohan excelled academically at Manchester Grammar and was top of his class in Latin, Divinity and English in his first year. He wrote a poem, 'The Blindness of Love', which featured in the school magazine, *Ulula*.[13] Aurobindo was a keen poet as a child too and produced a poem entitled 'Light' which was published in the *Fox Family Magazine* in 1883.[14] In 1884, William Drewett and his wife emigrated to Australia and so his mother, Elizabeth, took over care of the Ghose brothers and moved with them to London. Both Manmohan and Aurobindo won scholarships to St Paul's School.

Following school, Manmohan attended Oxford and then entered a career in education in India, while Aurobindo went to Cambridge and joined the Indian Civil Service before taking up a spiritual career. In 1911, Benoy was back in London as secretary to the Maharajah of Cooch Behar and continued a career in service for the Cooch Behar State until his death in 1947. Manmohan spent fifteen years in education in England and later told his close friend Binyon that he was 'four-fifths an Englishman, if not entirely one'.[15] Binyon agreed with this assessment in a letter to his friend, the poet Arthur Symonds, in 1890, remarking that Ghose only knew English and described him as English 'in everything but birth' although '"Oriental" in temperament'.[16] Manmohan only wrote poetry in English, rather than Bengali, and his literary inclinations were predominantly Western-influenced. He was the epitome of the 'Brown Englishman' that Macaulay had sought to create. As a child, he experienced a strong sense of isolation from his mother, who he did not see again because she died in India before his return. He later recalled that when he did return to India, he felt 'denationalized' because of his 'purely English upbringing'.[17] While their father had absolutely encouraged this English upbringing, it is clear that it created psychological and spiritual tensions for Manmohun and Aurobindo upon their return to India.

Womesh Chunder Bonnerjee was another prominent and highly anglicised upper-class Bengali who spent time in Britain. His father had converted to Christianity in 1847 and Bonnerjee, who was born in 1844, also broke away from his Hindu heritage. Brought up in Calcutta, he perfected his English by reading aloud every night. He married Hemangini in 1859 and following a few years working as a law clerk in Calcutta, Bonnerjee travelled to London to develop his legal education. He joined Middle Temple in 1864 and was called to the Bar in 1868. He made many friends in England and became determined that his children should be educated there from as early as possible to get the full breadth of an English education, learn English fluently from infancy and imbibe English ways and values.[18] He felt that the higher education that he had received in England was not enough for this. As Bonnerjee was now working as a barrister in Calcutta, he could not give up his profession or income but sent his wife and their three young children to England in 1874 to be looked after by Colonel Wood and his family, a retired army man who Bonnerjee had been introduced to through a solicitor friend. They had three children at the time: their son Kamilkrishna (Shelley) was 4 and their daughters Nalini (Nellie) and Susila (Susie) nearly 3 and 18 months-old respectively.

Unfortunately, Hemangini and the children did not get on with the Woods, who lived in Anerley in South London. Woods harboured racial prejudices and had only taken in the family for the money. He made it quite clear that he thought they were 'natives' and beneath his family. The Woods children were particularly cruel to the Bonnerjee family. Hemangini did not realise she was pregnant when she made the journey to England but in December 1874 gave birth to another son, Kalikrishna Wood Bonnerjee. In the autumn of 1875, Womesh sailed to England to bring Hemangini, Susila and Kali back to India, while the older children, Shelley and Nellie, were left with the Woods and their governess. Nellie was very young and did not realise that her mother was leaving her behind for a long time but in later memoirs recalled how the Woods abused her by locking her up in cupboards and using other physical punishments. She was made very aware that the Woods thought her siblings were inferior and dirty because of the colour of their skin. This was hardly the upbringing in English life that their father would have aspired to.[19] Despite this cruelty, the Bonnerjee children persevered with the Woods. In 1877, their parents returned to bring Susie for an English education. Susie seemed to get on much better with the Woods children.

In 1884, the Woods moved to Croydon, not far from Anerley, in South London and Nellie was enrolled in Croydon High School for Girls. The Bonnerjees also decided that Hemangini should settle in England with the growing brood of children being educated there and so, in 1888, she took up a house in Croydon with her nine children. Her eldest Shelley was now at Oxford; Nellie and Susie—both from the age of thirteen—and Pramila (Millie)—when she turned six or seven—attended Croydon High School for Girls; Kali and Kitty were taught by a tutor; Teenie was in kindergarten; and the youngest, Janaki and Fanny, were with Hemangini. Janaki also later joined Croydon High School when she was six or seven. Their house had a large garden and was near the high school and East Croydon Station.[20] It was a large three-storied house with ten bedrooms that included a tradesmen's entrance and a stable building, although the family did not keep horses. They were keeping up in a wealthy suburb and now had the luxury to engage in English pursuits without the constraints of the Woods family. Hemangini, who had very little education, was distant from her older children who she had little contact with and who had little in common with her, largely because education and Englishness had become somewhat of a fetish for them; they remembered little of Indian life. Janaki, who wrote a memoir in 1935, described her elder siblings as a 'race apart' from her mother and, indeed, they probably felt they were English despite all the trials of their upbringings with the Woods.[21]

Shelley and Kali's education at Rugby School epitomised their very English upbringing. Shelley joined Rugby in 1883 and Kali in 1889, while their younger brother, Ratnakrishna Curran (Teenie), joined in 1898. Shelley was very bright, a keen member of the debating society and was promoted to the sixth form as soon as he turned sixteen but got involved with drinking and gambling. He was threatened with expulsion, along with his classmates, but Hemangini managed to successfully appeal against it.[22] His Rugby connections remained important as he was a regular attendee at Old Rugbeian dinners in Calcutta once he had returned as a barrister.[23] When Ratnakrishna was at Rugby, he was also a keen member of the debating and chess clubs, even engaging in a debate in 1901 arguing that Rudyard Kipling was an overrated author.[24]

Janaki's account of her childhood emphasises the friendships she had with a whole host of her white British peers at school—children with the names of Janet, Lillian, Birdie and Aimee—which she started to attend at the age of seven. Although their father still lived and worked in India, Janaki's recollections reveal how typically English her childhood was.[25] This was a life of frocks, of teas, of school, of Church, of play and leisurely pursuits. Her sister, Pramila, for example, won an honourable mention and medal for a 'picture story wanting words' competition in a magazine called *Little Folks: The Magazine for Boys and Girls* when she was sixteen.[26] This was not the life of the colonies but the life of the metropole.

Despite the racism the older children faced from the Woods, the Bonnerjee children had little engagement with the politics of empire or nationalism or further contemplations on their own race. W. C. Bonnerjee though was one of the founding members of the Indian National Congress (INC) in 1885, the organisation that would eventually lead the fight for Indian nationalism. In 1885, it was a moderate organisation founded by a group of Indian, British and Irish men that included Bonnerjee, Badruddin Tyabji and Pherozeshah Mehta who had all studied law in London. Their aims were to lobby for more representation for Indians within imperial politics and they had no initial ambitions to dismantle the Empire. Bonnerjee was closely involved in the law and politics in Bengal but this did not seem to immediately influence his children. Janaki did marry a Bengali man, Prio Kumar Majumdar, who studied at Birmingham and was called to the Bar and they returned to India where her husband was moderately involved in politics. Christianity though was a key part of their lives with the Woods and then with Hemangini, who was part of the Plymouth Brethren, as the Woods were. Sunday morning services for the Brethren took place at the 'Iron Room'. Susie and Janaki later became baptised into the Church of England when they reached adulthood, rejecting the Brethren. Sundays for the Bonnerjees centred around trips to the cemetery to visit Kitty's grave—he died in 1890 at the age of 11 from pneumonia—and hymns but also socialising with other Indians (not necessarily Christian) who lived in London. Hemangini cooked Bengali food at home, which their English domestic servants also enjoyed, and so the Bonnerjee children lived a cosmopolitan life with influences of Bengali cuisine and culture alongside more dominant British and Christian experiences from the Woods, their schools and the long time they had spent living in London.[27] They were 'Brown Englishmen'—English in taste and values and yet, of course, still visibly brown with Indian cultural roots.

It is interesting then that Shelley's son, Kew Edwin, who was born in 1894, should change his surname from Bonnerjee to Shelley by deed poll in 1921, the year after he was called to the Bar. Surely this was the ultimate act of anglicisation? Shelley Bonnerjee had married Gertrude Eliza Johnson, the daughter of a professor, in 1893, the year he was called to the Bar. Kew was born in the UK but then spent a few years in India with his family before they returned in 1902. He attended Croydon High School for Boys and then went to Rugby in 1908, as his father had done, where he was a scholar, member of the debating society and sports captain.[28] In a report praising his shooting at Rugby in 1910, Kew was described as an 'Indian lad' and the first Indian to compete in the Public School shooting competition at Bisley.[29] He was very close to his grandmother Hemangini but, as stated, shed his Bengali surname in his adulthood. Kew later helped John Logie Baird form a new television company in 1944 and later became co-executor of his estate.

There are other children with anglicised lives connected to the Bonnerjees. Janaki's husband, Prio Kumar Majumdar, studied at the Bar in London from 1904 to 1907 and stayed at the boarding house of Ida Dutt. Ida Dutt's own life and family are extremely interesting and give us an insight into the varied lives of Indian children brought up in England at the turn of the century. Ida Dutt's father, Khetter Mohun Dutt, had married Ellen Anne Joy at the Holy Trinity Parish Church in Haverstock Hill, North London on 29 June 1866.[30] He was 26 and she was 20 and they were married in front of Ellen's parents. He was a medical man and the son of a gentleman; she was a spinster and the daughter of a clerk. They had six children together—Mabel Rani, Ida Shakuntala, Newton Mohun, Leila Juanita, Muriel Edith and Khetterina Marion. Khetter Mohun Dutt was a graduate of the Calcutta Medical College but it is unclear what profession he took up in London. He was described as a professor of languages on the baptism records for Ida in 1869, Leila in 1876 and Muriel in 1878.[31]

In 1870, newspaper reports revealed that Ellen had been admitted into a 'lunatic asylum' following domestic abuse from her husband. In March 1870, Dutt was tried at Marylebone police court for assault on his wife following a long history of abuse, but the case was dismissed. Dutt then applied, unsuccessfully, for custody of his children. Outside the court, Dutt assaulted the solicitor who had opposed his custody application and who had criticised him for abusing his wife. In September 1870, Dutt was brought to court again, this time the Clerkenwell police court, for assault on the solicitor, Thomas Braithwaite. Dutt was ordered to pay a fine and a bond to keep the peace for another six months.[32] An eyewitness to the fight wrote a letter to the *Morning Advertiser* to express their disgust about the leniency of Dutt's punishment. This eyewitness mentioned that at the earlier case in March, other Indian witnesses were called to attest to Dutt's poor character and that Dutt had assaulted one of those witnesses outside the court but they had not brought charges. The eyewitness, perhaps Dutt's father-in-law, told the paper that the judge had been too lenient on Dutt who had been excused because of his race. However, this letter-writer was keen to point out that 'Bengalis are educated from their childhood in the English language and understand English law as well as Englishmen, or better'. The writer also described Bengalis, in the words of Lord Macaulay, as 'feeble' and deceitful. Noting that the number of Bengalis in London was rising—perhaps an observation purely based upon their personal experience rather than particularly based on fact—the writer warned magistrates not to be fooled by their foreignness and to be vigorous in protecting against further assaults on women and children.[33]

In the 1871 Census, we see that Dutt was living with his three children (Mabel, Ida and Newton) and two servant nursemaids in Paddington without his wife. He died at the age of 40 in 1879 in London and by 1881, following Dutt's death, Ellen was reunited with all six children and living in Hackney, alongside her widower father, where she soon became a boarding-housekeeper.[34] In the 1891 Census, their fifth child Muriel was living as a 'scholar' at the Infant Orphan Asylum in Wanstead, Essex, at the age of 12. The Infant Orphan Asylum was charitably funded and accommodated children who were 'respectably descended' and could be admitted if just their father was deceased, until they were 15 years old. It is not clear if Muriel's other siblings spent time at the Asylum in their childhood as well. However, the lives of the Dutt children were not plain sailing. In April 1912, Leila was admitted to the London Bethlehem Hospital for 'mania'. She was 34 years old and had been living with her sisters in Finchley, North London. She had delusions about Christ and of her brother-in-law being burned at sea. She had run away from a previous nursing home and doctor's notes described her as 'excited' and a 'dark-skinned girl'. At one point during her stay, she had to be put in a padded room and her behaviour was volatile but she was discharged in March 1913.[35]

There was further press interest in this family when some of the sisters got married. In 1899, the youngest sibling, Khetterina Dutt, qualified as a woman clerk in the Post Office, following in the steps of her grandfather.[36] She married Lieutenant Abdus Sattar Khan from the Indian Medical Service in London on 5 January 1909 and the wedding reception was held at Westminster Palace Hotel where the Roy children were among the attendees (whom we will see more of later).[37] Meanwhile, Ida Shakuntala Dutt had married Mahimohun Ghose on 22 June 1908. He was the son of a barrister, Manomohan Ghose from Calcutta and had, like his similar namesake, been educated at Balliol College, Oxford, before becoming a member of the Madras Civil Service. At the time of her marriage, it was noted that Ida had a deceased father and was part of a family of boarding housekeepers in Hackney. There was ongoing press interest in the marriages of Indians who had spent much of their childhood in Britain. Badruddin Tyabji, one of the founding members of the INC alongside W. C. Bonnerjee, sent two of his daughters to boarding school in Haslemere in 1904. Tyabji himself had been sent to England at the age of sixteen to study at Highbury New Park College in London, where he excelled at French, Latin and elocution. One of his daughters, Nasima Tyabji, married Alma Latifi in London in August 1908 in a Muslim ceremony. As their marriage took place very soon after Ida's, it was reported at the same time, where it was noted that Nasima had by 'her long residence and education in England acquired a thorough knowledge of English.'[38]

To return to the Dutts, Khetter's only son, Newton, died in 1935 in Golders Green and was buried in Hampstead Cemetery alongside his mother.[39] He had been in India and returned in 1934 to live with his sisters Mrs Palit, Mrs Ghose and the Misses Dutts. He was involved in the development of the modern library movement in India as State Librarian of Baroda and reader to the Maharajah Gaekwar of Baroda from 1914 to 1931. He had several years' experience before this with the publishers Cassell's, George Philip and Son, Kegan Paul, Trubner and Co., George Newnes and Harper and Brothers and was the author of several books.[40] In 1939, Ida Ghose (née Dutt) was living at a farm in Llandeilo, Wales, as a widow with her unmarried sister Muriel and her son Joy Manny Mohun Ghose, who was born on 22 July 1909, and had been described in the 1939 Register as 'mentally deficient'. The register describes both sisters without jobs and professions. Mabel died in 1943, leaving all her possessions in her will to her sister Ida; Khetterina was to pass away in London in 1945; Joy Manny Mohun Ghose in 1951 and Ida and Leila both in North London in 1952. When Muriel died in 1956 in North London, her will and effects of £1582 were distributed to two women: Gertrude Beatrice Bovington and Margaret Ellen Staddon. A sad turn of events for a beleaguered family who, despite their anglicisation, did not have access to the privileges and support that elite Indian children enjoyed. Their lives help to reveal the different ways anglicised Indian children lived and loved in colonial Britain.

* * *

In 1892, Dadabhai Naoroji, another of the founding members of the INC, was elected as Liberal MP for Central Finsbury, in London. He had travelled to England in 1865 with his wife, mother, son Ardeshir (b. 1858) and daughter Shirin, who had just been born before their arrival. They lived in Hornsey Rise in North London. A businessman with a keen interest in economics, Naoroji was appointed professor of Gujarati at University College London and became settled into London life, establishing numerous associations and connections between British and Indian people. In 1886, he was unsuccessful in contesting the seat of Holborn on the Liberal ticket and the Conservative Prime Minister Lord Salisbury remarked that the British electorate was not ready to elect a 'blackman'. Naoroji's victory in 1892 was part of an election landslide for W. E. Gladstone but Naoroji only won by five votes. Following his success, some media commentators were keen to address Salisbury's comments while also pointing out that Naoroji had incredibly pale skin (he came from a Zoroastrian background in Bombay).[41]

Naoroji was an extremely prominent member of British society, highly integrated into English ways although also loyal to Indian interests, but beyond his political career, little is said about his children. Ardeshir and Shirin had a younger sister, Maki, born in 1868 in Bombay, by which time it appears the children had returned to India with their mother while Naoroji pursued his interests in London alone. However, there is an eleven-year-old child called

'Ardeshir Dadabhai' who was living with Naoroji in South Kensington according to the 1871 Census. The children were transient and difficult to trace in London, although Maki later trained in England as a doctor. What is particularly interesting is that one of their English servants named her own children after them, calling her children Ardeshir and Shirin.[42] In 1901, the census also reveals a Jae Ardeshir Dadabhai Naoroji, born in Mandvi, Cutch, in India, who was a fifteen-year-old boarder pupil at Leys School, Cambridge. There was another Indian pupil at Leys School at the same time: a seventeen-year-old called Coravanda Nanjappal Muttanah.[43] While there is no clear evidence that this pupil was related to Dadabhai Naoroji the elder, the names from the Naoroji family lingered in various traces across British life. We see this with Duleep Singh too. In 1865, the son of William Fernie, who worked as a ploughman at the Castle Menzies estate in Scotland, where Duleep Singh lived between 1855 and 1858, named his third child Duleep Singh Fernie after the maharajah.[44] India and Britain were, therefore, intimately intertwined through white and brown children at the heart of the Empire.

The anglicised ties and loyalties of some Indian children continued into the twentieth century. The sons from Indian princely families joined British schools throughout this period, such as Prince Nasir Ali Khan of Rampur, who was sent to England in 1894 at the age of eleven by his brother to prevent him from threatening the throne. Nasir married Dolly Parnell, an actress, in 1909, and they had a daughter, Betty, who was born in 1911.[45] A portrait of Dolly and Betty from 1918, when Betty was just seven years old, is held by the National Portrait Gallery.[46] Another example is Yeshwant Rao Holkar of Indore who was sent to Charterhouse School in 1923 at the age of fourteen. However, he felt discriminated against because of the colour of his skin, disliked the 'snobbish' nature of the school and therefore hated it and had few friends.[47] In 1926, Holkar succeeded to the throne and was known for his love of Western clothes, furnishings and cars. Meanwhile, in the 1930s, Jehan Warliker, who described himself as the Prince of Seesodia, embarked on a lecture series in America on topics related to India and yoga. In his adverts, he explained that he had been born in India but upon the death of his mother when he was six months old, he had been taken to England where he was first put under the care of an English nurse. The nurse baptised him into Christianity, without the knowledge or permission of his father. He later had a private tutor and was then admitted to Harrow School before studying at Cambridge. When he returned to India, after qualifying as a barrister, he was regarded as a polluted stranger because he had been abroad for so many years. He had an English accent, refused to embrace Hinduism and could not understand his family. Hence, he took up a life of further travelling and education before embarking on the lecture series.[48]

In subsequent chapters I will discuss the public-school lives of South Asian children in this imperial period further but it is worth emphasising the ways in which young South Asian children were being inculcated into parts of British life and culture, whether through education, religion, formal contracts or social circles. Their upbringing mirrored the white Indian children of Chapter 1 in many ways. These are unique stories of how children were at the heart of change in Britain and at the heart of the imperial endeavour. Their anglicisation and willingness to support the machines of empire were impressed upon them through their family influences and childhood. Christianity became an important route to anglicisation for some but not all.

The British Empire in India only worked because of 'collaborators', the 'Brown Englishmen', who were willing to engage with imperial structures and worked to become a part of the Empire. It needed loyal Indians to take up jobs in administration, law and education and Indian princes to willingly allow British imperial governance in return for minimal autonomy. In their anglicisation, however, many Indian children felt that they relinquished an ability to claim an Indian identity and lost ties with their families. The lengthy separation from family members did not help in this regard and has similarities with the experiences of the white children born in India who also faced similar estrangements. The British Empire would not have held strong across the nineteenth century and turn of the twentieth century without the opportunities for elite Indian children to be educated in Britain, shoring up the Empire alongside their white counterparts. The education system in Britain was central to this.

While not all families with South Asian heritage returned to India in this period, their anglicisation was important in upholding the connections between Britain and India and in encouraging British public interest in India and the Empire. Their cooperation was a necessary veneer over full understanding of the horrors of empire that affected the larger population of the subcontinent who would never have access to the kind of means and education of these privileged few. Understanding the history of these children helps us to better understand the development of imperial rule in the subcontinent and the ongoing legacies of empire for India and for Britain.

4

THE NATIONALISTS

In Britain, the public school system is notorious for its elitism and for its production of the British ruling class. Between 1721 and 2025, twenty British prime ministers have been educated at Eton, seven at Harrow and six at Westminster. Others like Tony Blair, Rishi Sunak and Clement Attlee attended independent boarding schools. British public schools were and are seen as institutions of political training for the young, designed to create 'leaders'.[1] It is embedded in their architecture, their uniform, their houses, their mottos, their prefect systems and their sports fields. Middle- and upper-class Indian parents were keen that their children should have the best educational and political opportunities if they travelled to England—otherwise why else leave India? And so, by the turn of the century, an increasing number of Indian children were attending British public schools. At least 11 Indian boys had attended Eton before 1919; at least 15 had attended Rugby before 1939; and at least 29 had attended St Paul's School before 1945.

In the university sector, Oxford and Cambridge have a similar reputation. In 2019/20, there were over 530,000 international students in the higher education sector in the United Kingdom. Over 55,000 were from India.[2] Although the UK remains a popular destination for students from India, as well as Pakistan and Bangladesh, in the early twenty-first century their travels have been hampered by increasingly hostile visa regulations and costs. There has, however, been a long-standing connection between students of Indian origin and British universities. In the early twentieth century, the largest foreign student population at British universities were Indians. In 1922, there were over 1,300 Indians studying in the UK. The three most popular subjects were law, engineering and medicine. The Majlis society, a group solely for Indian students, named after the Persian word for assembly, was founded at Cambridge University in 1891. An Oxford Majlis was founded in 1896. London University (later to be renamed UCL) also had a Majlis and Indian student societies sprang up across Britain from the late nineteenth century. These were often breeding grounds for Indian nationalism and anticolonial thought. The reason? It was often the first time that young Indians had met other Indians from different provinces and cultural backgrounds to themselves. Despite their differences they found common ground in their 'Indian' identity. Studying in the relative freedom of Britain, they began to question the premise of empire and to discuss the possibilities of forming independent nations. They also had lots of free time.[3] Choudhry Rahmat Ali, who is credited with coming up with the name 'Pakistan' and a leading proponent of the Pakistan movement, studied at Cambridge University in the 1930s. Mohandas 'Mahatma' Gandhi studied at the Bar in the 1890s. Mohammad Ali Jinnah, the first president of Pakistan, also studied at the Bar in London in the 1890s. Jawaharlal Nehru, the first prime minister of India, studied at Cambridge in the 1910s.

South Asian migrant children who studied at British schools were swept up in the nationalist movement. Age is, and was, no barrier to understanding political subjection and political possibilities. While public schools were hothouses for creating and perpetuating a British elite, one that governed the British Empire, what is remarkable is that these schools also became incubators for Indian anticolonial nationalists. The first prime minister of independent India, Jawaharlal Nehru, fierce anti-colonialist and leader of the Indian National Congress, was a student at Harrow from 1905. Founded in 1572, this was the same school that Winston Churchill attended in 1888, before vehemently opposing Indian independence as prime minister between 1940 and 1945. This was a school that celebrated Empire Day and had an annual Empire calendar.[4] Nehru was fifteen when he joined Harrow and was conscious of the differences between him and his peers immediately. Although he felt that he fit into school life fairly quickly, he always had a feeling that 'I was not one of them'. He found it frustrating that he was interested in politics and wanted to talk about India and the Empire but his classmates were less interested in contemporary affairs and particularly less aware of how the Empire affected their everyday lives. They were more interested in games.[5]

Nehru's father, Motilal, was a nationalist and member of the leading political party for Indian nationalism, the Indian National Congress (INC). Founded in 1885, the INC was initially a moderate group that demanded greater representation for Indians within the imperial system but by the end of the First World War was actively demanding self-rule for Indians. The family originated from Kashmir but Motilal had a successful law practice in Allahabad. They were a wealthy family, immersed in English ways: eating with knives and forks, wearing Western clothes, conversing in English and often socialising with British people in India. Their large palatial house in Allahabad, known as Anand Bhavan, contained furniture and furnishings from Europe, employed almost a hundred people and had high ceilings, pillars and an extensive library. Motilal had been keen for his son to be educated at an English school. He felt that an English public-school education would be of immense social and political benefit for Jawaharlal and make him a 'real man'.[6] Aged 15, he was already relatively old when he joined Harrow as a boarder. He travelled by ship with his parents and younger sister, who then left him at school and returned via a holiday on the continent. He was soon inculcated in Harrow life as a 'Harrovian', donning the straw boater hat, tie, waistcoat and blazer and being recruited into the practice of 'fagging': a public-school practice where younger boys acted as servants for older boys. It often involved bullying, beating and sexual abuse. Nehru's experiences seem relatively benign—he had to carry messages, light fires and turn on baths for the sixth formers after football.[7] He also took up the name 'Joe'.

'Joe' Nehru was lonely at Harrow. Writing to his father in December 1905, he mentioned that he had 'as yet failed' to find a close friend and saw 'no indications pointing to it'.[8] At the annual speech day, other boys would have family to see them but Nehru felt that he was the exception and spent most of the day in his room.[9] He joined in football, cricket and other games but his passion was in reading and general knowledge. He kept up with news about India by reading *The Times*. In January 1906, Nehru was reading about how the *swadeshi* movement, a movement that rejected all British and foreign goods in India in favour of home produce, was spreading across India including Kashmir.[10] His father also kept up him up to date with his activities with the INC. As a boy, Nehru was critical of some of the violence within the movement and allied himself with his father's moderate views. Nehru also took an interest in British and wider world news, including the 1905 General Election and the aviation activities of the Wright brothers who were in negotiations with the British War Office between 1905 and 1907 to sell their powered 'flying machine'.[11]

Nehru is a famous example of an Indian child migrant and much has been written about his life. What has been less written about is that there were other Indian boys at Harrow at the same time. They included sons from the Baroda, Kapurthala and Hyderabad royal families and yet there was no-one for Nehru to talk to about Indian news and politics. Although Harrow tradition—including its school song—demanded loyalty, and Nehru had imbibed many of these traditions, after a couple of years he was very keen to leave as he felt that the environment was restrictive and he had outgrown it.[12] In the holidays, Nehru would meet with his older cousins and their families who were studying at university. Nehru was not exempt from cultural forces and family pressures. In the early part of 1907, when Nehru was seventeen, his father tried to get him to marry.[13] Nehru resisted until 1916 but his father and other Indian relatives were trying to convince him to agree to a 'match' while he was still a school student.

Nehru was not oblivious to the issues of race and racism in British society. A major case at the time was the arrest of George Edalji, a British-born man of Parsee origin, for maiming cattle. His father,

Shapurji Edalji, was Indian and an Anglican vicar in the parish of Great Wyrley in Staffordshire. George Edalji was born in 1876 and had attended Rugeley Grammar School as a boy. He then studied law and had his own law practice in Birmingham. The Edalji family were often harassed locally because of their race and would often receive anonymous letters. In 1903, after livestock were mutilated in Great Wyrley, anonymous letters were sent out accusing George Edalji of these crimes. He was arrested, even though he had an alibi and no motive, and sentenced to seven years in prison. He was released in 1906 after the novelist Sir Arthur Conan Doyle took up the case in the press as it was very clear that the young solicitor Edalji was very unlikely to have been involved in the case. As Nehru pointed out to his father, 'I am sure he was convicted simply and solely because he was an Indian'.[14] There was no explanation for his release and only after further pressure on the state was he cleared of the crimes in 1907. Edalji was not allowed any compensation.

At the end of his school career, as a prize, Nehru was given the first volume of G. M. Trevelyan's historical biography of the Italian nationalist Giuseppe Garibaldi. As a soldier, Garibaldi had played a leading role in the unification of Italy in the mid-nineteenth century and Nehru later claimed that his fight and leadership inspired him in his nationalist career.[15] Nehru went on to Cambridge to study law and was called to the Bar. He returned to India in 1912 to take up a career as a barrister. At Cambridge he met more Indian students but tried to keep out of discussions around Indian politics. He had also kept in touch with his old Harrow classmates who led him into expensive habits and large debts. Upon his return to India, he soon became dissatisfied with his new life and the monotony of his new job. He found it difficult to fit in after seven years in England. In contrast to his experiences at elite educational institutions in Britain, where he managed to function alongside British peers without too much friction, it became clear that, in India, the British and Indians were more uncomfortable in each other's company.[16] He realised that the British official class was narrow-minded and that the Indian intelligentsia was cut off from the Indian masses. Nehru began to attend Congress meetings and gradually became more absorbed in politics, moving into a leadership position that took him all the way to becoming the first prime minister of independent India.

Nehru returned to India in 1912, just two years before the First World War started and seven years before the Amritsar massacre, when at least 379 civilians (likely many more) were killed and over twelve hundred wounded by the 1,650 bullets fired by colonial troops on a closed-off market square over the duration of ten minutes. This would prove to be a turning point for many in the Indian nationalist movement but the first two decades of the twentieth century were also a vibrant time for Indian students to meet in Britain and forge common alliances over the cause of nationalism. In 1911, Renuka Ray, who would later become a prominent Indian nationalist and socialist, travelled to London with her parents, Satish Chandra Mukherjee and Charulata Mukherjee, siblings and maternal grandparents. She was 7 years old. Her grandfather, Prasanno Kumar Roy, had been appointed advisor to Indian students by the Indian High Commission in London and they lived in Kensington. Renuka and her siblings attended Kensington High School for two years. Kensington High School was located on Cromwell Road, on the same street where Renuka's grandfather worked. Famous alumni of this independent girls' school included Emily Wilding Davison, the suffragette killed by the King's horse in 1913, and Eleanor Rathbone, a prominent suffragist and one of the first women MPs in the United Kingdom. Renuka's brother, Subroto, who was just a baby at the time, would later become the first Indian Chief of Air Staff; he returned to England for studies at a school in Hampstead when he was sixteen and then, at the age of eighteen, was one of the first six Indian boys selected to undergo two years of flying training at the Royal Air Force College, Cranwell. The children did not live in London for long but they met much of the Indian community in London through their grandparents. Indian university students would often visit their house in Kensington to eat home-made food, debate and sing songs. Jawaharlal Nehru was among those visitors.

As children in London, Renuka and her siblings would visit the homes of their white schoolmates and attend their birthday parties. They were welcomed and socialised fairly freely, which made for a shock when they returned to India and were not allowed to socialise with British families and white children in the subcontinent. In India, class and race hierarchies determined relations between Indian and British people. Elite British families would live in opulent colonial houses with servants and a clear sense of racial distinction.[17] For people like Nehru and Ray it was this stark difference which shocked them into fighting for social and political equality in India upon their return.

Nehru's nationalism was not solely engendered by his time in Harrow. He was heavily influenced by the leadership of Mohandas Gandhi in India after 1915 and his experiences returning to India after his time in Britain. In 1921, he was arrested for his participation in the nationalist movement and for urging the boycott of the visit of the Prince of Wales to India. At trial in 1922, he admitted that Harrow had taught him to be 'prejudiced' in favour of the English and he was 'perhaps more an Englishman than an Indian'.[18] Then, in 1935, while Nehru was in prison for sedition and inflammatory speeches, he wrote his autobiography and looked back at his time at Harrow (and Cambridge). Despite sitting in a prison administered by the British imperial state, Nehru did not wish to blame British people for the injustices of imperial rule. He knew that he owed too much to Britain in his 'mental makeup', for his 'habits of mind' and the 'standards and ways of judging other countries as well as life generally'.[19] He knew that he had gained a lot from his education in Britain and had lots of British habits and sympathies but there was no escape from the inherent injustices of British rule in India. Indian nationalism was in many ways characterised by this admiration for Britain at odds with the desire to rid India of British rule. These dilemmas continued to dog Nehru in his political career as disillusionment with the British over the Kashmir crisis in the 1940s and beyond, for instance, had to be reconciled with his many close friendships with British people and then resurfaced in India's negotiations to remain a part of the Commonwealth as a Republic in 1949.

Why should British public schools create Indian nationalists, then? Indian children who spent many childhood years alongside British children at elite schools had the unique experience of getting to see how British people lived their everyday lives first-hand, to see that their peers—for no reason other than ingrained racial ideas about empire—were able to take up roles in power over their own country. In being away from the subcontinent, many also got a better chance to see India from a distance, to be more aware of their racial identity and thus also felt the need to contemplate their national identity. In schools that would celebrate Britishness through their classes, their sports, their pomp and ritual, young Indian boys and girls became acutely aware of different types of hierarchies, of the weaknesses of Britain, that the Empire was held together by a string (by a minority of British people and a financially fragile system) and that there was no ingrained reason or human difference between Indians and British people that meant that Indians were not fit to rule themselves. Far removed from India by distance, many of these children wanted and needed to 'prove' their Indianness. They may have been brought up in Britain but they knew they would never be accepted as British. There was a chance they could be accepted as 'Indian' and they began to see, understand and articulate what that 'Indianness' could mean for the subcontinent and its peoples. Given their upbringings, they also had the tools to negotiate with the British. They knew them too well to be fooled by diplomatic missions or misunderstand British political ambitions. British India at this time was a huge, diverse place—the size of continental Europe without Russia—multiple vernaculars, cultural traditions, religious traditions, climates and landscapes. To bring this vast country of millions of diverse peoples together, the Indian nationalist movement had to articulate an inclusive broad-brush idea of Indianness. Much of this became beset with religious identity but, on the surface, the Indian National Congress wished to be a secular (non-religious) organisation that brought together people with a shared history and a shared land, with the aim of having shared values going forward. Indian children who had lived and studied abroad had many of the tools of articulation, debate and political understanding to lead in those ideas and that movement.

* * *

'Empire Day' was celebrated in British schools on the anniversary of Queen Victoria's birthday. The exact form differed between schools but often took on the form of a historical pageant; it was designed to educate children of the importance of empire and their duties towards it. The Batley Pageant in 1907, for example, had children dressed up as vanquished Zulu, Māori and Kaffir warriors. By 1907, over twelve thousand elementary schools had celebrated the day in some form.[20] On 1 July 1914, a 'missionary pageant' was held in Offley Parish in Hertfordshire. Children dressed up in 'African and Indian robes' for the pageant and their faces were blackened.[21] This process of 'blacking up' was not unusual nor was it done solely in the presence of white children. Neil Bruniat Bonarjee recalls dressing up as a Black African in a Pageant of Empire in 1915 at Dulwich College, London, when he was about fourteen. The boys wore black swimming costumes and miniskirts with plaited straws and carried massive clubs; all the other boys in the group, apart from Bonarjee, 'blacked up' with burnt cork.[22] In 1926, for the fancy dress dance at Sherborne Boy's School in Dorset, the seventeen year old M. K. Sahebzada dressed up as an Indian prince, while his classmate, called Woods, blacked up and wore a pith helmet.[23] Sahebzada would go on to become a prominent member of the Communist Party of India.[24] The idea that 'blacking up' only offends modern sensibilities does not hold water when we look at these earlier examples. Bonarjee clearly felt uncomfortable and discussed this in his autobiography. These examples also show the ways in which young children in the early twentieth century were groomed into accepting stereotypical ideas about race and ethnicity and encouraged to mimic and ridicule people of colour. When South Asian children were a minority in British schools, there was little they could do to challenge these unacceptable practices. These examples, however, reveal the ways in which racial hierarchies were ever-present for these young migrants. The injustices of empire were never hidden from view, not even in Britain.

Before joining Dulwich Preparatory School in 1910 aged 9, Neil Bruniat Bonarjee studied at Miss Robert's Kindergarten in south London with twenty or so other boys and girls. He had been taken to England with his older brother and sister in 1904 when he was not yet four years old.[25] In the Christmas play one year, he was given the part of King Alfred the Great and had the lines: 'I shall never give in, for I am a true-born Englishman'. On saying these lines, Bonarjee stopped to address the audience and break the fourth wall: 'I'm not really, you know. I'm an Indian'. His remark brought the house down with laughter. The audience were delighted by the young boy's interruption to remind them that he was not really an Englishman despite his breeding. As Bonarjee explained, it was unlikely that he made this aside asserting his Indianness because of a nationalist fervour but because, as he told his mother afterwards, it was wicked to tell lies.[26] But he did understand something about nationality and his place in the Empire at this young age.

Patriotism, that is English or British patriotism, was instilled in the young boys at Dulwich Preparatory School, including Bonarjee, mainly through their English literature and history lessons. It was here that the realities and contradictions of empire, and his own 'difference', became apparent to Bonarjee as a young boy. In history, for example, Bonarjee learnt that the 'English had conquered India entirely for the benefit of its inhabitants and had built up an empire there almost against their own wishes'.[27] He was taught that Indians did not generally have nice characters, as they practised barbaric customs such as sati (the immolation of widows). He was taught that the British were in India by divine ordinance, setting out to civilise Indians as part of their mission. This ideology of the 'civilising mission' was a common refrain for imperial supporters, depicting Indians as savages who needed the moral guidance of the superior Christian empire to progress. Empire was depicted as the 'white man's burden' and focus on the divine mission diverted attention from the expansionist, exploitative, brutal side of the imperial project.

It was brought home to Bonarjee at an early age that there was a clear distinction between his English peers and himself 'inasmuch as they had got something which I had not, namely an Empire. They possessed, while I only belonged.' Bonarjee accepted this without qualms or resentment at a young age—it was simply how the world he had been born into worked. Imperialism was the order of the day for Bonarjee and he voiced that his 'only regret was that I was not a part owner of the Empire as the other boys appeared to be'.[28] The realities of empire were brought home to Bonarjee in ways that would not have been as obvious had he grown up in India. There he would have been more evidently a colonial subject and seen racial difference play out in power relations in public through policing and in institutions like schools. Instead, at Dulwich Prep, on British soil, where for all intents and purposes he was an equal with his fellow pupils, his education constantly reminded him, if society did not in other ways, that he was a subject of the Empire and that he was seen as politically and racially inferior to his contemporaries. However, just as imperial ideologies were being imposed on Bonarjee as a young boy, so he and other young Indians in Britain had a part to play in shaping imperial ideologies. By his very presence on British soil and as a pupil at school in England, Bonarjee was an influence on his white contemporaries. Indian child migrants at public schools in the 1910s were shaping empire and its future as much as they were being shaped by imperial Britain.

Neil Bonarjee became acutely aware of racial difference as a child in Britain not merely through his school lessons but through the press and wider public culture as well. In December 1908, the African American boxer Jack Johnson defeated the Australian Tommy Burns to win the Heavyweight Championship. This momentous sporting achievement was overshadowed by racial prejudices. Bonarjee remembers people talking about the need to prohibit matches between Black and white boxers because they worried that the prestige of the white man was suffering by losing to Black men. It brought home to Bonarjee, at the age of eight, the idea that white skin was an advantage in his world and how important British people took skin colour in determining human relationships. He was also affected by stories about the Yellow Peril and Fu Manchu in his teens. In 1911, he would see press reports about the Delhi Durbar. This was a ceremony that was used to display the splendour and reach of the British Crown over its Indian empire, hoping to inspire more loyalty among its Indian subjects but constantly emphasising difference. He could hardly be immune, then, to how ideas of racial superiority shaped British culture and politics. Nor could he be inattentive to his own position as a brown-skinned boy within the dominant racial hierarchies of the day. All this while still just a child grappling with life in school, a distant father and emerging adolescence.

One day in the playground at Prep School, a boy called Tipple whose parents were in service in India, shouted at him, 'Hi, you Bengali babu', before descending into loud laughter. Bonarjee had never heard that phrase before, nor did he understand exactly what it meant, but understood immediately that it was intended to be derogatory. Hurt by a boy he had thought was his friend, Bonarjee started to fight with Tipple and had to be taken in to see the Master. When he asked them to explain why they were fighting, neither boy said anything and consequently the Master was not made aware of the racial undertones of the bullying Bonarjee was experiencing.[29] It is probable that he would have just ignored him, had he known, but the anecdote serves to indicate that Bonarjee already knew there was little point in raising racist bullying with his schoolmaster.

After Dulwich College, Bonarjee studied history at Hertford College, Oxford (from 1919). Immediately following his degree, he became assistant master at Dulwich College Prep School, returning to his alma mater and the town in which he had spent the best part of his childhood. Despite his highly anglicised upbringing, he ultimately 'returned' to India and joined the Indian Civil Service (ICS) in the United Provinces (UP) in 1924. It was a rocky road in the ICS as his commissioners criticised him for his 'nationalistic' tendencies and Bonarjee found it difficult to get on with some of his British superiors: 'I knew too much about the English and the result was that I was not always ready to give the same respect to the English that quite possibly other Indians were.' Despite his concerns and sympathies for Indian nationalists, Bonarjee stayed in the ICS to satisfy his parents; he had joined to prove that he was 'as good as' the 'English', as he had been brought up in the 'English way' and therefore intended to fulfil his obligations by remaining in the service.[30] He had a successful career in government service despite, or perhaps because of, his nationalist sympathies and was appointed chief minister of the United Provinces upon Indian independence. A young boy who studied at a quintessentially British public school grew up to reject a future in Britain, instead taking up a key political role in the emerging Indian nation.

Dulwich College was an attractive place for overseas parents to send their boys for study. Founded in 1619, it was in many ways a typical English public school with boarding arrangements and it had many international connections, especially with India. Bonarjee described it as more liberal than most.[31] It counts amongst its most famous old boys the author P. G. Wodehouse, whose father had been a magistrate in Hong Kong. Dulwich specialised in sending men into the imperial and colonial services but Bonarjee's headmaster Arthur Herman Gilkes also especially encouraged boys from all over the world to attend the school. The first Indian pupil to study at Dulwich College was Rustomjee Bahadurjee in 1890, who only studied there for a year, followed by brothers Moosa Ali Mirza and Hamid Ali Mirza from 1896. The Mirza brothers were sons of the last Nawab of Bengal, Bihar and Orissa—part of the Najafi Dynasty from Murshidabad—and had both been educated at Latymer Lower School in Hammersmith before joining Dulwich. Born in India, they settled in Britain where they later had children and subsequently died. Hamid Ali enlisted as a private soldier in the 8th Battalion, the Buffs (the East Kent Regiment) and served in the Great War. He was a prisoner of war from 1915 to 1917 and retired from the Army in 1920. He received 1914/15 Star, Allied Victory and British War medals.[32]

Another Indian pupil at Dulwich College, Nalinaksha Chintaman Bakhlé, was heavily involved in school activities during his time at Dulwich College (1917–23).[33] Bakhlé was awarded a school scholarship in 1917 and was one of the editors of the College magazine *The Alleynian* as well as being involved in the rugby, shooting and gymnastics teams and captain of the fives (hand tennis). He was a keen actor, often appearing in the Classical plays and coming second in a Greek prose competition in 1923. As such, he was fully immersed in school life. After Dulwich, Bakhlé attended Oxford on a scholarship and joined the Indian Civil Service but died of peritonitis in 1935, aged just 30, leaving behind two young daughters. He had been a huge success at the school both in scholarship and sports and was clearly a witty young man as his school poems attest. His brother wrote to the school upon his death: 'You will remember that while at school he held one or two records; I think, they were in shooting. ... Dulwich has lost a young man, who, had he lived, to the fullness of years, would have brought greater honour to the school.'[34]

This was the pull of empire and the influence of these Indian child migrants on it. They were significant participants in shaping and being part of how empire played out in public schools and this was key to creating the next generation of imperial servants. The boys who would go on to serve in the British Army, the colonial and Indian civil services and become the lawyers, judges, MPs, businessmen and lobbyists who would govern and maintain the Empire were growing up in these schools. Indian children were growing up alongside them. Public schools were crucial institutions that propped up and maintained the Empire. The boys learnt Classics and history that taught them to believe that Western civilisation was far superior and on a different plane to 'Eastern' cultures. They were encouraged to contemplate conquering far-off lands through their lessons and through the hotbed of competition at school. These were the routes to Sandhurst, Haileybury, Oxbridge and Westminster and they were the cocoons for the imperial officers, politicians, army generals and businessmen who would maintain, expand and continue to exploit and undermine their colonial subjects. It seems like a paradox or conundrum that these imperialist nurturing stations should also harbour colonial subjects—many of whom could be loyal imperial collaborators—but many became fervent anti-colonialists too. They were shaped by their times in these institutions just as much as their white peers. As so much of public-school life was predicated on observing and maintaining the British Empire and all its gentlemanly codes for the foreseeable future, their position as colonial subjects could not be forgotten, even as young children. And so, these childhood experiences are important for us to understand how the Empire continued to prosper and ultimately decline in the middle of the twentieth century.

* * *

One of the routes out of British public schools was into the imperial and colonial services. The Indian Civil Service (ICS) was a highly prestigious career choice for Indians. It was known informally as the 'heaven-born service' as it was a secure career path that offered power, chances for promotion and an ability to work alongside the

British and have a hand in the control of their own country. Boys like Bonarjee did follow this route into the ICS but they also exhibited strong nationalist sympathies. Motilal Nehru had initially wanted and hoped that Harrow would be an entry route into the ICS for Jawaharlal.[35]

Jawaharlal Nehru, Neil Bonarjee and Nari Rustomji were all involved in shaping the new Indian nation and have each left behind autobiographies which discuss their schoolboy experiences in England and their attempts to fit in back in India. Looking at the school records, shipping records and censuses, I have been able to piece together more of the activities about the Rustomji family and have found many other Indian boys and girls who were their contemporaries. Many lived in political obscurity but they reveal how dense the Indian child contingent was in Britain in the early twentieth century and how many attended British public schools.

Nari Rustomji's father and uncles had all studied at British universities. Both of his grandparents were Parsee businessmen and his father, Kaikhosru Jenhangir Rustomji, was trained in the law and was called to Middle Temple in 1911. Kaikhosru's two younger brothers Homi and Saros were both boarders at Bedford School, a public school in Bedfordshire founded in 1552. Born in December 1895, Homi, a keen boxer at school, boarded from 1909 to 1914. After Bedford, he went to Oxford and was called to the Inner Temple in 1919, practising as a barrister in India before serving in the army during the Second World War. Saros Jehangeer Rustomji was born in 1903 and attended Bedford School from 1914 to 1921. He went on to Oxford University to study law and was called to the Bar like his brothers. By 1940, he was acting manager of the Bank of India in Ahmedabad.

Nari Rustomji was born in May 1919 in Lahore. He had travelled to Britain with his whole family in 1927 by P&O ship as their parents had decided to educate their children in Britain. Nari was 8 but his brother Minoo was 11 (b. March 1916) and sister Thritti, 12 (b. December 1914). He was admitted to Bedford School Prep in 1927 along with his elder brother; his sister was sent to Bedford Girls' School. After a few weeks in a hotel, the family moved into a house in Warwick Avenue in Bedford, a less than fifteen-minute walk to

Bedford School. Bedford Girls' was a further fifteen-minute walk away. They had a car and a mongrel spaniel. Many retired British families from India lived in Bedford, a large market town just north of London. Bedford School was particularly favoured by British families in India and was well-known there. It may have been this connection that initially drew the Rustomjis to this town.[36]

Nari had a musical talent. He took up violin lessons with Alfred de Reyghere, a prominent Belgian violinist and conductor. De Reyghere entered Nari in for regular musical competitions in Bedford. In 1929, Nari came third in the 8–9 years' category; in 1932, he placed second in the 12–14 age group; and finally, in 1934, he won first prize in the 13–14 cohort. Nari also played at school and set up a chamber music club at Bedford School. He was often the star of the annual school concert and the school magazine, *The Ousel*, contained regular praiseworthy reports of his playing. In June 1938, the magazine described Rustomji's as the 'most remarkable performance of the evening' and in July 1938, the magazine lamented the fact that it was Rustomji's last concert performance for the school, discussing their 'profound regret' to 'say goodbye to Rustomji, to whose intense enthusiasm and outstanding musical gifts the success of these concerts is entirely due.'[37]

Nari was a keen violinist and singer but also a brilliant gymnast. He regularly performed for the school at the 'Assault-at-arms'— an annual display by the gym team followed by prizes and music— which he would open with circles on the horizontal bars. He was undefeated in the annual school competitions and was made vice-captain of school gymnastics in 1937. Despite his musical and gymnastic exploits, he was a shy boy throughout his childhood. At school, he was embarrassed in the changing rooms; he felt very self-conscious about nakedness and was fearful of showing any sexual excitement. Although he often played the violin with girls, he remembers being shy and awkward with them and some of this came from his cultural upbringing.

Nari also excelled at his studies. He was awarded a junior scholarship in 1933, being particularly proficient in the Classics. In 1937, he was appointed one of the 'pro-monitors' of the school and he also took part in the school debating society. He was, then, a well-rounded pupil, who was involved in all aspects of school life and seemed to be a very popular pupil with teachers and classmates. His race or nationality was not something remarked upon in the school magazines and he did not seem to face any barriers to involvement at school. Although his ethnicity might not have been discussed overtly in reports, it was also something that Nari could not hide from. His cultural upbringing shaped some of his social experiences at school, such as his shyness about his body and around girls; it certainly was a key determinant in the academic ambitions his parents had for him.

His siblings also engaged in extra-curricular activities. Thritti, his sister, played the piano and Minoo, his older brother, was a keen boxer at Bedford School and was unbeaten as a flyweight in school competitions. He went on, as an adult, to train as a chartered accountant, working for the Tata Engineering and Locomotive Company before writing several books on management. He often collaborated with C. Northcote Parkinson, a well-known historian and management specialist who put forward Parkinson's Law— the adage that 'work expands so as to fill the time available for its completion'.

Minoo and Nari left Bedford School in 1934 and 1938 respectively. Nari gained a place at Christ's College, Cambridge, on a Classics and choral scholarship and was appointed to the ICS, returning to India in 1942. He retained close links to Bedford during his university days as he is recorded on the 1939 Bedford electoral register, aged 20, and gave the same address in Bedford to his ship the SS *Castalia* when returning to India in January 1942. There were seven other residents at this address in 1939, four of whom were women, one being the widowed Beatrice Greenfield, who was probably the landlady. In the 1939 register, his parents were living in Madeley Road in Ealing, West London, with Thritti. Kaikhosru died in 1943 and Homi appears in registers back in Bedford in 1945. She was at a new address but living with Thritti and Minoo along with two other Rustomjis.

Nari Rustomji, like Nehru, felt that he was very 'English' after his upbringing in Britain. He had lived for sixteen years away from India, twelve of which at Bedford, and described himself as 'de-tribalized'. He later said that he had no opportunity of meeting any other

Indians as a child in Bedford, although this was an exaggeration.[38] He would often see Parsee relatives and the family would sometimes visit Zoroastrian House in London for Parsee festivals and Sunday gatherings. Due to the sixty-mile drive, they did not visit often and Nari did not engage with 'Indian' culture or news much. In 1931, at the age of 12, Nari went through the Parsee initiation ceremony known as the Navjote or Sedreh-Pushi in front of 100 Parsees at the Hotel Victoria in London. Following a sacred bath and prayers, Nari received his sacred white shirt (sedreh) and sacred thread (kusti), which was wound three times around his waist. With all eyes on him, it was an overwhelming experience for a boy not used to a ceremony that would have been much more familiar had he been in India. He blushed a lot during the ceremony and was glad once it was over to get back into his usual clothes. Not only was it unfamiliar for Nari, it was also novel for the wider British public, as a *Daily Mirror* reporter enjoyed recording the event in detail for the paper.[39] It was events like this that brought home to Nari his feelings of being outside of 'Indian' culture but equally, despite his feelings of being 'English', that he was always set apart.

What is clear, though, is that Rustomji was coaxed into the Indian Civil Service by his headmaster and mother; he would have much preferred a career as a teacher. In that he shared many common features with Neil Bonarjee who had, as we saw earlier, left a teaching position to join the ICS. Rustomji was posted to Assam with the ICS but realised he knew little about India when he arrived. In 1948, he became government advisor for the Tribal Areas in the North-East Frontier Agency, a post he held for ten years, in an environment which was a stark contrast from the urbanised Britain of his childhood. It is also clear that the public schools that admitted Indian children expected that, having grown up as contemporaries of their white peers, they would turn out to be loyal imperialists who would use their education to further bolster the Empire. In exchange, they would take up similar coveted positions in imperial bureaucracy as their white British classmates, a vehicle for further buttressing perceived British values within the machinery of empire and reinforcing it among their Indian peers.

There was another Indian at Bedford at the same time as Nari but their paths at school did not overlap too much and Nari does not mention him in his autobiography. Mohammad Ahsanuddin Hussain, known as 'Nawab', was at Bedford School from 1930 to 1935. He was a keen tennis player and also played rugby. By the 1950s, he was living in Hyderabad. There had also been other Indians before them. Brothers Pran Kumar and Raj Kumar Mitter joined the school in 1914 with sisters Mona and Shushila attending Bedford Girls High School. Their father, Robert King Mitter, was born in 1865 and worked in the Indian Medical Service. Robert appears in the 1891 Census in London as a single man. He was then married to Benodini and the whole family lived together in Bedford between 1914 and 1920 until Raj Kumar left Bedford for Oxford. The boys' and girls' schools would have an annual debate and a 'Miss Mitter' spoke in both the 1917 and 1918 debates. Mona went on to study at Westfield College, a woman's only college in Hampstead, part of the University of London. Benodini died in London in 1924 and the two sisters returned to India in November 1924 on the SS *China*. Raj Kumar left in 1920 for Oxford and joined the Indian Civil Service and Pran Kumar left in 1921 and joined the Indian Police for a while. Raj Kumar sadly died in 1932 in India and his death notice was placed in the school magazine in 1934 while Nari Rustomji was still at school.

Although many Indian boys who attended British public schools did then take up roles in the Indian Civil Service, as barristers or in the army, and thus joined the professional classes of Indian colonial society—an elite that were collaborators with the Empire and bolstered the imperial tentacles across the subcontinent—their experiences in Britain also created social and psychological tensions that led many of these former public school boys to engage with the Indian National Congress. Securing a role in the new nation of India that had shed its imperial shackles was an aim for some. Although Bonarjee and Rustomji joined the ICS and were keen bureaucrats, they were both keen to engage with the Indian nation-state after 1947 and were advocates of supporting and promoting the rights of Indian people.

Nehru, Bonarjee and Rustomji, then, were architects of the new Indian nation in different ways. Nehru was its most prominent—he was immersed in the Indian nationalist struggle from 1919 onwards, a keen follower of Gandhi and a proponent of his strategy of non-cooperation as resistance. He became president of the INC in 1929 and sought to draw Congress closer towards internationalism and socialism, though not always successfully. As history records, Nehru was a central figure in negotiations with the British over independence and with the Muslim League over the partition of the subcontinent. There were other Indian children educated in Britain, including at elite public schools, who were immersed in British history and took up British values but still became anti-colonialists. They had seen the inherent injustices of empire more clearly from their education and time away from India. They had also learnt the tools to dismantle and undermine the Empire from within, through their better understanding of British people, knowledge of how to persuade them in debate and familiarity with their systems of governance.

Bonarjee, Rustomji and other Indians within the very ranks of the imperial bureaucracy sought to dismantle it from within and prepare the country for the end of British rule. These Indian children were alive to the issues of empire, race and democracy. Their migration, school training and experiences in Britain—a Britain they never intended to settle in—all helped to shape the dialogue around them and shape the new emerging nation of India out of it too.

5

THE SPORTING STARS

In July 2001, 10-year-old Azeem Rafiq arrived in London with his family as they sought asylum from Pakistan. In October 2001, the family were placed in Barnsley, Yorkshire, and before long Rafiq was selected to play for the Yorkshire under-12s' cricket team. Rafiq went on to captain the England Under-19 side as well as Yorkshire in 2012 at the age of 21. To observers this looked like a remarkable success for a South Asian child migrant who was now forging a promising career at the heart of what is often described as 'the English national sport'. Despite his early promise as a child, however, his adult cricketing career did not match the success of his childhood years. Instead, by 2018, Rafiq was compelled to lodge formal complaints about racism at the Yorkshire Cricket Club, including evidence of derogatory language, inhumane behaviour and an incident where his young teammates forced red wine down his throat—Rafiq is Muslim and does not drink alcohol—when he was fifteen years old. The publicity around the case forced Rafiq to leave the country permanently because of the abuse he faced for drawing attention to institutional racism at one of England's most popular and successful cricket clubs.[1]

In any industry, people of colour can be encouraged into success and then very quickly become dispensable when they are perceived to fall short; this phenomenon is acutely noticeable for careers where winning and losing is more starkly absolute and ideas about local and national identity are constructed and solidified along nationalistic and ethnic lines. In 2021, for example, three Black footballers, Marcus Rashford, Bukayo Saka and Jadon Sancho, who played for the England football team in the 2020 Euros, were particularly targeted for racial abuse when the team lost the final in a penalty shootout against Italy. In times of sporting success, players of colour have usually been embraced into the England national side but in times of defeat it is noteworthy how belonging has become more fragile and contingent upon notions of racial belonging. These kinds of tested loyalties were also apparent at the time of empire, where children of colour were embraced if they demonstrated loyalty to their schools through sporting prowess. The unique position of British subjecthood in this period—when Indians were British subjects and could technically represent 'Britain' (or usually 'England') in national sports teams—shows how intimately tied the role of sports and national identities were. Without these children, whose sporting successes trumped race, these dualities would not have been apparent.

Sport can be a site of animosity and debate about identity and youth identities have often been bound up into sporting allegiances. In 1990, the Conservative MP Norman Tebbit infamously questioned the loyalty of British children of South Asian and Caribbean heritage who supported India, Pakistan or the West Indies at cricket rather than England. While these children were being encouraged to follow the sport by parents and other members of their community as a way to retain cultural links with their 'homeland'—and were naturally keen to support winning teams: India, Pakistan and the West Indies all enjoying success in this era—the whiteness of the England squad, along with the frequently nationalistic and jingoistic rhetoric of supporters, often felt very alienating.

Sports in the nineteenth and early twentieth century were not divorced from the politics of empire either and by exploring the historical lives of sporting schoolchildren, we can see how questions of belonging were played out over a century ago. While a site of nationalist exclusion, paradoxically sport functioned as one of the few arenas in which racial barriers could be broken down in colonial times; membership of a sports team was one way in which racialised young people were allowed to belong. Indian pupils were encouraged to profess loyalty to their schools, especially if attending public schools, and inculcated into school societies and games. They were often happily assimilated but this was contingent on continuing 'success', which in turn created its own tensions. These sporting histories emphasised the fragility of imperial belonging for many children in Britain.

* * *

The life of elite British colonialists in the Empire, especially during the nineteenth century, had been one of recreating public-school ideals and pursuing a life of leisurely pursuits in clubs, sports and hunting. What was empire itself if not a type of 'sport' for the British? Indians soon saw how sport was valued by British imperialists and learnt to follow in those footsteps, first in the clubs and schools set up in India but also in the pursuits of their children in public schools in Britain. Organised sports, and 'playing by the rules', were central to the ethos of British public schools and shaped the identity of elite British men—especially those who would go on to serve and prop up the Empire. Sports and games were an important form of control, mirroring the structures and hierarchies inherent in imperialism, while also being closely tied to national identity and belonging. It was believed by many within the public school system that games inspired virtue, developed manliness and formed character. While girls also engaged in school sports, these ideas were more acutely imposed upon boys. These values were closely tied to imperial ideologies; J. C. Welldon, the headmaster of Harrow from 1881 to 1895, believed that English success in the British Empire was because of sporting 'sovereignty'.[2] Public schools in India were founded in the nineteenth century along British lines too and sports helped to cultivate what J. A. Mangan has characterised as 'games ethic': the inculcation of perceived British values of loyalty, obedience and teamwork as part of an imperial mission that sought to entrench colonial hierarchies and mould allegiance to empire. Teaching sports to 'natives' in India became part of the civilising philosophy of British imperialism.

As the popularity of athletics clubs grew across India, however, Indians were able to ally concepts of manliness and athleticism with developing narratives about Indians' fitness to rule and desire for national independence.[3] Indian children who were swept up into the British public-school system, then, were also drawn into the cult of sports and the imperial mentality behind it.

Kumar Shri Ranjitsinhji, who had studied at Cambridge following schooling in India, was a model for young sporting Indians in Britain to emulate. Ranji, as he was known, not only played cricket for Cambridge but went on to represent England too. He was born in 1872 and in 1878 became the heir apparent to the Nawanagar throne. Ranji was educated at the elite Rajkumar College in India where he honed his cricket skills. In 1888, aged sixteen, he travelled to Britain before attending Trinity College Cambridge in 1889. Ranji was the first Indian to earn a cricket 'Blue' for Cambridge, which was recognition of competing at the highest level for the university. However, his inclusion in the Cambridge team was not without controversy. Initially other members of his college cricket team ignored him, however once they realised what a brilliant cricketer he was, they were keen to become friends with him. Ranji began to play for the county team of Sussex from 1895, becoming the first Indian to play for a major county. The following year, he made his debut for England in one of the most high-profile test matches going: an Ashes test against Australia.

Cricket was one of the most essential sports in epitomising English masculinity and 'gentlemanly conduct' at this time. As C. L. R. James, the West Indian writer put it later, cricket trained English boys in the 'public school code'.[4] This code was about self-control, patriotism, militarism and imperialism and thus enforced hierarchies of race within it.[5] Although cricket is now famously popular in India and Pakistan, the first Indian cricket team, a Parsee team that toured England, was not established until 1886. By 1911, India had its own national cricket team which toured England.[6] Before this then, Ranji's only opportunity to play on the international stage was via representing England. In 1906, following the death of the princely ruler of Nawanagar, Ranji finally became princely ruler himself. One might assume that an Indian royal would be unable to represent another country: that an Indian, and a prince, could represent England in this sport was remarkable. His sporting prowess superseded his racial background and that allowed Ranji to become an extremely popular sporting hero among the English public, although stereotypes about his 'Oriental' background were common in press reports about his play.

Ranji was popular in children's magazines such as *The Captain* and the *Public School Magazine*. Articles about him, posing in his cricket whites or leaning upon a car, in children's publications were important for strengthening the links between empire and Britain for young readers.[7] When C. L. R. James (b. 1901) had been at school in Trinidad in the early twentieth century, he had read boys' magazines like *Boy's Own Paper* and *The Captain*, in awe of English cricketers and had been steeped in that middle-class culture.[8] Other middle-class 'gentle' sports like tennis became popular in India by the mid-nineteenth century. In 1908, Cambridge student Sirdar Nihal Singh was the first Indian to play at Wimbledon, which had only started as a championship in 1877, playing there again in 1909 and 1910. Leela Row was the first Indian woman to win a singles match at Wimbledon in 1934.[9] Indian children playing sports at school in the United Kingdom were not expected to become international sporting stars but their engagement with these sports formed part of an acceptance of their class status within Britain.

Duleepsinhji (Duleep), Ranji's nephew, followed in his footsteps in England. Duleep was sent to Britain in 1921 at the age of 16 and studied at Cheltenham College before also matriculating at Cambridge.[10] At Cheltenham, Duleep was a member of the first Cricket XI from 1921 to 1923. As the cricket almanac *Wisden* noted: 'in his third and last year at Cheltenham he came out at the top of the batting table with an average of over 52 and was probably the best schoolboy bat of the year'.[11] Harry Altham, a Surrey and Hampshire cricketer, praised his natural gifts and stated that there was a 'certain ease and maturity about all his batting methods that stamps him as of a different class from the ordinary school batsman'.[12] Duleep was accepted and allowed to succeed as a teenager within British school circles and appreciated by commentators because of his sporting skills but he was never quite allowed to forget his difference. He became the second Indian to play cricket for England in 1930 (by this time India had its own national team). When critics suggested that Duleep play for India, Ranji is said to have protested: 'Duleep and I are English cricketers'.[13] Success in sports was an important way for these Indians to resist imperial stereotypes and yet hammered home the complex loyalties and identities inherent within the subjecthood of empire.

Four of Ranji's other nephews studied as children at Malvern College, a boarding school in Worcestershire in the 1910s: Hamatsinhji, Digvijaysinhji, Raisinhji and Rajendrasinhji. They were all appointed school prefects: Hamatsinhji (Hamat) and Digvijaysinhji (Digvi) in 1914, Raisinhji in 1915 and Rajendrasinhji in 1916. They all played cricket, with Hamat putting in some particularly successful performances for the College as a batsman-wicketkeeper but also having a reputation as a successful football player.[14] Hamat and Digvi were keen racket players and Duleep also played rackets for Cheltenham.[15] National newspapers frequently commented on the sporting results from British public schools because there was interest in the ongoing careers of young athletes and so we can find the names of these young Indians frequently appearing in the national press. Digvi won many racket competitions at Malvern including the 'Prichard Racquet' in 1913. The *Daily Mirror* noted his wrist power and 'splendid eye' with keen interest as he was the heir to Ranji's throne.[16] One of the matches Digvi played for Malvern was in the Public Schools competition in April 1914 at Queen's Club, which was reported upon in the broadsheet *The Times*. Digvi and his partner Naumann won their first round against Eton convincingly but lost in the second round to Charterhouse. Noted for his quickness, Digvi was singled out for his lack of accuracy and the *Times* reporter ultimately blamed him for the loss.[17] In success there were no issues, but in defeat, the swords came out.

In March 1916, Hamat competed in the Ledbury Run where he placed 8th—a remarkable feat considering that the course was affected by snow and floods. In the same year, he won the Public Schools' Singles Handicap Racquets competition at Queen's Club, beating competitors from Radley, Wellington, Eton and Cheltenham. The success of these Indians at sport was something the whole school took pride in. In 1944, the *Malvernian* remembered the success of Digvijaysinhji, Hamatsinhji and Rajendrasinhji in the Prichard Racket between 1912 and 1917. Remarking on how players needed quick eyes and feet, the school magazine noted 'how the "fly-eyed" Indians' excelled at the game. Pride in these pupils also stemmed from their connections to the sporting hero Ranji and the recognition of their princely status.[18] It was a boost for these schools to have young Indian pupils with these kinds of connections. At the same time, sporting success was an important way for children to be allowed to integrate into English school life.

In June 1918, Rajendrasinhji, who now played for the Malvern Cricket XI as a bowler and was lauded as an excellent fielder, played against Shrewsbury. In the opposing team was a batsman called K. S. Bahadursinhji. Bahadursinhji had succeeded to the throne of Palitana at five years old, in 1905, and was a page to Queen Mary during the 1911 Delhi Durbar. In 1913, he was taken to England under the guardianship of Mr and Mrs Tudor-Owen, who were also in charge of the minor Nawab Sahib of Junagadh. After a year at a prep school in Rugby, he joined King Edward VI Public School in Shrewsbury in 1915 where he stayed until 1918. He quickly gained a place in the Cricket First XI, playing for four seasons, and got the chance to play at Lords, the 'home' of cricket, twice as part of the public schools' competitions.[19] According to the society magazine *The Tatler*, his peers found it too hard to pronounce his long surname and so he was known as B. Palitana on their scoresheets.[20] These young Indian children could never quite hide from comments about their race. To provide an example, E. H. D. Sewell, a former cricketer turned sports journalist, remarked that Bahadursinhji's quickness of eye was the 'peculiar property of batsmen of Aryan stock'.[21] Bahadursinhji was also a member of the fives (hand tennis) team—a sport mainly only played at British public schools—but his cricketing prowess at Shrewsbury merited the most attention, as he was not the greatest scholar. The school magazine congratulated 'K. S. Bahadursinhji on an innings exceptional in Public School cricket' in a match against Repton in 1918, where he scored a remarkable 300 runs: 'Among his best shots were 16 "fours," and this is probably the finest innings ever played on this ground in inter-school matches. We should like to congratulate him on his magnificent performance.'[22] In 1925, a note in the *Daily Express* remarked upon the fine forms of Bahadursinhji at Shrewsbury and Rajendrasinhji and Hamatsinhji at Malvern back in the 1910s, revealing how these sporting achievements were well regarded beyond the confines of school communities but also how these young Indians were always viewed as a group rather than individuals.[23]

Bahadursinhji returned to India and Palitana in 1919 but, during his five or so years in Britain, he was presented to the King and Queen twice and was later awarded a KCIE (Knight Commander of the Indian Empire) in 1939 because of his elite connections. Seen as loyal to the imperial crown, the experiences of these young princes like Bahadursinhji and Digvijaysinhji were different to those middle-class Indians who also attended public schools at this time. Their success in sports was important—more important than the scholarly education they undertook, especially as they were not destined for professional careers that depended upon their scholastic achievements. As mentioned previously in Chapter 3, after 1858, Indian royal families had a unique position of privilege and service to the British Crown, where they were keen to strengthen imperial ties through education and sporting links to Britain. These royals' engagements in sports proved their manly aristocratic loyalty and that they could inhabit the best of British upper-class social norms.

Ranji's other nephews did not pursue sporting careers beyond school but did maintain their loyalty to their alma maters and the Empire. In 1933, following the death of Ranji, Digvi became the Maharaja of Nawanagar. He joined the Old Malvernians for their annual dinner in 1935 and pledged to pay for the lighting for the two new racquet courts at the school. A tablet recording his generosity was put up in the courts.[24] His cousin Rajendrasinhji, meanwhile, went on to serve in the Second World War and, in April 1941, was the first Indian to be awarded the Distinguished Service Order (DSO)—being the first Indian to do so in the Second World War— for 'courageous leadership and determined action' in helping to extricate the 3rd Indian Motor Brigade when they were surrounded by Axis tanks in Libya. Digvi's brother Hamat had also become an ambassador. Digvi returned in 1942 for the annual prize-giving, though this had to take place at Harrow because of the war. He was greeted with a Guard of Honour, the first time the school had done this for an individual. In his speech, he noted that: 'He loved Malvern and his study there; he had learnt to play the game, and had tried to be worthy of Malvern'. He also professed his loyalty to Britain and to the war effort, casting aspersions on the Indian National Congress.[25] Clearly some Indian children educated in Britain would feel very loyal to Britain—a loyalty that had been strengthened through sporting ties and that would continue beyond independence in an Indian nation that boasted many anglophiles and lovers of English sports.

* * *

In the early twentieth century, sports were important for middle-class Indian children at British schools too, not just those from princely families. Take, for example, Mirza Rashid Ali Baig, who was born on 23 March 1905 in Bombay and known as Rashid. His father, Mirza Abbas Ali Baig, was the Oriental Translator to the Government of Bombay. In 1910, just after the death of King Edward VII, the Baig family moved to London and found a house near Wimbledon Common. In 1917, Rashid's elder brother, Mirza Osman Ali (b. January 1904), was admitted to Clifton College, a boys' prep school in Bristol. The whole family moved to Bristol and Rashid joined the Clifton College junior school while their younger brother, Mirza Sikander Ali, joined the prep school. They had a fourth brother, Enver, who was only a baby—he later joined the preparatory school in 1924. Their father, Abbas, bought a house in Clifton, Bristol, that they stayed in until 1924, by which time all four boys were in boarding school or university.

Clifton College had been founded in 1879 and was located in spacious grounds with large red brick buildings, just behind Bristol Zoo. Osman and Rashid were both admitted into the School House, which was the oldest house, and at the time overseen by the headmaster. Joining in war time and as boarders, Osman and Rashid were confronted by food affected by rationing—cold lumpy porridge in the morning, chicory coffee and horse for lunch. As with other public schools of the time, there was a practice of 'fagging' to inculcate younger boys by making them run errands for the older 'monitors'. Sport was fundamental to the school with cricket, 'rugger', fives and squash among the games played competitively between houses and other public schools. They had cold baths and the 'spirit of manliness' was encouraged as part of the school's ethos. One of the houses, Polack House, was exclusively for Jewish boys. Unfortunately, this separation appeared to encourage antisemitism rather than encourage inclusion and celebration of the large contingent of Jewish members.[26]

Clifton College became a popular school for Indian families in the early twentieth century. It had longstanding links with India; the College archivist, Dr C. Knighton, estimates over 1,700 pupils who studied at Clifton before 1947 had some connection with India, whether through the Indian Civil Service, Army, law, church or other profession. Edwin Montagu, who was secretary of state for India between 1917 and 1922 and instrumental to political reforms in India, was at Clifton from 1891 to 1893. Francis Younghusband, a famous Indian Army official and 'explorer' of Tibet, had been at Clifton from 1876–1880. Alongside these famous Indian links, several well-established Indian families sent their sons to Clifton College. The first known Indian pupil at Clifton was Jaswant Sinha, son of the ruler of Tajpur in West Bengal, who joined the College in 1892 (until 1894). His school report noted that he had 'no bad habits beyond dullness and carelessness' although initially he was 'reported naturally lazy and bad tempered; but is learning self-control'. Bomdi Sri Ramulu joined Clifton in 1899 and left in 1903. He was a keen sportsman, playing cricket as a strong batsman in his House XI for three years and the School XIs of 1902 and 1903. Ramulu was in the House XV for two years and in his House Rackets pair and First Fives pair and won the School Bat Fives singles. He finished third in the Short Pen (cross country race) of 1901, 9th in the Long Pen of 1902 and 6th in 1903. Ramulu was awarded a 'Cap' in 1902 by his House in recognition of his sporting achievements. He went on to play cricket in Madras when he returned to India.[27] Just before the Baigs, M. H. Kidwai, the *taluqdar* (landowner) of Gadia joined Clifton from Cirencester. He attended Clifton from 1910 to 1917, playing cricket for the Wiseman's House second XI and later found success writing Urdu poetry.

Another family with several siblings attending Clifton were the Habibullah family. Isha'at Habibullah was born on 21 March 1911 and brought up in Lucknow where his father, Sheikh Mohammed Habibullah, was a *taluqdar* of Awadh and later vice-chancellor of Lucknow University. Sheikh Mohammed Habibullah had chosen Clifton for his sons because he was friends with Sir Harcourt Butler in India and the Butler family were associated with Clifton's governing body. Isha'at and his two older brothers (b. 1909 and 1910) were taught first by an English governess in India and then all sent to England in 1920. They travelled with their father—their mother and baby sister remaining in Lucknow—and were met at Dover by E. E. Long, the former editor of the *Indian Daily Telegraph* and his wife, who took them to Brighton. Isha'at and his elder brother, Enaith (Bubbles), the middle child, initially went to a prep college in Rottingdean in Sussex, which was the same town where Rudyard Kipling lived. The brothers remember seeing Kipling at their school. Most of the boys at Rottingdean had never met an Indian before and the Habibullahs became 'mascots' in their classes with much amusement over their English accents and amazement that they were not allowed to eat pork but were served kippers or haddock as a substitute.[28]

In 1921 Isha'at joined his eldest brother, Ali Bahadur (Sonny) at Clifton College, with Enaith joining in 1922, following a spell at Monkton Rectory School in Dorchester. Before they had left for England, the brothers met with Jawaharlal Nehru, who was then an upcoming member of the Allahabad Court Bar, for his advice about school life in England. He told them to 'expect nothing extraordinary, except a gnawing loneliness.'[29] Isha'at and Sikander (Siku) Baig became good friends at Clifton College and the Habibullah brothers would join the Baig brothers at their house in Clifton every Sunday for lunch. Lady Baig would feed them Indian meals of biryani, korma and kebabs.[30] When one of their friends, Howard Faulkes, the son of Major General Faulkes, decided he wanted to become a Muslim and was taken by Lady Baig to a mosque to convert, he became a sensation at school. In the holidays they stayed with Reverend Lionel

Harrison, the vicar of Winterbourne Monkton in Dorset; then later with Mr Ingleby, a widower and headmaster of a prep school in Berkshire; followed by an Irish vicar and his two sisters in Kingston-upon-Thames. At the same time as the Habibullahs were at Clifton in 1921, there was another Habibullah—Mir—who was studying civil engineering at Bristol University, but it does not appear as though he was a relation.[31]

At Clifton, the Habibullah brothers were known as 'the Hallelujah Chorus'. The three brothers attended church with the rest of the school every Sunday, although one day a visiting missionary criticised Islam and Isha'at walked out of the chapel. Their friend, Rashid Baig, has suggested that the average boy at Clifton would not have attended chapel if it were not compulsory and that the school actually encouraged him to become agnostic.[32] In April 1924, the Habibullah parents and their 5-year-old sister, Tazeen, came to visit them. The boys were delighted to see their mother who had become like a 'dream' to them and she was overjoyed to hear that they could still speak Urdu. The parents stayed in Dorchester over the Easter break before moving to a house near Bristol during term time and London in the summer, while the children remained with their guardian, Reverend Harrison, a mile and a half away, to maintain the familiarity of their holiday arrangements. They managed to celebrate Eid all together that year in London.[33]

Sonny Habibullah was a keen sportsman and made captain of the house cricket team and the school XI. He was also a member of his school house's fives team.[34] Enaith played cricket for the School House. As Isha'at put it: 'Being at public school is inextricably related to playing games. I had not the slightest potential, but I played them all'. Isha'at also remembers overhearing a master say, 'It's all very well to have these *café au lait* gentlemen make centuries on the cricket pitch, but I would rather have an Englishman making nothing at all.' Isha'at was fourteen and it was his first clear realisation of racial prejudice.[35] The comment also exemplifies the tensions around sports in Britain for children of colour that resonate with the contemporary examples I offered at the start. Isha'at was not involved in sports but was interested in acting, drama and classical music. He was also very academically minded and was the only boy in his year to receive credits in all eight subjects for the School Certificate, so did not need to take the higher school certificate. Meanwhile, Enaith won a prize in the Royal Drawing Society annual exhibition in London in 1927 when he was sixteen years old.[36] The three brothers tried to succeed and integrate the best way they could at school whether it was through sport or other extra-curricular activities. However, it was clearly through sport that we see more praise and attention heaped on the boys and more communal belonging as opposed to individual success. Isha'at later described himself as a 'glorified black Englishman' back then; this may well have been the case but clearly there was enormous peer pressure to fit in during his childhood there.[37]

Another contemporary of the Baigs and Habibullahs at Clifton was 'Russie' from the Talyarkhan family. The family arrived in the UK in 1922, travelling from Bombay with five children. In September 1924, Mrs Talyarkhan put out an advert in the *Western Daily Press* seeking a house parlourmaid for their residence at 10 College Road, Clifton, and so clearly the family were relatively settled in the city while the children attended school.[38] The oldest son, A. F. S. Talyarkhan (b. 1897) played for the local Bristol cricket club, The Optimists, in the 1920s. Known as Bobby, he became a well-known Indian cricket commentator. Rustom 'Russie' Fardoonji Sorabji Talyarkhan (b. 28 August 1907) attended Clifton from 1922 to 1925. Prior to joining Clifton, he had spent a short time being tutored at Chancery Lane, London. He was a keen cricketer and runner who studied law and qualified as a barrister before going into business. Russie's two sisters, Lulu and Frene, went to a nearby girls' school. One of his sisters was involved in a Bristol badminton competition in March 1925 at the Drill Hall in Old Market Street.[39] His youngest sister Frene, who was born in 1914, went on to become a successful journalist and editor. The Talyarkhan family returned to Bombay in 1925 without Russie, who stayed on at Cambridge. Interestingly, they returned with an ayah who may have been with them during their time in Bristol. We do not know where she came from or why she returned with them. Had she been with them in the UK the whole time, even though they advertised for a parlourmaid? What role might she have taken on, given that none of the children were babies?[40]

Although I focus on elite sporting children in this chapter, it is worth reiterating the entangled lives of South Asians in Britain along diverse class lines, such as the ayah who worked for the Talyarkhans above. When they lived in Wimbledon, the Baig family had a dressing man and cook called Abdul. According to Rashid, Abdul married Sikander's (English) nurse. In the 1911 Census in Wimbledon, when the Baigs were resident there, with Sikander just one year old and Enver yet to be born, I have also found someone called Abud Din Abdullah, who was 23 and born in Bombay. The other female servants were Kate Grove, Florence Pell and Mabel Chilman, who were all British born, and Kisori Dataram, who was Indian born and marked as the nurse. Either way the census reveals the wealth and status of the Baig family who were able to afford a sizeable domestic retinue. Following his marriage, Abdul received a contract to cater for Indian soldiers in camp and hospital in England during the First World War. He then started marketing Abdullah's curry powder and opened an Indian restaurant in London that was popular with Indian students. Soon after, he set up the firm Messrs A. Abdullah & Sons who were importers and exporters in Wormwood Street.[41] Following census records it is likely that this family lived in Finchley, north London, in 1921 with the head of the family, Abbud Bin Abdulah-Koreish, 33 years of age and born in India, noted as a restaurant proprietor. His wife, Clarisse Ethel, was 31 at the time and born in London. From the records, we can see that they had five children, two of whom—Abdullah Aziz, 8 years old and Aziza Clarisse, 6—were born in Wimbledon. They were followed by Abdul Hamid, 5 years old, born in Finchley; Alia Bebe, 3, born in Chelmsford; and Osman, 8 months, born in Finchley. While it is difficult to trace this family further, it is clear to see that their lives would have contrasted heavily with that of the Baigs at Bristol; their children did not attend public school or have the same elite sporting opportunities. They serve as another example of the diversity of childhood experiences for children of South Asian heritage, long overlooked by history books.

As we can see, the Baigs and Habibullahs were part of a wider history of South Asian children who would leave imperial footprints on British public schools. Even at Clifton College, there were numerous Indian boys in attendance. We have comparatively less access to their feelings about identity where they have left few recollections and were not engaged in sport, however they include boys like Sailendra Chandra Gupta, who attended from 1907 to 1910, and Zain Maurice Yusuf, his contemporary, both of whose fathers were in the Indian Civil Service. Yusuf had previously studied at Mowden School, run by Bernard Snell in Brighton, and his mother, Lizzie Grace Cargill, was English. Nirmalaya Chunder Sen (known as 'George', or 'Georgie'), the grandson of well-known Brahmo Samaj reformer, Keshub Chunder Sen, and son of N. C. Sen, the educational advisor to Indian university students in London, boarded at Clifton from 1926 to 1929. His school reports noted that his English was weak when he joined, that he was well liked and 'intelligent but not distinguished'. The Baigs had known the Sens when they lived in London and had perhaps recommended Clifton College to them. Homi Sorabji Batlivala was at Clifton from 1922 to 1926 and his school report noted that he got on well with English boys.[42] His sister, Bhicoo Batlivala ('Bee'), who I will discuss further in a chapter on leftists, was educated at Cheltenham Ladies' College, where she played polo and tennis, going on to become a well-known figure in British 'society' and a leading women's rights campaigner in India.[43]

The focus on sports at Clifton College is all the more relevant because of the famous poem by Henry Newbolt, a Clifton alumnus from the 1870s. His poem 'Vitai Lampada' ('The Torch of Life') written in 1892 transposes the sport (cricket) played at Clifton to the battlefields of empire. It has a memorable line, 'Play up! play up! and play the game!', which evokes and equates the supposed ideals of manliness and duty inherent in both sports and the spoils of empire. Although the poem was written at the time of the Boer War, it became popular during the First World War, where the 'Honour' of England was evoked further. The young South Asians who were also encouraged to 'play the game' could not help but be caught up in these contradictions of loyalty to school and 'England' while never quite being 'English' enough.

A trawl through the registers and school magazines and records of other notable public schools draws out more instances of young Indians engaging in school sports and being lauded for their efforts. Shumshere Singh, the third son of Kanwar Sir Harnam Singh of Kapurthala, joined Rugby School at the age of 14 in September 1893. He was in the Cricket XI from 1896 and the Rugby XV from 1895.[44] As a member of the cricket team, in 1896 alone, Singh had the opportunity to play against Balliol College, Oxford, where he scored a 'valuable 29', Oriel College, Oxford; Liverpool Cricket Club, with a 'patient' 34; and against Marlborough where he kept wicket.[45] Shumshere married Juliette Alice Maud Anderson d'Auquier, the daughter of a reverend, in London in 1906.[46] His son, Hector William Shumshere Singh, who was born in 1909, joined Rugby in May 1923 but did not have such an illustrious sporting record.[47]

Jumping to the 1930s, Danial Latifi, who had previously been educated at Hall School Hampstead and later became a member of the Communist Party of India and the Punjab Muslim League, was a keen runner at Rugby.[48] His contemporary Satyendra Nath Mitra, the son of the high commissioner for India in London, joined Rugby in 1933 and was a successful member of the School Fives (hand tennis), as well as a hockey player.[49] Elsewhere, Sorab Pestonjee Patuck (b. 1910) was a boarder at Bedale's co-educational Boarding School in Petersfield, Hampshire, from at least the age of eleven. He played cricket for the school and was goalkeeper for the football team, his exploits in these and involvement in athletics during sports days prominent in the school magazine, *The Bedale's Record*, across the 1920s, before he moved on to Cambridge in 1928.[50]

It seems that sports were important tools through which Indian children could navigate and negotiate challenges to their cultural identities and, perhaps, also ones that enabled survival. Their understanding of the rules of the game, and the cultural capital accrued from engagement, helped them to navigate silent codes around class. Hassanali Verjee was born into a South Asian business family in Mombasa, Kenya, in 1904. In August 1920, when Hassanali was 16, his father took advice from a colonial agent and sent him to England along with five cousins. Five of them were admitted to Brynmalyn School in Weston-super-Mare and one was sent to Bournemouth. Hassanali remembers how his cousin, Gulamali, was accustomed to using water to clean himself after using the toilet and how he was bullied when his classmates found this out. Brynmalyn had an initiation ritual at the time of scorching new boys' bottoms against an open fire, although Hassanali used his boxing skills to avoid this. He was a good cricketer and became a member of the school's first football XI. As he put it, this 'made me a popular student and dispelled any initial hostility towards the Asian boy from far-away East Africa.'[51]

* * *

As professional sports grew in India, children educated in Britain were increasingly able to represent India on the international stage rather than only seeking validation and acceptance in England. In 1926, Iftikhar Ali Khan Pataudi was sent to England at the age of 16. He was a keen cricketer and continued his cricket education at Kent with England batsman Frank Woolley, before proceeding to Oxford in 1927. Following Ranji and Duleepsinhji, Pataudi also came from a princely background—he was the prince of Pataudi, near Delhi—and played for the England test cricket team, touring Australia in 1932–3. He returned to India in 1934, then deciding to represent India at cricket—the only test cricketer ever to play for both England and India.[52] He also played hockey for the Indian national team at the 1928 Olympics in Amsterdam, alongside another former child migrant, Jaipal Singh, who had studied at Darlington Grammar School.[53] During the time of empire, in the sporting realm, citizenship and subjecthood could be fluid for mobile, upper-class South Asians who were British subjects. They could represent England on the international stage and were accepted onto the national team relatively easily without losing loyalty for an 'India' that did not yet exist in statute. They could move across dual identities for England and India as they were not yet being forced to choose sole citizenship. Looking at these children's sporting lives in Britain, then, is revealing of the ways in which identities were being formed and manipulated at the time of empire and how racial distinctions were not always as stark as we might assume from the vantage point of the twenty-first century.

We see changes though, after Indian independence, with Iftikhar Ali Khan's son, Mansur Ali Khan Pataudi, who went to Lockers Park Prep School in Hertfordshire and then Winchester College as a schoolboy from 1954 to 1959. Mansur was only eleven years old, and in England, when his father, Iftikhar, died in 1952. He went on to become one of the most successful Indian cricket captains of the twentieth century, having been appointed such at just 21 years old. Despite his upbringing in England, Mansur was described by Indian bowler Bishan Bedi as the first captain to give the players a feeling of 'Indianness' as he encouraged players to overcome regional rivalries and differences.[54] The ability of sport to bring diverse people together in support of a national team or player is testament to the historical power and influence of sport on broad populations and its huge influence on young bodies and minds.

Education and sport were important parts of developing elite British manhood and morality in the imperial era. Success at school sports allowed young South Asian boys to feel like they belonged and were accepted and yet the individual desire to win also fostered a sense of pride in being 'Indian' through achieving success despite the barriers they had to surmount. It was not only one way traffic; there were sports and games that Indians introduced to Britain like polo and chess. The rules of badminton were also developed in India and snooker was invented in India by British soldiers.[55] The loyal, almost 'British', Indians were the children who got stuck in and imbibed imperial values, especially through sports at school. This was all related to class and notions of masculinity; they could prove themselves to be the 'right sort' of Indian, who was not a threat or too alien, and—like the 'Brown Englishmen' before them—loyal to the Empire. By the early twentieth century, though, they were making their own waves. They were not just novel brown boys at school but growing in number and relevance within the British public school system and becoming mainstays of the establishment. They had to be accommodated within sporting teams and within the country's sporting imagination and, as the confines of these teams started to burst at the seams, these children began to imagine new futures where they could continue their pursuits and values back in India. There they would get more adulation and scope to pursue careers without the competition and constraints of imperial institutions.

These Indian children influenced British children and British sporting life too. The sporting and school exploits of Indian boys came face to face with the literature that young British children were reading in the early twentieth century. For example, Frank Richards (Charles Hamilton) wrote a series of stories for *The Magnet* about a fictional Greyfriars School, beginning in 1908. In the sixth story, 'Aliens at Greyfriars', a new boy comes to the school called Hurree Jamset Ram Singh, the prince of Bhanipur. A product of racial slurs and fun because of the way he talks, Hurree makes friends with the main characters of the series, including the infamous Billy Bunter, after he fights back physically against a school bully by use of an 'Indian wrestling trick' (helped by the fact that he also has lots of money).[56] In later stories, Hurree proves himself to be the best at bowling in cricket and skilful at chess. Hamilton later wrote in his autobiography that he had wanted to include an Indian boy who was an equal friend to the English schoolboys to show his young readers about the unity of the Empire and help rid the young of colour prejudice. The stereotypes about Indians with olive complexions were hardly without prejudice but the stories reveal how ideas of imperial loyalty and fraternity were being taught to young children in Britain and how South Asian child migrants were an integral part of those narratives.[57] Nationalism, via the mediums of politics and sport, was being heavily developed in India by Indians whose imperial footprints as children lay in the training and ethos of these British public schools.

6

THE SUFFRAGISTS

The British campaign for the right for women to vote began in the late nineteenth century and by the 1910s dominated conversations around women's rights. Women were asserting themselves as equal adults, chafing at the ways in which they were portrayed as girls without political understanding or the right to adult citizenship. The suffrage movement was part of a wider impetus, especially among middle-class families, for girls to be educated and financially independent. Young working-class girls during this period did go to work, often in factories or domestic service, living quite independently by the time they were 15, and political agitation was increasing around property, marriage and voting rights for women. Girls were brought into these debates from childhood. This was evident in the development of academically minded girls' schools such as Cheltenham Ladies' College and North London Collegiate School.[1] Advances in girls' education and debates around the political status of girls affected Indian girls who were migrants in Britain. They now had greater opportunities to engage with schools but also to engage with political campaigns that would affect their future citizenship in Britain and India. The position and role of Indian girls in Britain in this period was crucially important for ongoing debates around Britishness and the future of the Empire.

Women were enfranchised in the UK and Ireland in 1918 following a lengthy struggle by British suffrage campaigners, both the militant 'suffragettes' and the more 'moderate' suffragists. When women were enfranchised in 1918, there were some restrictions. Only women over 30, those who lived in registered property that was of a higher value than £5 in rent or graduates of universities could vote. It was not until 1928 that all women, irrespective of property or education, could vote, though there were no exclusions based on race, unlike Australia or South Africa where racial exclusions were written into the franchise. Indeed, in 1918, any British subject who met the residency qualifications was allowed to vote. In practice, this meant that any Indians who were resident in Britain, and who had registered to vote, would be allowed to vote, as they were subjects of the British Empire. The legacy of this remains enshrined in the voting regulations for the United Kingdom at the time of writing. Any Commonwealth citizens who meet residency qualifications are allowed to vote in UK elections; they do not need to have British nationality.

The right to vote in Britain, then, was entwined with imperial citizenship and subjecthood but the fight for women's suffrage was also entwined with struggles across the Empire and with Indian children who grew up in Britain. The most famous South Asian child migrant involved in the British suffrage movement was Princess Sophia Duleep Singh. Sophia was not only a descendant of the royal family of Punjab, as the fifth child of the Maharajah Duleep Singh, but also the goddaughter of Queen Victoria. Despite her background, she became actively involved in social welfare with female suffrage forming one part of this portfolio. Sophia was born in Norfolk in 1876 and had very little formal education as a girl. Her mother was often ill and depressed and died in 1887 when Sophia was just nine years old. Her father was often away having affairs or getting involved in financial difficulties. Queen Victoria showed a lot of interest in her and often sent her toys and gifts, like dolls and a miniature dinner set.[2] Her brothers had all been sent to Eton and her older sisters Bamba and Catherine had also had more formal education, attending Somerville College, Oxford. Sophia was not supported in her education in the same ways as her siblings but after her mother's death was enrolled into a day school in Brighton and had a governess—a German woman called Lina Schäffer—while under the guardianship of Arthur Oliphant. After her father's death when she was seventeen, Sophia was given deportment lessons to ready her for entry into British aristocratic life.[3]

In adulthood, Sophia became highly politicised. She joined the Women's Social and Political Union (WSPU), the leading British militant suffrage organisation, at the home of Una Dugdale in 1909 and became an active campaigner at the Richmond branch in Surrey. On 18 November 1910, Sophia took part in the first suffrage deputation, known as 'Black Friday', to the House of Commons. There she joined Emmeline Pankhurst, Elizabeth Garrett Anderson and nearly 300 other campaigners to urge Asquith's government to pass a limited suffrage bill, with the protest soon descending into police brutality and arrests. Sophia was not arrested on Black Friday but became actively involved with the Women's Tax Resistance League (WTRL). The WTRL's main form of resistance was to refuse to pay any taxes, ranging from income tax or property tax to dog tax or carriage licenses. They argued that as women did not have the vote they should not have to pay taxes. Bailiffs would impound objects from those who refused to pay taxes and then WTRL members would buy back the items at public auctions amid huge publicity.

In May 1911, Sophia's refusal to pay licenses for her five dogs, a carriage and servant led to a fine of £3. In December 1913, she was fined £12 10s. for refusing to pay for the licenses for two dogs, a carriage and a servant. In 1911, she refused to sign the census, defacing the form with 'No Vote, No Census', so a registrar had to fill it in for her. The census boycott had been organised by the Women's Freedom League as a non-violent form of political resistance, which incurred the threat of a £5 fine or a month's imprisonment. In the same year, she picketed Downing Street to demand votes for women, as part of an organised effort by the WSPU to picket various Cabinet members' houses.

Her elder sister, Catherine Duleep Singh (b. October 1871), was likewise involved in British suffrage, though to a lesser extent. She was a member of both the National Union of Women's Suffrage Societies and the WSPU but appeared to shun the militant side of the movement. Catherine attended various rallies and fairs, which included speaking at a suffrage fete in Nottingham in November 1912. She appeared at an 'Oriental Fete and Eastern Bazaar' organised by the London Society for Women's Suffrage in 1912, where those present wore 'gorgeous oriental dresses' and 'eastern attire'.[4] She had a long-lasting relationship with the family's German governess, Lina Schäfer, whom she first met when she was 15. Their relationship has been described as 'intimate'.[5] Catherine lived with Schäfer in Kassel, Germany from 1908 and so was rarely in Britain to be involved in suffrage activities. Schäfer died in 1937 and Catherine returned to Britain. In her will, she requested that a quarter of her ashes be buried as near as possible to Schäfer's coffin.

* * *

Due to her childhood of privilege and leisure, an outside observer perhaps would not have predicted that Sophia Duleep Singh would grow up to become an equal rights activist. In 1934, she listed 'The Advancement of Women' as her only interest for the *Women's Who Who*. At the same time, there were Indians who had spent their childhoods in Britain who began to engage with the fight for suffrage in the subcontinent. Like the children who developed into Indian nationalists, time in Britain as a child encouraged young South Asian girls to think more deeply about political inequality and political futures. Rajkumari Amrit Kaur was an Indian princess who grew up to become a suffragette who would work tirelessly for the Indian cause. Her fight was focused on the Indian struggle for equality in the 1920s and 1930s, leading up to independence. It was a time where it was not uncommon to find English-educated Indian princesses turned women's rights activists.

In 1921, the first women were given the right to vote in India—in the provinces of Bombay and Madras. The other states soon followed. Women were awarded the vote along the same terms as men, that is, if they owned a certain amount of property. By 1935, all provinces in British India had enfranchised women along these lines. In practice, this meant that less than 5 per cent of Indian adult women had the vote and in some provinces less than 1. In the 1910s,

'20s and '30s, Indian women travelled to Britain to petition British politicians and the state about Indian voting rights. As India was still governed by British politicians and the Crown, they were compelled to come to Britain to fight for this right. Indian women and girls continued to campaign after 1935 for full adult suffrage as Dalits and other minorities were excluded alongside women. Full adult suffrage was only introduced in India in 1949, after independence. Rajkumari Amrit Kaur (henceforth Amrit Kaur) was one of the key players in these campaigns.[6]

Born in Kapurthala Palace in Lucknow in 1889, Amrit was the first Indian to study at Sherborne School for Girls in Dorset, which she joined in 1902.[7] Having led an enclosed life in India, she was very shy at first and unfamiliar with games and sport. When she left in 1906, however, she was Head of School and captain of hockey, lacrosse and cricket.[8] There are photographs of Amrit from 1904 and 1905 with her hockey team and class.[9] She sits to the side though; as such an integral member of the school, she should have been front and centre. Was it a product of her race and ethnicity that led her to sit to the side or did she shun the limelight precisely because of her aristocratic privilege? Sophia Duleep Singh was known to be shy and reticent about public speaking despite her political convictions. Was Amrit also shy? Despite her upbringing and wealth—and despite her seemingly successful time at an English boarding school at the heart of elite British society—Amrit Kaur became a prominent Indian nationalist and women's rights campaigner in India. In her later life, she often shunned the help of British reformers and was keen to assert Indian independence and advocate for Indian women's abilities to lead their own societies and reform agendas. It is interesting that both Sophia and Amrit should follow this path.

Amrit Kaur had first visited Britain in 1902 at the age of 11 or 12 with her father, Sir Harnam Singh, the son of the Sikh Maharaja of Kapurthala and a convert to Christianity, in order to attend the coronation of Edward VII. She stayed on at Sherborne, living with a group of other girls in the headmistress's house during the term and spent holidays with Mary Kinnaird, the founder of the Young Women's Christian Association (YWCA), and the Wingfield-Digbys, the owners of Sherborne Castle. She had also spent some of her childhood in Ramsgate in Thanet, Kent, on the east coast of England, living with the family of Rev. K. B. Whiting, who was Vicar of St Luke's.[10] After leaving Sherborne, she had a few months of further study at Royal Holloway College for Women—although she did not sit any exams there or at Oxford—where she met Neil Bonarjee. She returned to India in 1908 and was soon drawn into nationalist politics.[11] Her parents died in 1924 and 1930, leaving her independently wealthy and unmarried.[12]

Amrit became heavily involved in the Indian suffrage movement in the 1920s and 1930s. In 1931, she gave evidence to a government committee in India looking into questions of the franchise in India, arguing that all women should be given the vote. She returned to London in 1933 to present demands on behalf of Indian women to a Joint Parliamentary Committee for Indian Reform. During her time in London, she met with many women's groups like the British Commonwealth League and attended afternoon parties held in her honour. Kaur utilised the help of British women to publicise the Indian women's fight but she disagreed with some of their strategies, especially the idea that the women's vote should be granted in stages. She argued that all women, irrespective of wealth, education or religion, should be given the vote. Kaur also served as one of Gandhi's private secretaries for 16 years and was an active member of the non-cooperation movement. She became a prominent women's rights activist in India, especially after 1926, and was the first Minister of Health in independent India in 1947 as well as the first female cabinet member of independent India. In doing so, she shed much of her aristocratic privilege but life at an English boarding school had certainly helped set up networks for later life and laid the foundations for her nationalist sympathies. In 1945, she was part of the Indian delegation to create the United Nations Educational, Scientific and Cultural Organization (UNESCO). At that meeting, which was held in London, she told other delegates: 'Children know no barriers of race or creed. Let us not educate them to know them'.[13]

Amrit's niece, Beryl, also studied at Sherborne and Amrit and Beryl were both successful tennis players.[14] Beryl was born in 1908 and her mother was Juliette Alice 'Maude' Anderson D'Auquier, daughter of the Reverend Emile Cornet d'Auquier, sometime headmaster of South Eastern College and curate of St Luke's Church in Ramsgate, Kent. In 1906, aged 21, Maude had married Shumshere Singh in London. Shumshere (b. 1879), or 'Shummy' as he was known in the family, was Amrit's older brother and was sent to England as a child too, joining Rugby School in 1893 at the age of 14. He went on to St Bartholomew's Hospital in London where he qualified as a surgeon and then joined the Indian Army Medical Service, serving in the First World War.[15] Their brother Inderjit may have studied at Harrow, though the records are unclear. Born in 1883, Inderjit died on 23 November 1914 at Festubert, Pas-de-Calais, France, when he was 30 years old. He was killed in action as an army doctor for India during World War I while attending to the wounded in a house completely destroyed by the enemy shells. Rajkumari Amrit Kaur died in New Delhi in 1964.

Rather confusingly, her namesake and another princess— Amrit Kaur, the Rani of Mandi (b. 1904)—was also educated at a British boarding school and engaged in the Indian women's rights movement at the same time. Her father, the Maharaja Jagatjit Singh of Kapurthala, was a cousin of Rajkumari Amrit Kaur's father but, unlike him, had not converted to Christianity. He sent his five sons to school in England, as well as his daughter, who went to the boarding school Clovelly-Kepplestone in Eastbourne. There, the Rani of Mandi read Shakespeare and Voltaire and was a member of an all-girl jazz band. She had an arranged marriage in 1923 to an Indian prince and then became involved in the Indian women's movement between 1926 and 1931. It had become a responsibility for English-educated and elite Indian women to engage in a movement that was keen to raise the minimum marriage age for girls and to ensure that all girls had access to education. The suffrage issue was slightly more divisive but the Rani of Mandi was one of the presidents of the All-Asian Women's Conference in Lahore in 1931 and enjoyed the participatory role of women's activism. Amrit Kaur of Mandi had two children and then moved to Paris in the 1930s. She was arrested in Occupied France by the Gestapo in 1940 for selling her jewellery to help Jews leave the country. She died in London in 1948.[16]

* * *

Another schoolgirl who was actively involved in the Indian fight for female suffrage was Avabai Mehta. Born in Colombo in September 1913, Avabai's family was originally from Bombay and of Parsee origin. Her father had been posted for work in Colombo. Her mother, Priojbai Mehta, was keen that her daughter should have the education she never received as a girl. She became further fixed on this point when she met the Irish revolutionary Annie Besant in Colombo, who saw Avabai and told her mother: 'You must educate your little daughter in England'. The fourteen-year-old Avabai and her mother, who had little command of English, sailed to England in 1928. Avabai's teachers and classmates, who had never known anyone to go to England for education before, sent them off with a tea party. Luckily, they had the financial means and Avabai's older brother, Pirojsha, who was nine years older and already settled in England studying at Cambridge, met them upon their arrival.[17] They lived in a flat in Adelaide Road in North West London, not far from Swiss Cottage and Primrose Hill, throughout their time in Britain.[18]

Avabai attended The Brondesbury and Kilburn High School for Girls from 1928, aged 14. It had been founded in 1892 as a demonstration school for the Ladies' Training College (later named the Maria Grey Training College). The council started aiding the school from 1909 and Avabai's brother, Pirojsha, had met with the headteacher before his sister arrived to check that the school was suitable. Avabai recalls that she faced both overt and covert discrimination as a student, being singled out as different and as the 'inferior subjects of a grand empire'. Friendships ensued, however, and she stated that on a personal level people were generally friendly, although 'a barrier between white and brown skins was maintained'.[19] The discrimination was a given, not to be questioned.

When they first came to London, Avabai and her mother attended various clubs and meetings for Indians. These included the National Indian Association, set up by Mary Carpenter back in 1870, which facilitated social interactions between well-meaning British liberals and Indian visitors to London, and the 'Sisterhood of the East' group for women which often met in Mayfair. The Mehtas were Theosophists, so they also met with Theosophical Society contacts. They both soon became heavily involved in suffrage societies.

On Adelaide Road, Avabai often visited the house of their Spanish neighbours, the Perez sisters, who held tea parties and were musically minded. At their house, Avabai met a young Devika Rani, another schoolgirl. Devika Rani went on to become the first Indian female star of Indian cinema. She was the poet Rabindranath Tagore's great-niece and daughter of the first Indian surgeon general, M. N. Chaudhuri. Devika Rani had moved to England aged 9 where she was forced into self-reliance early at boarding school. One morning she had asked for eggs for breakfast and in response had been locked up with only bread and water. She resolved never to ask for anything again. She felt stupid in class and was very conscious of her Indian identity.[20] Devika did, however, go on to attend South Hampstead High School and win a prize for a theatrical portrayal of Cleopatra before securing a scholarship to the Royal Academy of Arts in London.[21] During her summer vacations she worked for Elizabeth Arden as a makeup apprentice for women in London before her break into cinema.[22] Avabai also enjoyed visiting the cinema and theatre regularly in London with her mother.

Avabai's school was over two miles away from her home, so she probably took some form of public transport every day. She excelled at English in school and she was strong in French and history too. Avabai had to get used to new aspects of school; in her memoirs, she mentions that she found it complicated to navigate between moving rooms for her different subjects, as in Colombo they would stay in the same classroom all day. She also had to learn to deal with the cold and the compulsory edict to go out in the playground at break time, whatever the weather. Despite the changes, she thoroughly enjoyed the two years she spent there. Avabai learnt much later that the principal of Kilburn High School for Girls, Miss Johnstone, had announced to the whole school at assembly before Avabai joined that 'an Indian girl was joining them and they should all help to make things easy for [her] (show no racial prejudice)'. As she was not Christian, the headmistress said that Avabai did not need to attend assemblies but Avabai was used to them from school in Colombo and decided to attend. They would sit cross-legged on the polished parquet flooring. In one assembly, they were told to pray for India, which annoyed Avabai as they were directed 'to ask God to guide the

Indians properly' in their freedom fights. Avabai's mother insisted that she wear saris to school, which immediately accentuated difference while also soliciting a grudging respect for her individuality. She was allowed to wear the sari but had to wear a gym tunic and stockings for gym class once a week. She wrote that comments 'such as "How is it your finger nails are pink just like ours?" showed racial ignorance or prejudice, but there was never unkindness.' There was one other girl who had an Indian father but had been born in London and therefore 'counted as English'.[23]

At around the age of 16, Avabai joined the London Committee of the Women's Indian Association, through the invitation of Dorothy Jinarajadasa, a leading Theosophist. The Women's Indian Association had been set up in India in 1917 and one of its key aims was to enfranchise women in India. A London committee had only been recently set up as more Indian women found themselves in London and they wanted to gather interest and support for their cause in Britain. Avabai was the youngest member and she was soon travelling by herself by bus or train to various meeting places to give talks about the need for the Indian women's franchise. In June 1932, she attended the British Commonwealth League (BCL) conference and presented a paper on 'Women's Suffrage in India'. She had already attended the BCL conference in 1929. Avabai also met prominent suffragettes such as Charlotte Despard (founder of the Women's Freedom League), Florence Underwood (general secretary of the Women's Freedom League), Monica Whately (Labour councillor) and Margery Corbett Ashby (president of the International Women's Suffrage Conference). She visited the League of Nations in Geneva twice on behalf of the All-Asian Women's Conference—the first time in 1935, aged 22. Avabai also became heavily involved in another women's rights group, the Six Point Group. She was later an instrumental figure in family planning initiatives in India.[24]

In October 1931, the eighteen-year-old Avabai met Mohandas Gandhi in London at a celebration for his 62nd birthday. She also met Sarojini Naidu, a poet, suffrage campaigner and prominent nationalist from India who had been educated at Cambridge University; she was Gandhi's right-hand woman, with whom Avabai was enthralled. Given all of her contacts with British and Indian political activists in London it was no wonder that Avabai should become a firm supporter of Indian nationalism and Indian female suffrage. She also became a barrister, joining Lincoln's Inn and passing all of the bar exams by the time she was 19. However, she was not allowed to be called to the Bar until she was 21 and so had to wait to be called to the Bar in November 1934, eighteen months after completing her exams.

* * *

There were other Indian girls, earlier in the twentieth century, who, like Sophia Duleep Singh, had been drawn into the British suffrage movement. We have already encountered Neil Bonarjee in Chapter 4, now we turn to look at Dorothy (Dorf), his elder sister (b. 1894). Later to become a poet and artist who settled in southern France, Dorothy spent her childhood in London, living in Dulwich with her family. By all accounts, she was a creative and talented teenager. In 1912, at the age of 16, she had won a prize from a children's literary competition, run by the magazine *The Gentlewoman*, for a fairy tale she had submitted.[25] Two years later, while attending Aberystwyth University in 1914, Dorf was awarded an oak chair for winning the Eisteddfod (the Welsh music and poetry competition) for a poem she wrote about Owain of Wales. It was rare to win the competition for a poem written in English (rather than Welsh) and she was the first woman and first non-European at Aberystwyth to win this competition.[26] Dorothy was a trailblazer, becoming the first woman of any ethnicity to obtain a law degree from University College London, in 1917.

Dorothy and her mother were involved in suffrage activism in Britain. They both attended meetings of the British Dominions Woman Suffrage Union (BDWSU) in 1917, alongside other Indian women like Sophia Duleep Singh.[27] These meetings were organised by and for women from other members of the 'white Commonwealth' (Australia, New Zealand, Canada and South Africa) to meet and discuss common female suffrage struggles with British women. A series of 'Indian teas' were put on for Indian women which the Bonarjees attended, however at these meetings there was little to no discussion of how Indian women might become enfranchised in India itself.[28] Dorothy Bonarjee did speak at a BDWSU meeting in 1919 and signed an Indian Women's Franchise Address in the same year with her mother, which demanded equal franchise rights for Indian men and women in the subcontinent.[29]

Dorothy's cousins were also involved in the fight for suffrage in Britain. Susila (Susie) Bonnerjee (b. 1872), whose family we met in Chapter 3, was the daughter of the prominent Indian nationalist and reformer W. C. Bonnerjee.[30] Brought up in England from a very young age, she attended Croydon High School and then Newnham College, Cambridge, where she studied natural science. She then enrolled at the London School of Medicine for Women and was attached to the Royal Free Hospital, gaining her medical degree in 1899. Susie moved back and forth between India and Britain, returning to Britain in 1906 after her father's death and taking up a private practice in Ealing, West London. There she became a suffrage campaigner and secretary of the Ealing Branch of the Church League for Women's Suffrage (CLWS) in the 1910s. Members of the CLWS had to be Anglican or of related faith. On top of this, Susie was honorary secretary to the Indian Women's Education Association (IWEA) in 1911. She died in Lahore in 1920.[31]

The IWEA consisted of a group of Indian and British women in Britain who raised funds to bring women over from India to be educated on teacher training courses in Britain. The Association had many connections with the British suffrage movement. Another honorary secretary of the IWEA, Bhagwati Bhola Nauth, had been involved in the 'India section' of the June 1911 Suffrage Coronation Procession in London.[32] Her son, Veshasher Bhola Nauth, was a contemporary of N. B. Bonarjee and boarded at Dulwich College from 1912–17, having arrived from Oakfield School, Rugby. Nauth was a school prefect and a member of the rugby first XV like Bonarjee. Following a year at Cambridge, he trained for the Indian Army and was one of the first Indians to be granted a King's Commission. He was appointed second lieutenant in 1920, seeing active service in the Middle East during the Second World War. He died in 1950 after a short illness.[33]

Leilavati Mukerjea, daughter of Lolita Roy and a former student at St Paul's Girls' School, was a member of the Indian suffrage contingent at the Coronation Suffrage Procession in 1911 with her mother. Leilavati had married the Indian civil servant S. V. Mukerjea in London in December 1910.[34] It is likely that her two sisters, Mirabai and Hirabai, were also part of this procession. The procession was organised to celebrate the coronation of George V and use it to spur and publicise the women's demand for the vote. In order to demonstrate the potential reach and power of the British women's vote, an empire procession was included with representatives from the four nations of the UK in national dress and Australia, New Zealand and South Africa—all represented by white women—marching behind flags emblazoned with symbols from these countries (such as the kangaroo). Women from other colonies were apparently not found or invited but Indian women, including Leilavati, were in attendance, clad in saris and marching behind a flag bearing an elephant.

St Paul's Girls' School in Central London was founded in 1904 and was a relatively new school when Leila attended. She joined the school with her sister Mirabai in September 1905 and they both joined the fifth form (traditionally for 15-year-olds). Leila left in July 1907 with Mira departing the next summer. Their sister, Hirabati, joined the autumn after Leila left and stayed on for at least three years. She was a keen violinist who was awarded £5 for the Alice Lupton Senior Music Prize in 1907.[35] Mrs Roy had invited her illustrious friends Princess Sophia Duleep Singh and Atiya Fyzee—who was studying at a London teachers' training college at the time—to attend the Prize Day, where Mira also won a prize of several books.[36]

Lolita Roy, Leila's mother, had settled in England with her six children—three boys and three girls—with the firm intention of ensuring that they all received education in Britain. They had a servant at their London home and connections with Princess Sophia as well as an elite Indian set in London. They were not royalty or aristocrats but comfortably upper middle class. None of the sisters took any university entrance exams or seemed to pursue higher education despite their mother's role in the IWEA. Nor did any of the sisters take up prominent or traceable activities in suffrage or political activism during their adult lives. However, the connections and engagement of the Bonnerjees and Roys reveal how actively engaged young Indian girls in Britain were within the women's movement and the major women's political struggle of the time. They were not immune to or ignorant of these issues and played important roles in developing the women's suffrage movement in Britain and in India.

There were other daughters of Indian suffrage campaigners who went to school in Britain. Mrinalini Sen's three daughters, Srilata, Arati and Anjali, were born between 1906 and 1909, and had anglicised names that they used more frequently—Violet, Pansy and Rosie. Their father was the government-appointed Advisor to Indian Students, based at 21 Cromwell Road in London, and their house was a popular meeting place for Indian visitors and students in London. Their mother was actively involved in discussions about suffrage in London, promoting the cause at Indian teas with the BDWSU like the Bonarjees and Sophia Duleep Singh. In 1920, Mrinalini attended the Geneva conference of the International Alliance of Women for Suffrage, alongside other Indian delegates including Herabai Tata. She was also vice-president of the Bengali women's society, the Bangiya Nari Samaj, from 1921, which campaigned for women's suffrage. The three sisters were well known within Indian society in London and, in 1928, Frank Owen Salisbury painted a picture of them together known as the 'Sen Sisters'. Following Salisbury's death, the painting was kept at the Museum of Modern Art in New York from 1954 but sold in private auction for £96,000 in 2005.

Many Indian girls studied at St. Paul's like the Roy sisters; it seemed to have gained a reputation among Indian women activists as a conducive place for their daughters. Dhanvanthi Rama Rau, who was married to the deputy high commissioner for India in London, was very active in suffrage circles in Britain and Europe in the late 1920s and her daughters Premila and Santha were at Hall School, a Quaker school, in Weybridge. They joined in 1929 as the first Indians and stayed until 1934. When Dhanvanthi enrolled her daughters in the school, she had an interview with the Principal Miss Gilpin who was concerned to know: Could they play the usual games? Did they need any special instructions with their food?[37] In April 1931,

Dhanvanthi graced the front page of the suffrage newspaper *The Vote* for a discussion about the Indian suffrage struggle. The photo captured her with her two daughters, both kitted out in short-sleeved dresses with bobbed hair, alongside the caption 'Mrs Rama Rau and her little daughters'.[38] Both girls enrolled at St Paul's in 1934 where they studied for five years. Santha Rama Rau, the youngest, became a prominent writer and playwright in the 1950s and 1960s.

Leelamani Naidu, the daughter of prominent nationalist and women's rights campaigner Sarojini Naidu, went to St Paul's Girls' School as well, some time in the 1910s/1920s. Indeed, Sarojini Naidu was a hugely positive influence on Indian women in general, including Indian schoolgirls in Britain, and we have already heard of her influence on Avabai Mehta. As Gandhi's adviser, Naidu visited Britain often to attend political delegations and negotiations relating to suffrage, and to nationalism more broadly, but also to recover from chronic illness. She was a figurehead for Indian activists in Britain who would flock to meet her and gain inspiration from her calls for non-cooperation and independence. She also instilled independence in her daughter Leelamani and would encourage her daughter to stay in school hostels rather than with her mother.[39]

Padmini Satthianadhan, who studied at North London Collegiate from 1919 to 1923, remembers meeting Naidu often in London with her mother, whilst she was a schoolgirl. Padmini was the 14-year-old daughter of South Indian writer and women's rights activist Kamala Satthianadhan. Padmini came from a family with connections to England. Her maternal grandfather had converted to Christianity at the age of 19. Her uncle, Noble Krishnamma, born in 1887 in Madras had been sent to Merchant Taylor's School at the age of 12. When he first arrived in England, he lived in a boarding house in Norwich under the care of Major Fanning and his family.[40] His other brother, John (b. 1884), had been sent to England at the age of 12. Padmini had only ever been home-schooled in India so North London Collegiate was her first experience of formal education. She returned to India to continue her studies and edit *The Indian Ladies' Magazine* from 1927 to 1938. She later wrote several books and biographies about women in India, including a biography of her mother published in 1956.

To add another layer of connection, Padmini Satthianadhan lived on Adelaide Road, the same road—and perhaps the same property—as Avabai Mehta. Padmini had lived there in 1919 while attending school, later moving with her mother to a house in Denning Road, Hampstead. Avabai was there from 1928 while attending her school in Kilburn. Different generations of Indian girls, then, traversing the same streets a decade apart from each other, engaged with Naidu, women's rights and Indian writing in their own ways and would go on to change the course of women's politics.

* * *

The British suffrage movement is a key part of British history. It is taught in schools and remembered in films and books. Indian children were involved in this history. Indian girls in Britain were becoming inspired by the equal rights movement; their education, travels and connections helped them to forge roles within the British fight and translate this campaign into the Indian context. Indian girls in Britain were shaping women's politics both in Britain and in India, just as Indian children of all genders were influencing the broader nationalist fight in India. In their childhood in Britain these Indians could not help but face their political subjugation as colonial subjects and as girls. Inspired by their difference and the major political questions of their age, they took things into their own hands for their future. It is crucially important then to consider the history of these children in British schools and how they engaged in political agitations around suffrage, whether this was through the WSPU and WTRL as Sophia Duleep Singh did or giving evidence to government committees in India like Amrit Kaur. Their presence, conversations and activism indelibly affected the rights of women. Their paths were connected and inspiring and through their experiences at school, home and in political spaces, they were able to use their migrant experiences in vibrant ways to further women's rights around the world.

1. Author's mother, uncle and grandparents in Staples Corner, London, c. 1955, © Sumita Mukherjee.

2. Dolly Parnell and Betty Naldera Ali Khan, 1918.
© National Portrait Gallery, London.

3. N. C. Bakhle, Form Classical Remove, Dulwich College, 1919. With kind permission of the Governors of Dulwich College.

4. A.B. Habibullah (Sonny), Watson's House Fives team, Clifton College, 1927. Courtesy of Clifton College Archives.

5. Rajkumari Amrit Kaur, Aldhelmsted Senior Floor, Sherborne Girls' School, 1905. Courtesy of Sherborne Girls' Archive.

6. 'Why not make your own dug-out?', *The Graphic*, 29 September 1917. Mary Evans Picture Library.

7. Kamal Chunchie and children, c. 1930s. Courtesy of Eastside Community Heritage.

8. M. K. Sahebzada, Fancy Dress Dance 1926, Sherborne School.
Courtesy of Sherborne School Archives.

7

THE CASUALTIES OF WAR

India contributed more men than any other colonies or dominions of the British Empire to the war effort between 1914 and 1918. 1,440,437 Indians were recruited into the Indian ranks during the First World War and a further 239,561 into the British Indian Army in 1914.[1] At least 50,000 Indians were killed and missing in the War and over 67,000 wounded but with so many unrecorded combatants the number may be much higher. Indian troops fought in major battles such as the Battle of Neuve Chapelle in France and the Battle of Kut-al-Amara, just south of Baghdad, losing their lives thousands of miles away from home. Captain Kalyan Mukherji had trained as a doctor in London and Liverpool before joining the Indian Medical Service and becoming encamped with the Indian Army in Mesopotamia. He wrote a letter from 'Aziziya in Libya, on 20 October 1915, which blamed patriotism and nationalism for wars and bloodshed. He was critical of the violence of Indian nationalism as well as of the War and put the blame sorely at the feet of the English: 'England is the educator. ... it's the English who have taught us this.'[2]

The sense of loss that the First World War created in Britain through a 'lost generation' of young men—those who survived and those who were left behind—with tragic repercussions for families, has been documented and recorded in British poetry, literature and films. The novel *The Testament of Youth* by Vera Brittain, first published in 1933 and dramatised on television, in radio and film, for example, captures the emotions of loss for a young generation, with its focus on white, middle-class Britain. But what of the loss for Indian families and for the children of empire? What changes did the war wreak upon that generation? Tragedy befell the lives of young Indians who had been schooled in Britain and got caught up in the war as well as a larger generation of Indians whose youth was shaped by the experiences of war.

For some young Indians, the adventure of war, as well as a sense of duty, inculcated through education in Britain, inspired them to join the war effort at a very young age, sometimes with tragic consequences. This sense of adventure was bound up with the wonder of travel and schooling abroad that had inspired middle- and upper-class Indians to travel to Britain in the first place. Hardit Singh Malik had insisted that he wanted to study in England from a very young age. Born in 1894 in Rawalpindi, Punjab, Hardit's father was president of the local municipal committee. Hardit's older brother and cousin had both gone to England for university studies and his parents reluctantly allowed Hardit to go to England at the age of fourteen, provided he proved his maturity by making all his own arrangements. In 1909, he sailed from Bombay, alongside the Thakore Sahib of Limbdi (a prince in Kathiawar, North West India) and his son, who was also going to England for schooling. After a two-hour train journey from Dover, he was met at Charing Cross Station by his older brother, Teja Singh, a student of civil engineering at University College London. From there they drove in a hansom cab to their boarding house on Upper Addison Road in West Kensington, where Indian students lived alongside students of other nationalities. The landlady Mrs French served boiled mutton for their first dinner, which Hardit found disgusting; it was a disappointing introduction to London life. Hardit had to attend school by himself and first joined Linton Preparatory School in Notting Hill Gate for a year under the headmaster, Mr Hardie. Hardie arranged for Hardit to then enter Clifton College, Bristol, but, after being forced to attend chapel, he returned to London the next day.[3]

Hardit was admitted to Eastbourne College (in the south coast town) in May 1910. There, he was not compelled to attend chapel but soon found himself drawn to the Christian hymns and services anyway. He spent three years at Eastbourne and during his holidays stayed either with his housemaster—Mr Atkinson, a clergyman of Blackwater House—and local families or sometimes with his brother and other older Indian university students. Hardit was an opening batsman for the Eastbourne First XI and once played a cricket match against Marylebone Cricket Club (MCC), one of the most famous cricket clubs in the world, which included the guest player Sir Arthur Conan Doyle, of Sherlock Holmes fame.

At Eastbourne, Hardit engaged in cricket and hockey but not rugby because of his turban. Indeed, on his very first night at Eastbourne, a group of five or six boys—led by an Irish boy called Dennys, whose father was friends with Malik's father—surrounded Hardit and ordered him to take off his turban so they could see what was underneath. Hardit refused, explaining that he was a Sikh, and threatened to kill the first boy who touched his turban: 'So they backed off, unsure of what this native might do'. Following this, whenever Hardit played sports, the other boys would immediately apologise if they bumped into him and knocked his turban.[4] There were two other Indians at Eastbourne at the same time, Narpat Singh and Dalpat Singh from Jodhpur. One of the teachers, Mr Arnold, a strict disciplinarian, used to ignore the three Indian boys, making clear that he could not tolerate any foreigners, Indian or otherwise; this formed a black shadow over their time at the school, although other friendships flourished.[5]

Hardit took part in the Officer Training Corps (OTC) at Eastbourne. The OTC was a school society that prepared students for the British Army, although it could be enjoyed on its own merit. The OTCs had been formed in British public schools in the wake of the Boer War (1899–1902) and pupils would wear military uniforms, perform drills and parades and practise shooting. This was also replicated at universities and by 1914, the Officer Training Corps had over 27,000 members.[6] Hardit enjoyed the drill practice, training and shooting, as well as the discipline of the parade, which inspired him in his later military career. He finished at Eastbourne in the summer of 1912 and went on to Oxford in the autumn to study history at Balliol College, starting two months before he turned 18. At Oxford, he socialised with other Indian students in the Majlis Society and played golf. He also enjoyed cricket with another Indian, Paramasiva Subbarayan, whose wife, Radhabai, was a prominent suffragist in the 1920s and 1930s and whose sons subsequently studied at Eton.

Hardit was not allowed to join the Officer Training Corps in Oxford, despite his Eastbourne experiences, because Indian students were barred. In testimony he later gave in 1921 to a government committee looking at Indian students at UK universities, chaired by Lord Lytton, he talked about this exclusion. The English boys at his school had shown no objection to his membership of the school's OTC and he did not understand the difference at university. He did not think that his English compatriots wanted these restrictions either but realised they were based upon political reasonings. Political concerns about only including 'English' boys were soon thrown out of the window, of course, when Indians were required—in huge numbers—to engage in the 'English' war effort. Reflecting on his public-school education further, Hardit told the committee that he thought Indian students at British universities got more out of their time there if they had been to an English public school beforehand. Schooling in England was necessary preparation to get used to the 'strange atmosphere' of Britain, as English students were much less serious in games and studies than their Indian counterparts. Hardit thought it essential that Indian school boys should be placed in the care of a family in England, though, if they arrived as children and felt strongly that his insistence to travel to Britain at 14 was worth it.[7]

Hardit also played cricket for Sussex in 1914—introduced to the club by a doctor at Eastbourne who was friends with the cricketer K.S. Ranjitsinhji. When war broke out, Ranji opened his house in Staines into a hospital for wounded soldiers. He donated troops from his state of Nawanagar. He also went to the Western Front. In August 1915, Ranji was involved in a shooting accident in Yorkshire and lost his right eye but continued to play for Sussex until 1920. His strong connection with Sussex therefore helped smooth the way for

Hardit. After the 1914 season, Hardit attempted to enlist into the British armed forces. He was not allowed to enlist: the War Office provisions noted that people of colour could only voluntarily enlist when numbers permitted and recruiting officers allowed it. The only opportunity for Hardit to engage in the war effort was to work as an orderly at the Brighton Pavilion Hospital that had been set up to care for wounded Indian soldiers from the Western Front. So, Hardit learnt French and stayed on in Oxford until he was allowed to enrol in the Crois Rouge Française in 1915 as an ambulance driver; it was not until 1916 that he went to France. He was soon allowed to join the British troops and joined the Royal Flying Cadets. He saw action in 1917 and 1918 as a fighter pilot and was wounded in October 1917 in France, being subsequently demobilised in 1919.[8]

One compatriot and colleague at Eastbourne, who played cricket alongside him, was Dalpat Singh (b. 1892). Singh attended between 1907 and 1911. His father, Thakur Hari Singhji, who died when Dalpat was young, had been aide to Maharajah General Pertab Singh, who sent Dalpat and his own son Narpat to Eastbourne. Narpat Singh, who attended from 1906 to 1911, was in Blackwater House with Dalpat, who was known as a great batsman. He scored 117 in a match against the Stoics in June 1911 and was also a strong bowler. Dalpat lived in England for 10 years and during the holidays the boys spent considerable time with the Reverend Owen Tudor at the Vicarage in the village of Willingdon, not far from Eastbourne. Dalpat was recorded as living there in the 1911 Census. Iris Butler, who we met in Chapter 1, met Pertab Singh and the boys as a child during the war—at the London house of her uncle, who worked at the India Office—and remembered how disciplined and obedient they were.[9]

Immediately after Eastbourne, Dalpat joined the Indian Corps. He had been commissioned in 1913 before starting with the Jodhpur Lancers in October 1914, serving initially as a scout in France. A story circulates that his benefactor, Pertab Singh, met him in France and was furious that Dalpat had seemingly forgotten Rajput greetings and only displayed 'English manners'. It is also reputed that he may have married a French woman during the War.[10] During Dalpat's time of leave from fighting in France, he would return to Willingdon

Vicarage. Owen Tudor's four sons—Claud, Lionel, Oswald and Roland—attended Eastbourne College and all fought in the War too. Dalpat later became a major in the Jodhpur Lancers during the First World War, taking part in India Corps' campaigns in France and Mesopotamia. He was awarded the Military Cross but died on 23 September 1918 from wounds inflicted during the Battle of Haifa.[11] In a death notice in 1918, it was noted that Dalpat had 'gained the affection and esteem of all who had the privilege of knowing him' at Willingdon Vicarage. Owen Tudor's wife, Brenda Grimston, had connections with India as well; her two brothers had served in the cavalry in India. Upon Dalpat's death, condolences were sent to Brenda from Major Harvey who remembered Dalpat as a 'most gallant boy', saying that she must 'feel proud to have brought him up' and acknowledging the important connections and influences this family had on him as a boy at Eastbourne without parents in England.[12] T. Dalpat Singh is recorded on the tablet in the archway of the memorial tower at Eastbourne College dedicated to those boys who lost their lives in the Great War. He is one name alongside 166 others.

* * *

One of the more relatively well-known Indian fighters in the First World War was Indra Lal Roy. He is remembered on numerous British websites commemorating the War. Born in December 1898 in Calcutta to a Bengali family, he had arrived in Britain with his three sisters, two brothers and mother in 1901. All six siblings studied at St Paul's in London; the boys were all keen sportsmen and the girls were keen musicians. Their mother, Lolita Roy, was heavily connected with other Indians in London and, as we have touched upon, became a prominent Indian suffragist who helped organise an Indian contingent of women for the 1911 Coronation Suffrage Procession. In the same year, Roy joined St Paul's School. Stories of his attempts to compete as a boxer, alongside the prolific boxing success of his elder brother Paresh, abound the pages of *The Pauline*, the school magazine.

Indra Lal Roy, known as 'Laddy' / 'Laddie Roy', famously 'forgot' his mother tongue when he was a boy in England as a result of not speaking it habitually.[13] At the outbreak of war, he was only 15 but determined to join the war effort as soon as he could. He left school in 1917 for Oxford but almost immediately enlisted in the Royal Flying Corps instead, pretending that he was already 18. Roy was rejected initially on grounds of poor eyesight but in response he obtained two other opinions, even selling his motorcycle to pay off the eye-doctors and the decision was ultimately reversed. Like Hardit, entry for Roy had not been automatic and he was excluded from the chance to obtain a commission in the Army. Mohandas Gandhi's newspaper, *India*, suggested it was a 'discredit' to the authorities that they did not allow young Indians, like Roy and Malik, these opportunities, unlike their British fellow-students.[14] Clearly their schooling in England had prepared them to feel willing, entitled and a sense of duty, even, to engage in the British war effort alongside their British peers. Despite the injustices of empire and subjecthood that the war highlighted, they did not, in serving, see their race or 'nationality' as a contradiction, instead wishing to prove their loyalty to Britain and their colleagues.

Before the war, at school, Roy had been a captain of swimming and a committed member of the OTC. Despite this loyalty to the school, and his immense immersion in all parts of public-school life, Roy could never escape his racial identity. Even in death, a report in *The Sportsman*, lamenting his loss in the war and highlighting his sporting achievements as Bantam Champion of St Paul's in boxing, captain of swimming and an excellent half-back in rugby, noted that he had a 'quickness of eye and hand, the prerogative of his race'.[15] Why was there a need to suggest that it was a feature of Roy's race that made him such a quick rugby player, especially after he had died? The difference was always there and always marked despite his service. Roy was also a scholar. As his obituary in the school magazine recorded:

> He combined in an unusual degree intense devotion to England and intense love for the country of his birth. It was a source of great pleasure to him that in his last year at School he was the first to obtain three distinctions never before obtained by an

Indian: he gained a stripe in the O.T.C., was elected Captain of a game, and was offered the King's Commission.[16]

He would carry on breaking records after St Paul's, and indeed after his death, as the first Indian to be awarded the Distinguished Flying Cross, which he was awarded posthumously in 1919.

During the First World War, Roy's career was marked further by distinction. He obtained a pilot's certificate in the Flying Corps and went to the Western Front in October 1917. In March 1918, his machine was brought down but he was rescued from capture in an injured and unconscious state. By May 1918, doctors had cleared him to return to the War, first as an equipment officer, and then he was medically passed to fly again within a few weeks. The 19-year-old brought down ten German planes in fourteen days before plunging to his death in a dogfight on 22 July 1918.[17] As his death notice in *The Times* put it: 'He was one of a number of ardently loyal young Indians studying here who, precluded until recently from any chance of obtaining commissions in the Army, have found scope for striking a blow for the Empire in the new arm of our forces.'[18]

The wider Roy family had strong links with Britain and politics. Having arrived to live in Ealing, West London, in 1901, where they had a governess, a cook and two other domestics including an Irish parlourmaid, they became fully ensconced in British public-school life. By 1911, they had moved to Hammersmith where the sisters engaged in suffrage activism alongside their mother. The three brothers were all at St Paul's and well known within the school, having come up through the prep school, been involved in various societies and shown strong commitment to the St Paul's ethos. While the women in the family were campaigning for women's rights, the male offspring were committed to military careers in service to the British Crown. Was this a contradiction? Perhaps not in the eyes of the family where activism and engagement were important—sitting on the sidelines would not do. Indra Lal's older brother, Paresh Lal, had also fought in the First World War and survived. He went on to become an important Indian boxer, helping to popularise it in the subcontinent; he had proved his early mettle at St Paul's, where he was described as a clever fighter who did not face any other boys who met his level of skill during school boxing competitions.[19] Paresh was known as 'Ghu Ghu' by his family and enlisted in December 1914 as a private in the reserve battalion of the upper-class Honourable Artillery Company. He was sent to the Western Front in early 1915, joining the 3rd Division in May 1915, and then serving with that unit in the Royal Naval Division from July 1916 to June 1917. Paresh was wounded in action in May 1917 but not hospitalised.[20] He died in 1979 in Calcutta.

Their youngest brother, Lolit Kumar, known as 'Maffie', trained in the military but died in 1920 at Sandhurst Academy, aged just 20. His obituary somewhat confusingly states that he died of blood poisoning after he caught a chill from 'over-exertion' playing football. *The Pauline* remembered him fondly: 'At school his kindly and genial nature endeared him to all his companions. He was a keen sportsman, of unfailing cheerfulness, and, like, his brothers, was distinguished for a more than ordinary devotion to St. Paul's.'[21] Lolit boxed and at an early stage was playing in the Novices Boxing Competition in December 1913 where he won the Bantams final with his speed and a straight left.[22] In April 1913, at the annual boxing competition, the magazine noted that L. K. Roy was 'probably the smallest boy who has ever boxed in the School competition: both showed a fast and enterprising style, which recalls that of Roy's eldest brother, and which bodes well for School boxing in years to come'.[23] Lolit would likely have represented the school at boxing, like his eldest brother, but no public-school competitions were held during the War. He did earn a Boxing Blue at Sandhurst though, winning the annual competition in 1920. Following the exemplary contribution of Indians during the War, Sandhurst Military Training College was opened to Indians. In 1918, ten vacancies were created for Indian candidates and Lolit Kumar was part of that first batch. Between 1918 and 1926, 243 Indians competed for 83 places at Sandhurst; 16 of those 83 had been educated as schoolboys in England. Only 44 of the 65 candidates eligible to do so had graduated by 1926. Lolit and another candidate had sadly died before graduating from Sandhurst.[24]

War brought casualties upon innocent civilians caught up in crossfires too. On 30 December 1915, the SS *Persia*, travelling to

Karachi and Bombay from London, was torpedoed by a German U-boat in the Mediterranean. Over 500 people were on board, of whom over 300 died, including a large proportion of the Indian crew from Bombay. The children on board all died almost instantaneously—with one three-year-old child, David Hutchison, surviving—and, of those who died, there were at least three young Indian school students: Bawa Mangal Singh, Bawa Pratap Singh, and Sita Ram Gupta.[25] The two Singh brothers studied at St Paul's School in London and Sita Ram, who was sixteen, studied at Clifton College in Bristol. The Singh brothers had intended to join the Indian Civil Service and both were heavily involved in sports, including boxing. In the school obituary, Mangal was remembered for his 'shy and retiring nature' and for being a 'true friend'. Mangal was also a member of the school OTC. Pratap had a 'buoyant, merry disposition' which made him a 'great favourite'. As a boxer, he had speed and strong swerving powers that led him to win the final Junior Bantam Class for those under 6 stone in the House competition.[26] The contrast between the sporting joys of young Indian children in Britain with the tragedy of their deaths is acute. They were an unknown lost generation.

Indian involvement in the war affected young people beyond the military scenes. We have a photo of an Indian family standing in front of an air raid shelter in Hither Green in southeast London from October 1917. The picture shows us a man in a suit and hat, a woman in a sari and two young girls in dresses.[27] Further photographs, held by Getty Images, present this Indian family by the air raid shelter alongside white families. A page in *The Graphic* from 29 September 1917 contains an image of some of the children, including the Indian children, crowding into the shelter itself under the caption: 'Why not make your own dugout?'[28] It explains that a city merchant in Hither Green had built the dugout because of the war and that it was designed to accommodate his family and friends during air raids.[29] The Indian family, then, were part of that friendly neighbourly cohort that were bound together in the defence of war.

The imperial scale of the War was evident to many British people. The High Master of St Paul's, on 28 September 1914, only a few weeks into the War, well before the death of Roy or the Singh brothers, offered an address to the school which acknowledged the

Indian contribution: 'Do you not feel a glow of pride when from every corner of this big empire came the voice of approval and the promise of help? They are free peoples, and need not follow where we lead. Not least I think of India, who offers her hundreds of thousands of men and all her resources.'[30] The school master did this to invoke the glory of empire among the young schoolboys and to extol its virtues and benefits. There were other ways in which this rhetoric became evident. Hilton DeWitt Girdwood was an official British cameraman for the War Office. His film *With the Empire's Fighters*, which followed various Indian regiments, was premiered on 11 September 1916, and Girdwood went on an extended 'lecture- tour'; he claimed to have given 866 lectures in Great Britain, reaching a million people, including 250,000 children. The film is lost but schoolchildren were invited to write down their reflections after watching the film and enter a prize competition. The essays from Constance Fletcher, aged 11, from St Paul's School in Preston; Isaac Silverman, aged 13, from Liverpool Hebrew Higher Grade School; and John Slater, aged 11, from St Augustine's Boys in Preston, survive. John Slater described how the film brought home to him the 'magnificent' way India was helping the 'Mother-Country in her hour of need'. He admired the patience of Indian soldiers fighting in trenches on the Western Front during the winter and remarked that the 'Indians are greatly devoted to their British officers and they also like children very much.'[31]

Meanwhile, the presence of Indian soldiers on the shores of Britain changed expectations and the spaces of encounter for British people. I have already mentioned the hospital that Ranji set up in Staines and briefly alluded to the Brighton hospital. In November 1914, Lord Kitchener, the Secretary of State for War—famously emblazoned on 'Your Country Needs You' posters—appointed Walter Lawrence as Commissioner for Sick and Wounded Indian Soldiers in France and England. He procured the Royal Pavilion in Brighton as a space that could be, and was, converted into a hospital for wounded Indian soldiers. In addition, hospitals were set up in Brockenhurst and Bournemouth. Photos and sketches of these hospitals show young Indian soldiers convalescing, with strict requirements to stay within the grounds of the hospitals unless taken out with guards or on special tours. Later concerns and restrictions were enforced about their contact with white nurses.[32] While they may not have been children as defined by modern ideas of age and adulthood, the ages of those recruited to the Indian Army in the subcontinent were not always known and there were likely many aged 18 or younger. While there were restrictions on their mobility, because of fears about race and social mixing, there were some occasions when local British communities could interact with the Indian soldiers. In January 1915, the *Brighton Herald*, for example, reported one interaction where after an Indian soldier picked up a white child, so many more mothers began to hand their children over to the Indian soldiers that it turned into a 'comedy that aroused pearls of laughter'.[33] Young white British children were being encouraged during the War, then, to empathise with and celebrate the Indian contribution to their national successes, victories and safety. When the War was over, why did these feelings of comradeship become forgotten? The potentially inclusive nature of Britain under conflict, with a shared sense of purpose across empire, was forgotten in peacetime when more parochial notions of imperialism and nationalism were re-strengthened through the rhetoric of remembrance and victory.

* * *

Although the Indian contribution to the First World War was part of a commitment to the British Empire, it marked a watershed period in Indian relations with Britain because immediately afterwards, in April 1919, the Amritsar massacre occurred. At least 379 unarmed men, women and children were shot upon by British soldiers and more than a thousand injured, contributing to Gandhi's rise to political leadership of the Indian National Congress in the subcontinent. The tragedies for Indian soldiers in the First World War were immense and had important repercussions on the Indian economy and society but young Indians were also affected by the Second World War as the theatre of war became much more global. Indian involvement in the Second World War became more politically charged than it had been in 1914. By 1939, the growing non-cooperation movement in India questioned why India should join an 'imperial war' and these concerns led to calls for the British to 'Quit India' in 1942.

The cases of Indians who were educated in Britain and who fought for the Allied Forces are few and far between as the contradictions of imperialism were heightened by this period and more acute for young Indians at this time. There were some exceptions, of course, such as Noor Inayat Khan.

Noor Inayat Khan was born to Inayat Khan and Ora Ray Baker, who had married in London in 1913. Ora, an American of Scottish heritage, changed her name to Amina Sharada Begum after marriage. Noor's father, Inayat, was born into a noble family in Baroda and had trained in music and Sufism. They soon moved to Russia and Noor was born in Moscow on 1 January 1914. When war broke out, the family returned to London and spent the next six years there.[34] Inayat was a musician who was well connected with European high society as well as Indian leaders, meeting with Sarojini Naidu and Gandhi in London. In 1915, he founded the Sufi Order in England and became a *murshid*, teaching and lecturing about the Sufi Order. By 1917, the family were living in Gordon Square, London with Noor and her two younger brothers and sister. Their house was frequented by visiting Sufis and Inayat was involved to some degree in politics, sympathising with nationalist developments in India. It appears Noor and her siblings had a lot of freedom and were relatively unsupervised in their early years. In 1920, the family moved to a village just north of Paris.[35] Noor started attending school in Suresnes at the age of 8. Her father died in 1927. Most of Noor's upbringing and childhood was in France but she had spent crucial early years in Britain before leading a highly cosmopolitan life in France where her father was always longing for connection to India and Indians.

In 1932, Noor enrolled at the Sorbonne to study child psychology and then started a career as a children's writer, including writing adaptations of Indian legends. She signed up with the French Red Cross in 1939 and then, in 1940, the whole family evacuated and relocated to Britain. Noor, who had been a child migrant, became involved in the Second World War from the British side. Despite her father's political allegiances and Sufi upbringing in France, she felt energised and compelled enough to fight for the British cause and Allied side during the War. Her cosmopolitan background was an asset but perhaps ensured that she did not feel a contradiction about

133

her allegiances or sympathise with an alien India that she had never visited. In recent years, though, historians have claimed her for her Indian heritage, reducing her to her ethnicity without interrogating whether she identified as 'Indian'. We should pause to ask, is this fair to Noor and her memory and her intentions? She joined the Women's Auxiliary Air Force (WAAF), training as a wireless operator and was soon recruited as a secret British Resistance Agent by the Special Operations Executive to work in France. She was captured and killed in Dachau Concentration Camp in 1944.

There were other former Indian school boys from English schools who fought in the Second World War. They include Rajendrasinhji, the prolific cricketer at Malvern we looked at in Chapter 5, who was commissioned into the Second Royal Lancers and won a DSO. He maintained his military career up until the Second World War when he was sent to North Africa in 1941 as a squadron commander. He returned to India in October 1942 and was promoted to Brigadier after the War.[36]

His older cousin Digvijaysinhji had taken up a military career after he left Malvern too but did not fight in the Second World War. After leaving school in 1915, he studied at University College London before being commissioned into the British Army in 1919. He retired from the army in 1931 and succeeded his uncle, the cricketer Ranjitsinhji, as Jam Sahib (prince) of Jamnagar in 1933. During the Second World War he sat on the Imperial War Cabinet and set up a refugee camp in Jamnagar for Polish children from Eastern Europe. When the children arrived, Digvijaysinhji is said to have told them that he was their father now and to call him 'Bapu'. The camp was said to house 1,000 Polish children, providing them with food, comfort and entertainment.[37] In October 1942, he returned to England to give a speech to the pupils of Malvern College. He explained that he had tried to be worthy of Malvern in his career and that he and other Indian princes were ready to fight for democracy and against Germany, even if Congress was unwilling. He noted that one million Indians were already fighting in the War, with another million to go.[38]

Meanwhile, the Second World War had also come to the streets of Britain, with the Battle of Britain in 1940, evacuation of children from major cities to rural areas and air raid sirens, drills and shelters becoming a major feature of British life. When I was a child, my favourite book was *Carrie's War* by Nina Bawden. First published in 1973, it told the story of Carrie and her brother Nick, who were evacuated to a Welsh town during the Second World War, and the friendships and adventures they got involved in. I had other favourite books that featured evacuee children such as *Goodnight Mister Tom* by Michelle Magorian (1981) and C. S. Lewis' *The Lion, The Witch and the Wardrobe* (1950). Were any Indian children evacuated during the War? With growing numbers of children of Indian descent in Britain, by 1939 there were children of South Asian heritage who were evacuated or knew evacuees, as my subsequent examples will show, although we do not know on what scale. The research in this area is limited, however, as consciousness and recognition of the multiracial background of 'British' children in this period remains partial. The novels I read about this period certainly did not feature children of colour but I have found some real historical examples. A pupil at Malvern College, Pratapsinhji, was an evacuee during the Second World War; the whole college had to evacuate to Blenheim Palace first and then Harrow School while the College was requisitioned by the Admiralty and the Telecommunications Research Establishment.[39] Maya and Chaya Bhattacharyya were twelve and eight at the outbreak of the War. Maya had been born in Assam and came to Britain with her mother and doctor father when she was three. Chaya was born in London in August 1931. They were evacuated from their London home to Berkhamsted in Hertfordshire during the War.[40] We will encounter another evacuee, Doreen Khan, in the next chapter.

The experiences of the Chowdhary family in Laindon, Essex, give some rare insight into other Indian children's experiences. Dharam Sheel Chowdhary was a GP in Laindon. His wife Savitri, who came to Essex in 1932, gave birth to their son, Vijay, in 1935 and their daughter, Shakuntala, in 1938. When Poland was invaded on 1 September 1939, Savitri remembers watching her children play outside with the neighbour boy, David, and recognising their innocence. The family built an air raid shelter in the garden; when the Battle of Britain started in 1940, they began to sleep regularly in the shelter until it got flooded and they had to move back into the house, with the children sleeping under the kitchen table. In the shelter, the family squeezed in with Mary, their maid, who slept on a top bunk, the children on the bottom bunk and the parents on the floor.[41] Both Dharam and Savitri enlisted as air wardens. The local authorities soon ordered evacuation and Savitri took Vijay and Shakuntala to St Austell in Cornwall. They stayed with the Kelynack family who had previously owned a chemist in Laindon. After a few months, air raids began to hit Cornwall too, so the three of them returned to join Dharam back in Laindon until the War was over.[42]

Savitri's accounts do not reflect on the tensions that Indian nationalists were feeling about the Second World War. Her husband was part of the Civil Defence Guard and she was engaged in local activities to support the wounded. While Savitri was also involved with the India League in London, headed by Labour activist Krishna Menon, who was vocal in support of Indian independence, the tragedies of bombing and the threat of war compelled her family to support their local community in the face of international conflict. Immediately after VE Day in 1945, Dr Chowdhary employed a new medical assistant, Dr Madan, a Punjabi who had come to Britain when he was 19. A Sikh, he had cut his beard and no longer wore a turban. He was married to Gwyneth and had two children. Savitri asked him: 'Do they know anything about their grandparents and other relatives in India?!' He replied: 'No not at all. I never talked to them about India. I want them to get thoroughly assimilated in this country. I don't believe that one can be loyal to two countries at the same time. I don't want them to be frustrated and belong to neither this country nor India.'[43]

Questions of loyalty and identity became acute during the War and its aftermath. Was British subjecthood incompatible with Indian identity? Where did Indian children sit within the narratives of war and where did the future for these children lie? The *Daily Mirror* produced a cartoon on 13 March 1946 which recognised the famine crisis affecting children globally—a housewife is putting food into her dustbin while a cloaked figure with 'World Famine' on their back asks: 'Madam, you have just killed two Chinese, one European and three Indian children—feeling good?'[44] Earlier, the Bengal famine of 1943 had highlighted the injustices of colonialism and the ways in which children are often innocent victims of war and geopolitical conflicts. About 3 million people lost their lives in the Bengal famine. But while the poor, hungry, Indian child was being invoked, what of the children of colour and empire within Britain? Did they fit into narratives of British victory on VE Day? While campaigns for independence had grown, no-one had predicted the speed with which this would happen or that, two years after VE Day, the new nations of India and Pakistan would be created, on 15 August 1947.

What does all this death mean? These children of empire lived in different countries from their birth and their parents. They went to British schools. They fought for the British. They gave their lives to a British war effort. How have they been remembered? Why are they not included in more British school lessons, films and novels about the Wars? In 2022, the Commonwealth War Graves Commission agreed to mark a grave for Lolit Kumar Roy. He had not fought in battle but had been training in Sandhurst to do so. His brother is remembered as the Indian World War I fighter pilot who died in the war but how should we remember Lolit? And Dalpat Singh in Palestine? And Hardit Malik, who fought but did not lose his life? Noor Inayat Khan has a statue in London, and a blue plaque, even though she spent little time in London in her life—why has she been accepted by English Heritage when others have not? The First and Second World Wars continue to loom strongly in the formation and rhetoric around British identity and belonging. Remembrance looms largely in the myth of British identity. These children of empire emphasise the instability of imperial and British identity both then and now, as well as the multiplicity of experiences which were shaped by race and age. We should not forget them.

8

THE LASCARS' CHILDREN

In 1968, the Conservative MP for Smethwick, Enoch Powell, infamously delivered his 'Rivers of Blood' speech where he warned that ongoing immigration to Britain was 'wiping' out the white population, with no spaces for white women in hospitals for childbirth and their children unable to find school places: 'It almost passes belief that at this moment 20 or 30 additional immigrant children are arriving from overseas in Wolverhampton alone every week'.[1] While citing the 'influx' of children from racialised backgrounds as a particular menace, he raised concerns about the racial make-up of a future British population. On the other hand, a year earlier, in 1967, the sociologist G. S. Aurora, in his study of Indian immigrants to 'Greenend' (a pseudonym for a borough neighbouring a big city in the UK), discussed how interracial relationships were a progressive sociological trend. Aurora suggested that they might grow, particularly as a result of those Indians who were keen to assimilate in Britain. Focusing on white European women having children with Indian men, he noted how children often made interracial relationships more secure and encouraged the men to become more 'European' in their ways through the influences of their wives and children.[2]

Throughout British history there have been clear disparities in responses to mixed race relationships. As Chamion Caballero has researched, interraciality in Britain goes back centuries and is not a modern phenomenon. While there has been some lurid interest in these relationships throughout history, they have also been so widespread as to be ordinary and unremarkable.³ When upper-class Indians, whether a man or woman, married white people in the nineteenth century and at the height of the British Empire, there was often opposition but also a long colonial history of this, as William Dalrymple has evocatively shown.⁴ We have encountered the Duleep Singhs and the Sake Mahomeds already; their interracial relationships were not prohibited. There are rumours that Queen Victoria may have forbidden Prince Victor Duleep Singh to have any children with his wife, Lady Anne Coventry, in 1898, for fear of diluting the race of the British aristocracy. This has parallels with rumours about concerns expressed by the Royal Family in the twenty-first century about the 'colour' of Prince Harry and Meghan Markle's children. Eugenic sciences in the early twentieth century took on a different tone when discussing lower-class children.⁵ For example, attention was placed on their intelligence and physical strength relative to other classes with racialised concern about the survival of the fittest. Eugenic reports of the 1920s and 1930s in Britain made much more of appearance, hair and nose features, health and the quantity or fractionation of race, i.e. whether someone was 'half-caste' or other derogatory and extremely offensive terms associated with slavery, such as 'quadroon' or 'octoroon'.

There were also more concerns around white women's sexuality when they engaged with lower-class Indian men. This anxiety was firmly rooted in ideas about sex and the control of women's sexuality more broadly. From 1870, British women who married foreigners automatically lost their British nationality and this was restated in law with the 1914 British Nationality and Status of Aliens Act which conversely allowed non-British women to become British if they married a British man.⁶ In 1913, the India Office— the government department that dealt with India matters—issued a circular to registry offices around Britain suggesting that Indian men were invariably polygamous and reminding them that British women who married Indian men would lose their British nationality.[7] These public concerns fed into the lives and experiences of children born from these unions in Britain. Much of this concern was centred around working-class children in British port cities.

South Asian sailors, known as 'lascars', were used in high numbers on merchant marine, trading and passenger ships between India and Britain for centuries and particularly from the mid-nineteenth century onwards. British maritime agreements dictated that South Asian lascars would receive between one fifth to one third of the pay of white seamen and they were forced into harsh roles, such as stoking the coal fires below deck, and into more cramped living conditions than their white peers. Many of these lascars would 'jump ship' in Britain and try to make new—often hidden—lives for themselves. By the 1840s, 3,000 lascars were arriving in Britain every year.[8] Their numbers increased over the nineteenth century with the development of steam technology and by the interwar period more seamen were settling down with white British women in Britain. Most of these men were Muslim and many of their wives converted to Islam. Very little has been written or researched about the children of Indian seamen who were born into mixed-race and mixed-faith families in Britain. As a result of their mixed heritage and lower-class and social status, these children were, of course, engaging with different racial politics to the public-school children discussed in previous chapters.

Census records also reveal that lascars on ships in Britain in 1901, 1911 and 1921 were often in their mid-teens, aged around 14, 15, 16 or 17 (along with much older seamen). For example, in 1921, the P&O SS *Nankin* was docked at Falmouth Docks in Cornwall and their lascars included the 14-year-olds Esmail Abdul Dawood, Moosa Mahd and Esmail Eussoof from Daman in India, as well as the 15-year-old Fazal Ahmad Baloor who was a fireman from the Punjab and the 16-year-old Fazal Ahmed Akmar who was a coal trimmer on the ship.[9] Though they might not have been regarded as 'children' by contemporaries at the time because they were working in hard manual jobs, they were still early in their life cycle and going through huge migration and upheaval at a young age. It was through this profession that young lascars found themselves in port cities across

England, Wales and Scotland. In 1861, 17-year-old Manill Daymane could be found lodging with shoemaker Robert Gillespy's family in South Shields.[10]

On 17 September 1940, the SS *City of Benares* was carrying evacuee children from England, sailing from Liverpool to Montreal in Canada when it was torpedoed by a German submarine. There had been 406 people on board, including 100 British, Australian and Canadian children, and 81 of those children lost their lives. The crew included 167 people from India and Goa, 101 of whom died. Most of the attention on this tragedy has been placed on the evacuee children but many of the lascar crewmen who died were also children. Twenty of the crew were officially aged between 14 and 17. The children aged 14 worked in roles such as cabin-boy, pantry-boy and pot washer. Derek Law has found an image of young South Asian boys serving tea to soldiers in London docks who look much younger than 14 and argued that we can assume that many lascar crews included boys who were younger, especially as birth records in colonial India were largely unkept.[11] The tragedy of the *City of Benares* proves how forgotten and hidden South Asian children's lives have been.

Life for lascars in Britain was not easy. They had to find places to stay and places to work. The Alien Restriction Act of 1919 required Black and Asian seamen to possess official documents proving their right to live and work in Britain; they would be treated as 'alien' by officials if they did not have them, even though subjecthood within the British Empire gave them a right to entry and settlement in Britain at the time. The Coloured Seamen Order of 1925 was also used indiscriminately to police and control Indian seamen.[12] The largest conglomeration of Indian lascars populated the East End of London around the East India Docks and areas known as Limehouse and Poplar. Seamen who docked in shops in the East India Docks were catered for by other South Asian landlords and cafes that grew in the nineteenth century, alongside mission houses such as Salter's Strangers' Home. There was a case in 1902 when a sixteen-year-old boy, Ankaram, from Madras found himself at the Strangers' Home. He was not a sailor and came from an educated background. It is unclear how he arrived in England but, when he turned up destitute at the India Office, they sent him to the Strangers' Home.

Ankaram was given lodgings at Dr Barnado's Home for Children plus dinner and keep at the Strangers' Home. The Home tried to find him employment as a cabin boy but, as a rule, there were very few opportunities for this role. Due to his class background, he was initially alarmed to be among sailors. He eventually found work as a cook's mate and attended evening classes.[13]

Many lascars moved to the industrial city of Sheffield, with its large steel industry. Gisalic Amidulla, for example, was a boiler firer at the Brown Bayley steelworks in the 1920s. He was married in a Christian ceremony to Maggie, whose family lived just round the corner from the steelworks, and they had four children. Amidulla died in 1931 from a heart attack, at the age of 37, by which time the family were living in a housing estate in Sheffield's suburbs. The family soon returned to Maggie's parents' home. One of their sons, James, followed his father into work as a furnaceman.[14] David Holland's study of Sheffield's South Asian migrants reveals that many Muslim men married white women in Christian marriage ceremonies, indicating that not all white women converted to Islam in such unions. Like Caballero, Holland has emphasised the ordinariness of some of these relationships and proven how difficult it is to trace the children of South Asian migrants in this period. It is difficult, especially if we remove the assumption that they retained distinctive links with South Asian religions and other community strongholds in Britain.

As mentioned above, when Indian women married white British men, they were deemed British but when Indian men married white British women, they did not become 'English' or 'British', although they still had the rights of British subjecthood through the Empire. Class dynamics played into these identities too. Diane Robinson-Dunn has argued that lower-class English women were not considered truly English because of their class and could become 'orientalised' via their relationships with Indian seamen. For example, Sarah Graham became known as 'Lascar Sally' because of her association with lascars 'whose language and habits she had acquired'.[15] Women in that area bore the names Mrs Mohammed, Mrs Peroo, 'Calcutta Louise' or 'Lascar Sally', demonstrating the rise of mixed-race relationships there and through the nineteenth century.[16] Lascar families, then, became characterised as 'other' and their children had to grapple with complex questions of nationality, class and religious identity. The imposition of a Muslim ethnicity upon them, through terminology such as 'Mohammedan' and the association in the British media that all lascars and their children were Muslim, marginalised them within British society, whether they came from South Asia or other parts of the world. This brought Muslim lascars together through new bonds; they formed communities centred around the *zawiya* and the local sheikh. The sheikhs played an important role in teaching Islamic tenets to their white wives and English-born children.[17]

In the 1950s, the sociologist Sydney Collins wrote some academic articles about 'coloured' children in Britain in the period 1949–1951. He argued that Pakistani families' migrants organised on the basis of religion, i.e. Islam, rather than on the basis of race. Discussing Muslim Pakistani seamen, Collins argued that the majority married white working-class women and their children were brought up Muslim because of the dominance of the father and because the women converted to Islam. In a rather generalising account, Collins suggested that religious institutions and instructions were formative for young British-born children, as well as socialising with white British children at school and their mother's families. He theorised that most of the boys born from these unions became seamen, like their fathers, and that the girls generally married young and usually into Muslim families.[18]

But what of the children and their lives? How did they engage with Islam or other religions? What did they make of their fathers' professions and sea journeys from the faraway lands of the Indian subcontinent and how did they navigate poverty and their lives in Britain's urban areas? Did they manage to reconcile their white British identity with their South Asian identity at a time when the Empire was at its height and, though common, mixed-race origins were marked out for intrigue, study and concern? Though, as we shall see, it can be difficult to answer these questions conclusively, there being few accounts of these childrens' inner lives, it is essential to pose them and parse what we can based on the evidence we have.

* * *

THE LASCARS' CHILDREN

> Chinks and Dagos, Lascars and Levatines, slippered about the faintly evil-byways that ran off from Bute Street. ... Children of the strangest colours, fruit of frightful misalliances, staggered half-naked about the streets; and the shop windows were decorated with names that were an epitome of all the clans and classes under the sun.[19]

How did white British children view 'lascars' and their children? Well, the quote above from Howard Spring's memoir of his infancy reveals the derogatory language in use in the early twentieth century. Ivy Alexander, who was a child in the interwar period, similarly recalled that, growing up in the East End of London, she was instructed to stay away from Victoria Dock Road which was frequented by '"black men" who wore their shirts outside their trousers'. They were lascars and according to Ivy they lived 'wretched lives'.[20]

Even before this, Joseph Salter—the missionary we encountered in an earlier chapter, who worked with Asian and African sailors in Victorian East End London—used colourful language to describe children of colour in the East End. In his 1873 book, *The Asiatic in England*, Salter discussed a visit to Bluegate Fields, an area near the east London docks known as a 'slum area', referenced in Oscar Wilde's *The Picture of Dorian Gray* (1890). In his writings, Salter depicts the children he saw, just released from school, as representing 'so many nationalities', and being 'distinctively' of 'foreign parentage'. He describes the anxiety and pity placed upon these 'innocent' children and uses stereotypical imagery, from the 'woolly hair' of Africa to the 'luxuriant flowing hair of Hindostan', suggesting that they unconsciously spoke using depraved vocabulary and that their faces unmistakably linked them to the Empire.[21] The children were marked out for their skin colour and facial features, with little consideration of the imperial politics and trade that had made their lives possible and necessary in Britain.

In March 1930, the *Daily Express* wrote about the lives of mixed-race children who lived in Crown Street, a road in Canning Town in East London. With an accompanying picture that had the caption, 'The great majority ... of the children ... are of every conceivable hue', the article narrates that Crown Street is a squalid thoroughfare known as 'The Street of Hopeless Children'. Suggesting that the population they had observed was of roughly 600 children, with 98 per cent of them having a white mother, they describe the children as 'poor little half-castes' who were looked down upon from childhood and therefore grew up with bitterness against the white race. The article goes on to detail that by 'nature they are children of sunshine, open air, and laughter', living in the cold and dirt of the East End slums, 'without race, with no country that they can call their own' and knowing only cockney idioms. The report tries to be sympathetic to their class and impoverished background but, instead of suggesting any solution, concludes that the prejudices they face will inevitably lead to desolate lives.[22] Crown Street was also known as 'Draughtboard Alley' because it was popularly described as having Black and white people living evenly across the street like a draughtboard.[23] The language around race and mixed-race children was often derogatory and also made a problem out of varied social relationships.

In 1930, a social worker, Muriel Fletcher, wrote a 'Report on an Investigation into the Colour Problem in Liverpool and other ports' for the Liverpool Association for the Welfare of Half-Caste Children. Fletcher's report focused on relationships between Black and white people and was particularly concerned with their children. She used derogatory language to discuss the men, women and children in these families and condemned these relationships. Although the report was not widely taken up afterwards, it did lead to several other reports on the conditions of port cities, seamen and relationships. In 1934, a Port Survey Officer, Captain F. A. Richardson, conducted a survey of London, Liverpool and Cardiff around the conditions of seamen's living quarters but took the opportunity to condemn white women who engaged in relationships with 'coloured' seamen and portrayed the children of these relationships, especially the girls, as leading tragic lives.[24]

While people of colour in interwar Britain were, of course, racialised in different ways—racialisation of Black people involving different tropes, for example—these reports indicate the general way in which people with authority and official positions were perpetuating concerns about race and imposing these concerns on children in Britain. In 1944, a committee of 'concerned residents' in Stepney, East London, including two South Asian men, S. D. Khan and Jamiab-ul-Muslimin, commissioned a report into the conditions of 'coloured' people in the Stepney area.[25] Phyllis Young wrote up the report and, like other reports, showed particular concern for 'half-caste' children, while also blaming white women for engaging in mixed race relationships. The report categorises children into three categories: (1) homes in which both parents are coloured; (2) homes where the parents are mixed; (3) homes of mixed marriages but where either parent is connected with promiscuous living. Young concludes that children in category 1 are the happiest but that children in 2 and 3 come under strain and have divided loyalties to their parents or, specific to the third category, are not looked after properly.[26]

Mixed-race relationships did not only have to be between South Asian and white people, of course. A former lascar from the Punjab, Rasool Khan was married to Elsie in Sheffield in 1928. Elsie's paternal grandfather was a Black African from Natal. Rasool was firmly Muslim and refused to engage with the Salvation Army, even though Elsie had been brought up within the movement. Rasool and Elsie had seven children in Sheffield and one of their daughters, Doreen, remembered how her family felt well integrated in Sheffield's East End. Her father was a trader and, as a child, Doreen and her siblings would help her father make kites that he sold in the summer, while at other times he sold confectionary. Rasool also performed as a magician from time to time and sometimes the children would dress up and assist in his performances.[27] During Eid, the family would share food with their neighbours and everybody knew each other.

During the Second World War, Doreen was sent as an evacuee to rural Leicestershire and it was there that she was called a 'piccaninny' and 'Topsy' (the Black character from *Uncle Tom's Cabin*), which she refuted by saying 'I'm an Indian'.[28] Doreen even wrote a letter to the *Sheffield Telegraph* when she was an evacuee, to discuss her experiences of evacuation, although she did not bring up these issues of race, instead just mentioning how she was missing her home in Sheffield: 'When we first came I missed the field days and entertainment. I expect you miss them now the war has started but that cannot be helped.' The correspondent suggested that 'Doreen's dad and mother are from the North-West Frontier of India, but both have lived in England for many years. As for Doreen she is practically a Sheffield girl now'.[29] Note how Doreen was only 'practically' a Sheffield girl, rather than one without question—her mother was, after all, born in Sheffield and not Indian but Doreen's race and belonging were brought into question, even at the time of national War.

* * *

One way of thinking about childhood and family experience for migrant families, and to gain more insight into their social lives, is to think about religious practice and observance. In 1877, there were 8,079 Muslim lascars and 900 Hindu, Buddhist and Christian lascars living in England.[30] The first formal mosques built in Britain were in Woking (1889) and Liverpool (1887). The Liverpool Muslim Institute included separate day schools for girls and boys and a boarding school for boys with purpose-built playgrounds and toilets. The Institute also founded the Medina Home for Children in 1896 to care for illegitimate children and so children were prioritised within its function and aims.[31] As the number of South Asians in Britain grew, more religious institutions were built to provide permanent physical spaces for families and communities to meet and grow. The East End of London was particularly popular for lascars and their children as a site of settlement and, throughout the 1920s, there were plans to build a mosque there to cater for these families. The Jamiat-ul-Muslimin, based at the East London Mosque, was a charitable society for the promotion of Islam founded in 1934, and was initially located at Canton Street, off East India Dock Road in London. Its membership consisted predominantly of working-class lascars, peddlers and other workers who inhabited the East End of London. Its key aims and objectives included raising funds for a Mosque in East London, opening a school for the training and education of Muslims and 'look[ing] after and provid[ing] for the education of orphans and other poor Muslim children'.[32] The East London Mosque was eventually founded in 1941 and continues to be an important site for families and children of South Asian origin in Britain.

While it remains difficult to trace many of the lives of these working-class children and how they engaged with these mosques, one interesting example is that of Adbullah Rahmatullah. He was born in 1902 and in September 1914, at the age of 12, started at the County Secondary School in Woking. Rahmatullah was a day scholar and the postal address he gave for his home was that of the Woking Mosque. His previous school was the Llandover elementary school in South Wales and in July 1915, after just one year at the Woking school, he was discharged and removed to South Wales. This may have been because of the First World War, as he returned to the school in 1919 and left in 1921. This information all comes from the National School Register, so it tells us little about his life, and some of it may be incorrect, especially as it notes that his father, the Maulvi Sadrud Din, was a 'Hindoo Merchant' which does not correlate with his Islamic surname or address at Woking Mosque. It may have been that 'Hindoo' was simply a conflation for 'Indian' and that the mosque was used as a proxy in the absence of a stable home address.[33]

Religion came into children's lives through multiple avenues, including mosques or institutions such as those run by Kamal Chunchie. Kamal Chunchie (b. 1886) was born into a Muslim family of Malay origin in Ceylon (Sri Lanka). Having enlisted in the army, he fought on the Western Front in the First World War in 1915. Two years later, he converted to Christianity and in 1918, he moved to London. In 1920 he married a white Welsh woman called Mabel Tappen, who had also served in the War in the Queen Mary's Army Auxiliary Corps. They had a daughter together, Muriel, born on 12 September 1920, and lived in a one-room flat in East London. In 1921, Chunchie became a Methodist minister for the Queen Victoria's Seamen's Rest in Poplar, East London, working to engage with and convert African and Asian sailors who lived in the docks. Through his work, Chunchie began to meet with a range of African and Asian seamen who lived in poverty and poor conditions in East London, meeting their (usually white) wives and children and becoming increasingly concerned for their welfare. He was particularly troubled by the lack of employment for the seamen and poor future prospects for their mixed-race children, who were often bullied at school. In 1923, Chunchie organised a day trip for Black and Asian families from East London—59 adults and 29 children—to visit Reigate in Surrey in an attempt to 'brighten' their lives. He soon set up a Wesleyan Methodist Church for 'coloured people' and a Sunday School for children. This led to the foundation of the Coloured Men's Institute in 1926 in Canning Town, which, until 1930, served as a centre for Black and Asian people in East London and their children.[34]

Accounts of Chunchie's work have emphasised his work with mixed-race families and children in the East End of London in the 1920s and 1930s but little account is given to these families, especially the children. Photos from the Coloured Men's Institute show a range of Black and brown children, some of whom were probably of South Asian heritage. Photos include children eating at the daily canteen in 1926 and on trips to a beach.[35] Kamal and his wife provided breakfasts to children at their Sunday Schools. His grandson recalls that his grandparents would receive wooden toys for the children of seamen which he kept in the garage while his grandparents tried to reconstitute the Coloured Men's Institute.[36] The faces and stories of these children reveal that the presence of children of empire was much more prevalent in the 1920s than many have realised. They lived side by side with children of African and Caribbean heritage and were forming nascent communities through the work of Chunchie and others. In 2021, the road upon which a newly built City Hall in London is found was named as Kamal Chunchie Way, following a public vote, in recognition of Chunchie's contributions to the area. It currently houses the Greater London Authority. Media focus on this new name concentrated on Chunchie's philanthropic work as well as his war service but, although the engagement with children is implicit in some summaries and photos of his work, surprisingly little has been said or researched about the families and children he engaged with to offer a fuller picture of the diversity of childhood experiences in interwar Britain. A notable exception is the work of Chamion Caballero, co-founder of the digital project The Mixed Museum.[37]

In an earlier period, the work of Reverend Ebenezer Bholanath Bhose, a Bengali Christian from Calcutta, who was a member of the Society for the Propagation of the Gospel, is notable. In 1874, Bhose married Emma Green in Marylebone in London and they had five children: Agnes (b. 1877), Emma Florence (b. 1879), Mary (b. 1879), Cyril (b. 1881) and Mabel (b. 1884). In 1881, Bhose was licensed to the curacy of St Andrews in Bethnal Green and, by 1887, he was appointed chaplain at St Luke's Lascar Mission in Victoria Docks. The vast majority of the sailors that came to St Luke's were Muslim. In his mission reports, Bhose noted the observance of Muslim festivals by sailors in the ports. The daughters all attended George Green School on East India Dock Road in the 1880s and '90s. Records show that they were academically gifted. In 1888, Emma Florence won a school prize for English, followed by one for French in 1889 and Scripture in 1890; in 1892 and 1893, Mary won the school prize for Modern Languages.[38] In February 1895, girls from the George Green Schools put on a night of entertainment to raise money for the Lascar Mission. It included music and singing and in the second half a comedy called 'Gaffer Grey's Legacy' which included Mary.[39] Florence died in 1897 and Cyril died in 1903 but the three other sisters all took up careers in healthcare—Mary and Mabel became public health inspectors and Agnes was a nurse. Mary also married a clergyman.

The facts of all of these lives are of interest partly because they show the ways in which children of South Asian heritage lived their everyday lives in Britain but also because they are indicative of the ways in which class, race and religion intertwined in this period and were experienced through the eyes of children. Aside from the lascars' children, as a point of comparison, it is worth considering children of dual heritage with other faith backgrounds and experiences. Shapurji Saklatvala was a Parsee from Bombay who arrived in Britain in 1905, when he was in his thirties, to manage the Tata company office in Manchester; he was the nephew of the industrialist J. N. Tata. In 1922, he was elected Labour MP for Battersea. He lost the seat in 1923 but regained it in 1924 as a Communist MP, holding it until 1929. Saklatvala had five children with his wife Sarah Marsh (often known as Sally) whom he had married in 1907—Dorab (likely b. 1908), Candida (b. 1909), Beram (b. 1911), Kaikoo (b. 1915) and Sehri (b. 1919). They moved to Manchester in 1909, living there for a couple of years and sharing a house with another Indian couple, Mr and Mrs Chaman Lal and their young children. From 1913, the Saklatvalas lived in Twickenham, often socialising with other Indian families and children who lived in London, with picnics in Richmond Park or visits to London Zoo.[40] In 1921–2, they moved to Highgate and at four years old Sehri, who has written a memoir of her childhood, started attending a convent school.

In 1926, Saklatvala was imprisoned for sedition after he gave a speech in support of the miners during the General Strike. A girl at Sehri's convent school taunted her in the corridor, sticking out her tongue and telling her that her father had been jailed for saying 'nasty things about the King!' Sehri's retort was: 'Oh no he isn't. He's in prison for sedition!'[41] Returning from a summer school in Paris in 1933, when she was just fourteen, Sehri was the only schoolgirl singled out by the Customs Officer at Dover. She had to unpack her suitcase in front of everyone while a detective presided over the search; her surname and connection to her father had marked her out and, as Sehri remarked later, this was intended to make things awkward and unpleasant for the family rather than because of any real perceived threat.[42]

In 1927, Saklatvala performed the Parsee ceremony of the Navjote for all five children. This is a religious ritual where children, usually between the ages of 7 and 15, are inducted into the Zoroastrian religion. It was believed that the year before was only the first time this ceremony had been performed in the UK, on Saklatvala's friend's children. Kew Gardens provided fresh pomegranate leaves for the ceremony and it took place in front of a large audience at Caxton Hall, Westminster, on 22 July 1927. The press were in attendance too and later Saklatvala was criticised by the Communist Party for participating in a religious ceremony. Sehri Saklatvala remembers that, during the 1920s, the Indian Social Club put on a Christmas party every year at the Savoy Hotel, where the children of members and their guests received gifts. They would sing songs like 'Oranges and Lemons' and 'Nuts in May'. A committed socialist, Saklatvala was keen that poorer children did not miss out. So every year through the Indian Workers' Welfare League, they put on a similar party for seamen's children, held in Poplar Town Hall. The children would all be given a toy and their mothers a packet of tea and other household goods. Sehri would help her parents make sandwiches and there would be cakes and sweets.[43] It is clear, then, that working-class children of South Asian heritage were being catered for by various organisations and that they were integral parts of British religious and social life.

Without focusing too much on sensational studies, the case of the children of Buck Ruxton reveals how many of the stories of children of South Asian descent from this period are lost. Some are lost because they simply lived ordinary lives and their stories were not recorded. Other names became more and more anglicised throughout the generations and so looking for South Asian names and histories, therefore, becomes harder. Others became lost within institutions like the three children of the murderer Dr Buck Ruxton. Ruxton was of Parsee and French heritage and married to Isabella Kerr. They had three children and lived in Lancaster. In 1935, Buxton murdered Isabella and the children's 20-year-old nanny Mary Jane Rogerson. Their bodies were only identified with the use of new forensic techniques such as skull photography, feet casting and the identification of maggots to ascertain the time of death. Rogerson's body was also identified as she had on her one of the Ruxton children's romper suits. Ruxton was found guilty and hanged at Strangeways Prison in May 1936. It was a public execution and pictures of the crowd actually show women sitting in the front row holding young children to view the spectacle.

Over 900 members of the public signed a petition asking for a reprieve for Ruxton for the sake of his children; this was not heeded. Yet nearly £200 was raised by Ruxton's solicitor and executor of his will following an appeal to help care for the children's futures. The three children—Diana aged 6, Elizabeth aged 4 and William (Billie) aged 2—were orphaned and sent to Parkside Children's Home in Lancaster during the trial where they were told simply that their father had gone on holiday. In June 1936, they were adopted by Lancashire County Council and then it is assumed that they were rehomed but little is known afterwards. It is likely that their surnames were changed but also that they were separated—although their mother did have two living sisters. As the *Daily Mirror* alluded to at the time, three children of colour could not bury their past as easily as other white children within the institution; however, as the case was so notorious, the Lancaster Institution apparently received offers from all over the country from people who wanted to adopt them.[44]

* * *

At the outbreak of the Second World War, 50,000 of the Merchant Navy's 190,000 men were lascars. However, after the end of the war and the partition of India and Pakistan, with the growth of the aviation industry, the need for lascar employment declined. Many had already settled in Britain but former seamen who now resided in East Pakistan were destitute and distressed until, in 1956, the Pakistani government agreed to grant 1,000 passports to 'distressed seamen' and their survivors or nominated dependents.[45] This generation was the core antecedent to the British Bangladeshi population in East London and other parts of the UK in the twenty-first century. But, as I have discussed, Asian lascar seamen had been settling with their families in Britain for decades before the 1950s and their children have often been forgotten by history.

We cannot consider the history of these children without being conscious of the intersections of race, religion, gender and class. As Caroline Adam's study of Sylheti lascar seamen in the East End of London reveals, these histories have been overwhelmingly male. As I mentioned earlier, very little work has been done to acknowledge the role of these seamen's children or the possibility of them being both vessels of and agents for discourses about race, religion, family and Britishness in the early twentieth century. While more contemporary discourses have grappled with issues of race and belonging in the context of larger-scale migrations to the UK than those within the remit of this book, in this period we can see the antecedents for those anxieties. We can also see how the focus on charity and welfare for deprived children was being crystalised in this period and how important understandings of race and migration were to these concerns. Following the Second World War, for example, the children of relationships between African American GIs stationed in Britain and white women were known as 'brown babies'. Government ministers expressed concern about these 'half-caste' children. While many lived happy lives, others were abandoned to orphanages or subjected to cruel racism throughout their childhood.[46] However, this concern about children of mixed heritage, especially centred around their welfare, was part of a longer trajectory whereby the presence of children of colour in Britain was forcing institutions to confront race and realign their ideas of British liberalism in the face of the realities of the Empire, interracial sexual relations and the world.

There are other forgotten South Asian children who remain silent in the archival records. These children were not merely passive victims but integrated children in everyday British urban working-class life in this period. They were not 'hopeless', nor did they need to be the objects of vague pity. We can see how indelibly linked the histories of India and Britain were through these children, who were the products of empire through its imperial trading routes. They exemplified the multiplicity of religious and cultural traditions through everyday physical and social encounters in the streets of Britain, as well as in more intimate familial settings, and were integral to all British social classes. These children reveal the problems with understanding Britishness historically, and in the contemporary moment, through rudimentary ideas about skin colour and race and highlight the longstanding influences of empire on ordinary families. Their very Britishness should never be denied, whatever their faith or the colour of their skin.

9

THE LEFTISTS

One of the founding members of the Communist Party of Great Britain (CPGB) in 1920 was Rajani Palme Dutt, who was born in Cambridge in June 1896. A committed socialist during his childhood, Rajani's upbringing in Cambridge reveals how the politicisation of young Indian children in Britain was not solely confined to the more mainstream liberal politics of nationalism or suffrage but could also take on more radical left-wing and anti-fascist causes. Rajani's father, Upendra Krishna Dutt, was from Calcutta and practised as a doctor in Cambridge. Upendra was known as a 'sixpenny doctor' as he only charged a modest amount and catered for poor patients in the area. Rajani's mother was Anna Palme, a Swedish writer from an upper-middle-class background—her father had been a county judge—related to the future socialist prime minister of Sweden, Olaf Palme. Rajani had little contact with the Swedish side of his family as they did not approve of Anna's marriage to Upendra.[1]

Rajani Palme Dutt was largely seen as an intellectual leader of the CPGB. His role in nurturing the CPGB across the 1920s and 1930s, as it sought parliamentary routes to power, was influential in inspiring Indian communism. It was also hugely important in the development of the British Left in this period more broadly, for relations between British communists and Russia and international communist networks. The spread of communism across Europe in the 1920s and 1930s, the Italian invasion of Abyssinia in 1935, the onset of the Spanish Civil War in 1936 and the rise of Nazism and Fascism in the lead up to the Second World War, all heavily influenced local and global political ideologies. At the same time, anticolonial organisation was developing with the transnational organisation the League Against Imperialism (LAI), founded in Brussels in 1927, with Jawaharlal Nehru a key member. The LAI had its roots in communism and, although it folded in 1937, was hugely influential in ongoing Global South solidarities throughout the rest of the twentieth century.[2] The generation of South Asian children in Britain that came after Dutt were motivated by anti-fascist and socialist influences. Living in Britain during this era, they were afforded opportunities to be politically radical and organise in ways that were not often possible in India under the draconian surveillance of colonial rule.

Rajani's name means 'night' in Bengali, given to him to reflect the time of his birth. He had two elder siblings: a sister Elna, who was born in 1891, and a brother Clemens, who was born in April 1893, both in Cambridge. Elna studied at the County School for Girls in Cambridge before joining the girls' boarding school Roedean School in Brighton on a scholarship in 1905; she would later secure a scholarship to Newnham College, Cambridge, in 1910. In May 1904, Clemens, who had been at Miss Hutt's Lyndewode House School, won a foundational scholarship to Perse School. In 1906, Rajani, who also studied at Miss Hutt's, joined Clemens at Perse having been on the reserve list for the foundational scholarship since July of that year.[3]

Perse School was a private secondary school founded in Cambridge in 1615. The headmaster when Rajani and Clemens attended was W. H. D. Rouse, who had been born in Calcutta and was a Sanskrit scholar before he took up the role. In 1904, Rouse opened Hillel House, a Jewish boarding house for the school. He actively encouraged overseas students to attend the school, although it is worth remembering that the Palme Dutts were of course British-born. In 1910, Rouse opened another new boarding house named School House and began advertising in India. An article in the Allahabad paper, *The Pioneer*, described Rouse's educational experiments and drew attention to the low fees at Perse compared to larger British public schools.[4] This opening up did not go without opposition. Rouse was criticised by the Cambridge Town Clerk in 1911 for admitting Jews and 'coloured races' but Rouse retorted by telling him to firmly mind his business.[5] Despite Rouse's recruitment efforts, only one Indian joined in 1912 and two in 1913—the first Indian admitted to Perse had been in 1907. Following the First World War, seven Indian pupils joined between 1919 and 1928.[6]

Clemens and Rajani flourished academically at Perse School. In November 1907, Clemens won multiple essay and subject prizes—in English, maths, natural sciences and modern languages. In November 1913, Rajani won the Mayor's Prize and was part of the singing and dancing entertainment.[7] He was also brilliant at Greek. They excelled in other aspects of school life too. In the sixth form, Clemens was a senior prefect, a member of the swimming sub-committee, curator of the museum and won colours for hockey and rugby. In the 1910 annual swimming competition, he placed second in the 220, 100 and 50 yards open.[8] Meanwhile, Rajani was a junior prefect, honorary secretary of the fives sub-committee and vice-president of the Debating Society. Perhaps setting him up for more serious topics in later life, in 1911, Rajani successfully opposed the motion that 'soup should be eaten not drunk'. By May 1913, his rhetorical skills were sharpened on more overtly political subjects, being singled out for special praise for his speech in opposition to the Insurance Act.[9]

Rajani also excelled at performance. At the 1912 Speech Day, he acted a scene from Schiller's *Wilhelm Tell* as the titular character, the school magazine, *The Pelican*, noting that he 'acted well'. Dutt was also honorary secretary of the Perse Folk, the folk dancing group that was undergoing a revival at the time. In May 1913, he formed part of the Perse Morris Men, a group who danced for the May Day festivals in Cambridge.[10] He was one of only six dancers, so clearly he enjoyed the pastime. May Day was celebrated as the start of summer in England but 1 May was also International Workers' Day, established in 1889 by the International Workers Congress. The different strands of the celebration, from festive Englishness to workers' rights, neatly epitomise Rajani's multiple influences as a child.

Dutt's parents may have come from relatively affluent backgrounds but the family did not possess much wealth in Cambridge and were extremely interested in politics and socialism. Rajani later said that he derived political inspiration from the 'mixed traditions' of his upbringing, his father's work with the working-class people of Cambridge and a 'strong current of hostility to the British Empire and to ruling class institutions in Britain'. His father had been a student at Cambridge and, when Rajani was a child, Upendra used to host Cambridge Majlis—Indian student society—meetings in his house. The house was visited by bright political sparks—Nehru called in, as did H. M. Hyndman, the founder of the Social Democratic Foundation (a British Marxist party), and Keir Hardie, the future Labour leader.[11] The rivalry between 'moderates' and 'extremists' within the Indian nationalist movement around the 1907 session of the Indian National Congress was discussed intensely at the Dutt house in Cambridge and Rajani recalled that this was 'my first political baptism'.[12] Not only was he becoming attuned to the very politics of Indian nationalism but also the spectrum and divisions within the nationalist and socialist movements, helping him to see his own individual path forwards through communism.

Rajani was also acutely aware of class and racial politics growing up. Not only was he aware of his Swedish family's disapproval of his parents' interracial marriage but he was also conscious of the prejudice within Cambridge, especially among upper-class circles, against his father practising as a doctor. Rajani recalled this prejudice and argued that he became very conscious of class in his early childhood. By all accounts, though, the Palme Dutt family were very close and affectionate, sharing diminutive nicknames like 'Ellie', 'Bocca' and 'Raji'. Their mother would mix medicines for their father and the children would get a penny for delivering them to his patients.

Through his travels around Cambridge meeting different people—his father's patients from working-class and less privileged backgrounds, elite students from the university and politicians who visited his house—Rajani became conscious of the disparities in wealth, living standards and employment between social classes in Britain.[13] He also engaged actively with the local community. His mother was a secretary of the Cambridge Women's Liberal Association and a keen supporter of women's suffrage.[14] In December 1906, Anna Palme Dutt helped to organise a Christmas party for local children through the Cambridge Women's Liberal Association. They catered for 48 children with music, games and teas. Rajani, who was only ten years old himself, dressed up as Father Christmas and handed out toys, sweets, crackers and oranges to the children.[15] It is a shame we do not have any surviving photographs of this scene.

A contemporary of Rajani's at Perse remembers that, at school, most children were aware of the major political events happening around them. These included the introduction of Lloyd George's National Old Age Pensions Act in 1908, the death of King Edward VII in 1910 and the Irish Home Rule Crisis between 1912 and 1914. Most schoolchildren were aware of the debates around free trade and tariff reform, with members of the Conservative Tariff Reform League arguing that Britain should abandon free trade and impose taxes on foreign imports to protect British and imperial trade. Meanwhile, the Labour Party was growing in strength and support.[16] According to Rajani's biographer, Elna, Clemens and Rajani were all committed socialists before they left school.[17] Rajani joined Balliol College, Oxford, in 1914 on a scholarship but was expelled in the summer of 1915 after he professed support for the Bolshevik Revolution in Russia. He was also a vocal conscientious objector to the War. While he was at Oxford, secret files were being compiled about him and his brother, Clemens, by the police, Home Office and India Office, noting that they were both ardent socialists and that their parents were pro-Germans (a common smear).[18] Later, during the 1930s, Clemens spent time in Paris and Moscow and married Violet Lansbury, the daughter of George Lansbury, the Labour leader. They had a daughter, Anna Elizabeth, born in 1936, and by 1939 were living in London. During the Second World War, Rajani and Clemens were monitored closely through telephone wiretaps, intercepted mail and undercover officers as the police feared their communist influences on Britain and India. Meanwhile, their mother,

Anna, did not wish to take in evacuee children or soldiers, so shut up their house in England and went to Geneva.[19]

Following the Dutts, the next generation of children who went to school in the 1920s and '30s were being inspired by the Communist Party. Mahmuduzzafar Khan Sahebzada was born in December 1908 in Agra. His father came from an aristocratic background but had defied his family to train as a doctor in Edinburgh. Sahebzada was taken to England by his father, when he was twelve, for his studies. He first went to Dulwich College Prep School, before spending a term at Dulwich College in 1922 and then joining Sherborne School in Dorset from January 1923–April 1927. His guardian in England was a doctor, H. Crichton Miller, who lived in Harrow. During his time at Sherborne School, Sahebzada was fully involved in school life. He was bestowed with a dark blue blazer with a gold XXX (thirty) on the pocket, awarded to the thirty best rugby players. He was a Physical Training (PT) class leader, a sergeant in the Officer Training Corps (OTC) and a member of 'the Duffers', a literary society founded in 1898 by Henry Robinson King for selected members of the sixth form. King, who was the school chaplain during Sahebzada's time, kept a diary and noted once in March 1927 that Sahebzada had written a very good paper on Keats which he had read to the class.[20]

Like Rajani Palme Dutt at Perse, school records from Sherborne highlight the variety of Sahebzada's school engagements and emphasise that children of South Asian heritage did not necessarily endure isolated school lives in Britain. Sahebzada was a member of the Archaeological Society, whose activities included an expedition to Salisbury in July 1926 where they visited the cathedral and enjoyed a nice tea. He was also something of an artist: the school archives have kept his sketches of Sherborne School's Abbey, part of an exhibition held by the Sketch Club in the autumn of 1926, for which Sahebzada won a school prize. In 1926 at a school fancy dress party, Sahebzada dressed in traditional Indian clothing, with a turban, jewellery and a long *sherwani*. Another classmate 'blacked up'; clearly the school was not immune to racial politics and it was clearly something Sahebzada could not avoid.[21] While photos from the Sherborne School archive show him constantly smiling, these official traces only offer us glimpses into the ways he navigated life in England as a young boy as, within a few years of leaving school, he became a very vocal communist who was extremely active in left-wing politics in India.

During his childhood, Sahebzada became acquainted with the Habibullah family, who were first at Rottingdean and then at Clifton College in Bristol, less than 50 miles from Sherborne. Isha'at Habibullah and Sahebzada then both attended university together, with Isha'at remembering how the Great Depression of 1929 had a huge impact on the lives of fellow classmates. Isha'at was also keenly aware that Sahebzada had been influenced by Marxist and Leninist ideologies by this time; he had started to impress upon Isha'at the need to direct his educational privileges into the cause for a progressive, forward-looking India upon their return.[22]

Sahebzada's first visit back to India was in 1927, following his graduation from Sherborne, and it was the first time he met his then seven-year-old sister Hamida. His time at Sherborne had been an idyllic estrangement from the normal daily politics of family life in India but he now came face to face with the realities of his future. He returned to England to study at Oxford and then returned to India in 1931 to take up a teaching role. He also worked for the Communist Party of India (CPI), a young party—with the main portion of its leadership drawn from relatively elite, educated families—inspired by the writings of Dutt and Nehru among others.[23] Upon his return to India after Oxford, Sahebzada wore a Gandhi cap and *khadi* (home-spun) clothes and insisted on speaking Urdu or Hindi—with an English accent—rather than English, thoroughly emerged as he was in the mileu's spirit of anticolonialism. Family members knew he was a very capable artist and had the privileges and potential to take up a career in the arts but he was committed to engaging with socialist politics and furthering political change in India. He felt strongly that his English upbringing compelled him to prove his commitment to Indian society. In 1934, he married the communist and feminist writer Rasheed Jahan and, in 1936, he visited London as one of Nehru's secretaries. There he met with the publisher Victor Gollancz to discuss ways to publish Indian editions of Leftist books. In the same year, Sahebzada became a founding member of the All-India Progressive Writers' Association (PWA), set up in 1935 by Indian students and writers based in London to encourage 'progressive' writing that dealt with social issues.[24]

* * *

In June 1938, two former South Asian child migrants, Jawaharlal Nehru and Bhicoo Batlivala, barrister and campaigner, travelled together from India to Spain in support of the Republican fight against General Franco in the Spanish Civil War. The Indian National Congress believed that there were strong parallels between the Indian fight for independence and the Republican cause in Spain and had set up an 'Aid Spain' campaign; Batlivala was travelling as Nehru's private secretary.[25] Following concerns about how close the two were getting—along with the reputation Batlivala had gained for engaging in extramarital affairs (although Nehru also had his own reputation)—once they reached London later that year, Batlivala no longer remained Nehru's private secretary and she settled back in London. Batlivala, who had lived in Britain from the age of 10 and been educated at Cheltenham Ladies College, now became an active member of the India League, a campaigning group for Indian independence led by V. K. Krishna Menon in London. In 1939, she married Guy Mansell and by 1943 they were living in Cobham, Surrey, with their two children.[26] A colonial official, who knew Batlivala from her time working in Baroda, stated that she had lived in England for sixteen years and was a victim of being 'denationalised'. When she had worked in Baroda she was unhappy and only wanted to socialise with Europeans but upon her return to England as an adult she seemed to have shifting allegiances.[27] These dual and duelling loyalties likely tormented people such as Sahebzada and Batlivala, who could not dissociate themselves from the urgent politics of the era and perhaps felt they could never quite fit in.

When Nehru was imprisoned in 1941, by the government in India, for his role in Indian nationalist agitations, Batlivala spoke at several Indian League meetings campaigning for his release, including one meeting alongside Parvati Kumaramangalam.[28] Parvati was a university student who had spent part of her childhood in England. In November 1941, the India League held a conference where they protested the sentencing of Surendra Mohan Kumaramangalam, the brother of Parvati, in the Madras Communist Conspiracy Trial. Menon's protest included the retort that S. M. Kumaramangalam was a socialist who had never identified with communism.[29] The Madras Conspiracy Trial had followed the Meerut Conspiracy Case, which began in 1929 when thirty-two people were put on trial in Meerut for being communists and smeared for attempting to overthrow the government. The trial lasted until 1933 and had been a clear warning of government desires to suppress communists in India. While the government portrayed Indian communists as violent, in studied contrast to the 'non-violence' epitomised by Gandhi, in reality INC members—including Nehru—also engaged in 'violent' activities.[30] However, the atmosphere of suppressing communism in India in the 1930s can be juxtaposed with the ways in which, in Britain, young Indians had relative freedom engaging in radical politics at this time.

Surendra Mohan Kumaramangalam (henceforth Mohan) was born to Paramasiva Subbarayan and Radhabai Subbarayan in London in 1916. As is traditional in parts of South India, although his birth was registered under the surname of Subbarayan, he soon took on the surname of Kumaramangalam. His older brother, Paramasiva Prabhakar, had been born in 1913. At the time, his father was studying at Oxford University and Radhabai soon spent time in Oxford alongside her husband. Mohan had another older brother, by two years, Jayawant Gopal, who was born in 1915 in Northleach, Gloucestershire.[31] Shipping records show that, in September 1918, the mother and two sons travelled back to India, although the boys soon returned to England to attend school.

All three sons attended St Hugh's prep school in Bromley, Kent, before being sent to study at Eton College in Windsor—Paramasiva in 1926, Jayawant in 1928 and Mohan in 1930. While Eton College had already admitted several Indian students by the 1930s the Kumaramangalam brothers formed part of a noticeable racial minority. In December 1930, a diarist for *The Daily Express* recalled the celebration of St Andrews Day on 30 November at Eton College. This was an occasion on which parents would visit the school and the Eton Wall Game was played—a tradition that combines a form of rugby with a curved brick wall that boys climb over in pursuit of the game. This was followed by a football match. According to the paper: 'Prominent among the boys was a little group of Orientals, including Prince Birabongse of Siam and two brothers named Kumaramangalam.'[32] As well as this, the brothers all engaged in cricket for their house teams and Paramasiva boxed for the school. Mohan appears to have been both academically and creatively gifted: in 1929, he played the part of the merchant in a school production of Shakespeare's *A Comedy of Errors* and was also a prize winner in Latin; in 1933, he was runner up in a maths prize.[33]

Mohan's Canadian friend, Henry Stanley Ferns, remembered his charm and social talents, refined by his time at Eton. One of his best friends at Eton was Robert Inskip, who later became the Viscount Caldecote—a title created in 1939 for Robert's father, Thomas Inskip, so that he could serve in the House of Lords as Lord Chancellor. Mohan's own family came from a landed background and he socialised at school with other elite boys.[34] Another of Mohan's best friends at school was Michael Barratt Brown, latterly an economist and activist. Barratt Brown came from a Quaker family and was a member of the CPGB in the 1940s. He recalled that Mohan lived with Arthur Gillett and Margaret Clark's Quaker family in Oxford during his holidays and developed strong left-wing views. Indira Nehru also spent her student holidays with the Gilletts.[35] At Eton, however, Mohan felt isolated. He was a quiet boy who did not profess his political sympathies. He left a year early because he was not made a school prefect and vehemently believed it was because he was Indian.[36] It is possible that Mohan's school experiences paid a part in the shaping of his political sensibilities and we certainly should not underestimate the importance of these formative experiences in moulding attitudes and responses to society. It could be that the Quaker tenets of spiritual equality played a factor in the development of Mohan's communist ideals.

Mohan's sister, Parvati (b. 1919), did not appear to take her early schooling in England, unlike her brothers, but when she was eleven years old accompanied her mother to attend the Round Table Conferences in London that began in 1930.[37] These were a series of conferences that gathered together politicians and chosen Indian delegates to discuss Indian constitutional reforms with a view to greater representation and independence for Indians. Radhabai Subbarayan was one of only two Indian women invited who presented and discussed their demands for Indian women to be enfranchised in any further constitutional reforms. Radhabai would go on to become a vocal suffrage campaigner in London in the 1930s on this issue, also engaging with the League of Nations. She attended the Round Table Conferences in 1930 and 1931 and thus was able to spend the school holidays with Mohan and Jayawant in London. Newspaper reports following Radhabai tell us that Parvati was a 'Blue Bird', which seems to refer to a role in a children's uniformed organisation or similar, and appears to have attended a Quaker School in England at some point during her childhood.[38] It also seems that Parvati went to Badminton School in Bristol in the 1930s, which is where Indira Nehru spent a year from 1936–37. These two women latterly became Parvati Krishnan and Indira Gandhi respectively, the names they are now both known by. Krishnan was a leader of the Communist Party of India and MP in Coimbatore, Tamil Naidu. She served in Indira Gandhi's cabinet and represented India at the 1975 UN World Conference on Women in Mexico City.

The 1930s saw a vibrant decade for the Left. Following the Great Depression of 1929 and the rise of fascism and Nazism, radically-minded people were interested in the growth of Soviet and Chinese communism, of the Spanish Civil War and Indian independence. These campaigns were closely linked in the minds of Indian students of the time. In May 1938, when he was 24, Mohan addressed the British Youth Peace Assembly and, in 1939, he visited Spain as a member of a delegation organised by the Student Committee of the British Youth Peace Assembly.[39] He was no longer a child but he remained committed to 'youth' politics and engaging with young people. Eric Hobsbawm, the well-known socialist historian, was friends with Mohan, Parvati and Renuka Ray at university in the 1930s.[40] V. G. Kiernan, a communist and historian who knew Kumaramangalam when he was at Cambridge, has suggested that for some Indians at Cambridge in the 1930s communism was just youthful dramatising but for others it became a lifelong career. This lifelong commitment was held by Mohan Kumaramangalam, who in later life joined Indira Gandhi's Congress government but was always suspected by his detractors of remaining a communist. As a lawyer, he refused to take on cases for landlords.

The Subbarayans' house in Madras had been kept in an 'English style'; when Mohan returned to India, he was more fluent in English than any Indian language and was thus known as an 'Angrezi-wala' in India (or 'English chap'). Employed on English language publications, there was envy towards 'Angrezi-walas' as well as scorn and people like Mohan, who were deemed and also felt only 'half-Indian', became ardent Bolsheviks as a means of rising above these kinds of criticism.[41] Parvati, who had studied at Oxford, was a lifelong communist, who married another communist from South India.[42] Their parents, the Subbarayans, had not been communists and although engaged in politics were conservative in some of their ideas of political change. Yet, the children's exposure to radical politics in England, and the freedom away from their parents' political set, politicised them in unexpected ways. This was the same for Sahebzada. Unlike the highly anglicised children of the nineteenth century we encountered in earlier chapters, these young Indians threw themselves into ideas about, and advocacy for, broader democratic rights and access to state institutions for all, conscious of the politics of class despite their own elite status.

* * *

Of course, not all South Asian children became communists in the 1930s but it is notable how politically engaged with leftist and progressive politics many young migrants in that decade became. Santha Rama Rau was six years old when she first arrived in England with her elder sister Premila and parents in 1929. Her father, Benegal Rama Rau, attended the first Round Table Conference in London, one of three that spanned 1930–2 to cover negotiations and discussions between Indian and British delegates on the future of the Indian constitution. Santha recalls that one of her mother's main concerns was what clothes to bring for the girls to wear and in the end she had a family tailor make them some dresses.[43] Santha and Premila initially attended Hall School in Weybridge. Premila was a boarder; Santha was supposed to be a day student because of her young age but soon insisted that she wanted to be a boarder too, so that she could stay on for the after-school activities. It was a private school run by a Quaker committee and the sisters were the first Indians to have attended. The teachers and staff became quite enamoured with Santha because she was so young and treated her as somewhat of a novelty.[44]

In 1934, at the end of the Round Table Conferences, Benegal was appointed Indian deputy high commissioner in London on a three-year term. Premila gained admission to St Paul's with Santha following a couple of years later.[45] Santha started to become a keen writer, a profession she was to take up as an adult. She would contribute poems and short stories to the school magazine, *The Paulina*.[46] As Santha recalled, 'The only thing that set us apart in our own minds was that we would return to India to live, that eventually our loyalties would be tied to a country that was growing daily less familiar'.[47] Yet, over the course of the late 1930s, before the outbreak of the Second World War but with rising nationalism in India, Santha was constantly surrounded by news of, and references to, Indian politics. Her father's role dictated this but it was also evident that politics was inspiring her generation immensely at that time. At school they were asked to support the international youth camps of the League of Nations. Premila had felt very strongly about the Spanish Civil War in 1936 and Santha had fallen in love with the story of a Spanish man who had written poetry and died in the War. Their engagement with the anti-fascist politics of the time was common for many young people; although, indeed, many young people were also engaged with fascism as these competing international groups and movements, especially across Europe, were vying for the attention of young recruits. Santha recalls a visit to France one summer where they had come across groups of Hitler Youth on an organised walking tour.

In 1938, Benegal Rama Rau was appointed Indian high commissioner in South Africa. As he and Dhanvanthi decided to leave the sisters in England to continue their education, they arranged for Premila and Santha to stay on at their flat in London. At the same time, the Rama Raus took in a young Jewish refugee and music student from Vienna, Lilian Ulanowsky, who provided some companionship and guardianship for the sisters. Premila was now studying at Newham College, Cambridge, but Santha was still at school at St Pauls. Later, in 1939, Lilian's brother, Peter, who had been interned at the Dachau Concentration Camp, was released and came to stay at their London flat. At home in London, they took in refugees from Dachau and elsewhere, like their British friends.[48]

In the summer of 1939, Premila and Santha visited their parents in South Africa for a holiday. With the outbreak of war, Santha was unable to return to England to complete her education and the whole family returned to India. Santha was now grown up and had to navigate Indian society after more than ten years away. People made assumptions that—because of her English accent—she was pro-British. Despite having a primary focus on anti-fascism, she had adopted, as she put it, 'the usual unclear English attitude about India'—a conflict between loving India and benefitting from the Empire and recognising its injustices alongside the demands of nationalists. It took a few years for her, however, to recognise the need to prioritise the fight against the fascism of imperialism in India ahead of other anti-fascist global causes.[49]

* * *

An interesting aspect of the socialist organising in the 1930s was that it was committed to international cooperation. The British Empire itself was of course a huge international entity that connected people from various continents including Asia, Africa and Europe. Over the 1930s, international labour organisations and communist groups were networking globally as they understood that their fights were universal and not restricted to parochial nation states or declining empires. The fight for Indian independence was also not divorced or immune from the larger anticolonial drive across other parts of the Empire. Meanwhile, migration by South Asian children was not only happening linearly to and from Britain but also to other parts of the international world. Beyond Britain and beyond India, the global politics of anticolonialism and socialism was shaped by people who had been migrants as children. Take, for example, Sinnathamby Rajaratnam, who was born in Sri Lanka to Tamil parents in 1915 and then raised in Malaya. He went to a mission school in Seremben where he learnt English, was taught about Christianity and met boys from a range of ethnic backgrounds as was common in colonial Malaya. He studied in Kuala Lumpur, then Singapore, before enrolling as a university student at King's College London in 1937 where he met other like-minded students from South Asian backgrounds. He returned to Singapore in 1948, later co-founded the People Action's Party, and was one of the leading figures behind the independence of Singapore in 1965.[50]

It is important to point out, amidst these profiles, that not all South Asians became left-wing or anticolonial in this period. In these same decades, the rise of global fascism was synonymous with the rise of the Hindu right wing (the RSS being founded in 1925), religious factionalism and ongoing conservative support for the Empire within India. Indian independence still felt like a long way away by the end of the 1930s. Recent twenty-first century Conservative politics in the United Kingdom has demonstratively shown that people of South Asian heritage who grew up as children in Britain—such as Priti Patel or Suella Braverman, both Conservative Home Secretaries between 2019–2022 and 2022–2023 respectively, who have been vocally hostile to immigration and socialist liberalism—do not automatically take on socialist ideologies purely because of their own racial background. What we have seen with the Palme Dutts, Sahebzada, the Kumaramangalams and the Rama Raus, though, is the duality that concerned South Asian children in the 1930s, torn between integration in Britain through their schools and strong friendships and loyalties to a distant home in India, both sitting alongside the urgent political fervour that inspired the young.

The growing urgency of Indian nationalism and anticolonialism was felt even by Indian children who were at school in Britain and the moral fight for independence engulfed the young as they saw the parallels between dismantling the British Empire and dismantling other manifestations of global fascism, evident in the need to challenge authoritarianism and limited freedoms for ordinary people in both. Using the tools they had learned in British schools to aid the anticolonial struggle, these young children subverted their highly anglicised experiences in Britain and utilised them to fight for radical change both inside the Empire and outside, in the broader anti-fascist socialist campaigning they were involved in. They helped to build left-wing coalitions, such as the CPGB, CPI and LAI, that played significant parts in dismantling the Empire, not only in the Indian subcontinent but also in other parts of Asia and Africa, and played an important role in forging ongoing global solidarities of anticolonialism that shaped the nature of decolonisation across the Global South and new forms of cooperation for decades beyond them.

10

PARTITION

As India gained independence on 15 August 1947, an interim government had been set up with a Constituent Assembly. Its members, led by Dr B. R. Ambedkar, wrote up a new constitution that was instituted on 26 January 1950, leading to the first full general elections in 1951. Within the Constituent Assembly, between 1947 and 1950, at least six members had been educated as children at school in Britain. They included the first prime minister of India, Jawaharlal Nehru, who we have already encountered, and the first minister for health, Rajkumari Amrit Kaur, the suffragist whom we have also already encountered. In addition, Major General Himatsinhji (b. 1897) had been educated at Malvern College and represented Saurashtra (formerly Kathiawar). He had served in the Indian Army and was military advisor in chief between 1947 and 1950.

Jaipal Singh was a member of that government who came from an Adivasi (tribal/indigenous) background in Bihar. Born in 1903, he had been taken to England in 1918 at the end of the First World War by Canon Cosgrove, the principal of his school in Ranchi. Singh had a close relationship with the Canon following his baptism into Christianity in Ranchi. In England, he stayed with him while he was educated at Darlington Grammar School and was then sent to

St Augustine's College, Canterbury, to train for the priesthood. After two terms there, he moved to St John's College, Oxford, in 1922. There he was a keen member of the debating society and played hockey, later representing the Indian hockey team at the 1928 Amsterdam Olympics.[1] Following an illustrious and varied career—and a first marriage to Tara, the daughter of Janaki Majumdar (née Bonnerjee) whom we met earlier—he became the president of the All-India Adivasi Mahasabha in 1939, a large political party for Indian Indigenous Peoples. The term 'Adivasi' had been mobilised in the 1930s as part of a growing political movement within India that sought to campaign for the rights of indigenous Indians who were often excluded, ignored and oppressed by both the colonial state and elite high-caste Indians. They were a varied group of peoples with roots often in the hills or forests. Though we know very little about his time at Darlington Grammar, as an adult Jaipal Singh had a reputation for flying expensive aeroplanes and staying in luxury hotels. He did not see this as a contradiction or hypocrisy while campaigning forcefully for the rights of indigenous people, which included the demand for a separate state of Jharkand. The debating skills he honed at Oxford certainly helped his political career as he actively campaigned for the rights of tribal peoples to be enshrined within the new constitution.[2]

Muhammad Ismail Khan, representing the United Provinces (later known as Uttar Pradesh), was born in 1887 and had been educated at Tonbridge School, Kent, later going on to become vice chancellor of Aligarh University.[3] Muhammad Ismail Khan's father was close friends with Jawaharlal Nehru's father and Khan had been sent to boarding school at Tonbridge from the age of twelve. Despite his family's closeness with the Nehrus, Khan became an important member of the Muslim League—a rival political party to Nehru's Indian National Congress—and was a key thinker behind the Pakistan Movement. Upon independence, however, he decided to stay in India. While Tonbridge School has no records relating to his stay there—there are few left from this time—he was a remarkable politician who was instrumental in both the creation of Pakistan as well as trying to protect Muslim interests in a newly independent

India. We can wonder about how much his statesmanship was influenced by his childhood upbringing as a boarder in Britain.

Another member of the Constituent Assembly was Tajamul Husain (b. 1893), representing Bihar, who had been educated at King's College School, Wimbledon. Of Muslim background, he was president of the Bihar Provincial Shia Conference and had been a member of Bihar Legislative Assembly from 1935. In the Central Assembly, Husain was a keen proponent of secularism, arguing that religious instruction should not be given in schools and that religion should be practised only privately.[4] He was the son of Nawab Sarfaraz Hussain Khan, a member of the Indian Legislative Assembly and a leading member of the Bihar Provincial Congress. Also known as Tajammul Hosain Khan in school records, Khan had attended Burlington House School in Richmond before joining King's College School in 1911 at the age of 16. According to school records, he was born on 26 April 1864, and his guardian while at King's was Miss Beck, the secretary of the National Indian Association in London—an organisation set up in 1870 to foster social relations between Britons and Indians in Bristol and London. Husain left the school in 1912 but made an impression during his two years there. He was a keen member of the school museum project, in charge of the 'Oriental section', and when he left the school in July 1912, he instituted a Challenge Cup for swimming, donating a trophy for the prize.[5] He went on to study law at Queen's College, Cambridge, and in the 1914 issue of the School Magazine it was noted that 'Sammy', as he was sometimes known, had sold his motorbike and car and so was no longer the 'public danger' he once was.[6] All this points to someone who seemed to be quite popular at school and university, who led a privileged life and yet returned to India, like Jaipal Singh and Rajkumari Amrit Kaur, to take a leading political role in overseeing India's transition to an independent nation.

The independence of India in August 1947, however, was not merely a positive story of a new generation of Indians forming a new government and creating a new nation or the children of British public schools taking on prosperous political careers and playing their part in it. Independent India was born out of one of the bloodiest catastrophes of the modern era. It was only in February 1947, a mere six months before independence, that the British government announced that they would grant Indian independence and that this would take place in June 1948. Secret negotiations between Indian and British politicians soon led to the decision to partition the subcontinent into India—and a new nation of Pakistan, separated into West and East Pakistan despite sharing no borders. In the face of political pressure and rising violence, the date was brought forward to August 1947. This was a completely rushed and incomplete decision, with minimal information passed on to the general populace. On the day of independence and partition, people in the subcontinent had very little concept of what partition meant practically for their citizenship or national identity, nor did they know where the new boundaries lay, as the new borders were only announced on 17 August, two days later. Some princely states like Hyderabad, Junagadh and Jammu and Kashmir were undecided at this point. Although there were many factors that determined the mechanics of partition, the basic public understanding was that this was based on a religious division of the subcontinent and so there followed a mass exodus of millions of Hindus, Sikhs and Muslims from the new countries of India and Pakistan. It is estimated that 6 million Muslims left India, 4.5 million Sikhs left West Pakistan and under a million Hindus left East and West Pakistan. This led to mass confusion, looting, violence and murder on an unprecedented scale. More than a million people died; many others were subject to the most horrific crimes of violence imaginable.[7] With such a seismic turn of life-changing events, South Asian families both in the subcontinent and in the diaspora were indelibly affected. How children lived through that violence and migration, came to terms with new identities and witnessed that tumultuous history is explored further in this chapter.

* * *

While India and Pakistan were going through partition, Britain was recovering from the effects of the Second World War. The post-war period in Britain was characterised by rebuilding, labour shortages and the emergence of the newly created National Health Service (NHS). Rationing remained in effect in some form until 1954 but, in the meantime, the school leaving age rose from 14 to 15 in the spring of 1947.[8] During these years, political attention was also placed upon the rehabilitation and rehousing of refugees from post-war Europe, while labour migrants from the Empire were given the freedom to move to Britain to help with the rebuilding efforts and to bolster the new NHS. The arrival of the HMT *Empire Windrush* from the Caribbean on 22 June 1948 is widely recognised as marking a new era of post-war Commonwealth migration to Britain. The increase in the size, scale and diversity of post-war migration to Britain has shaped British immigration policy and culture ever since. Where did new Indian and Pakistani refugees and migrants fit into this picture? What of the children of the new countries of India and Pakistan who became refugees in the subcontinent or those who left the subcontinent in the wake of independence? There were some continuities for those children we have looked at in previous chapters—elite children who continued to engage with elite schools, the children of former seafarers and those born in Britain—but, as the size of migration from South Asia increased in the post-war period, there were new relationships to navigate and different identities that emerged in the wake of changing British laws.

The 1948 British Nationality Act offered British subjects of empire the right to British citizenship and the support to arrive in Britain to help with the rebuilding of houses, transport, health service and welfare. Labour shortages in foundries and steel mills and other major industries such as textiles provided attractive jobs to male South Asian workers. South Asians had to navigate new identities as British citizens—rather than the former 'subject' status of empire—as well as understand that the pre-1947 'India' no longer existed. Many now had 'Pakistani' identities (but not citizenship), though they had never lived in or visited the new country. Indian and Pakistani government decisions about citizenship laws were not concluded until the 1950s and so, in the interim, the UK government became concerned about conferring British citizenship upon South Asians who had no other citizenship ties.[9] Children navigating these new identities were part of a changing world with shifting political and diplomatic alliances as the Cold War started to overshadow global politics, while the prospect of a diverse and vibrant multicultural Britain loomed with a changing migrant population from across Europe and the Empire. South Asian children became part of a larger struggle for British subjecthood as the state also often failed to follow through on their promises and as new racist and anti-racist coalitions reshaped British politics and society.

Despite the British Nationality Act, for example, very few passports were issued to Indians between 1947 and 1950 and getting a passport from Delhi could take up to two years. There was also confusion about how to apply British citizenship to people living in the subcontinent, including people of Anglo-Indian or European heritage, leading to obtuse discussions about race. The high commissioner in Delhi suggested in 1951 that children who had European heritage but just one Indian ancestor (such as one Indian great-grandparent, for example), and who maintained strong links with the United Kingdom, could be treated as a 'pure European'.[10] In those early post-partition years, migration patterns followed those of before the war, with continued migration by seamen and some elite families for education, but after 1952, the size of Pakistani and Indian immigration to Britain became more significant. In December 1958, the Home Office announced that there were 55,000 Indians and Pakistanis in the United Kingdom.[11] However, in 1958, Prime Minister Nehru stated that only 5,000 Indians had travelled to Britain between 1955 and 1957 with passports issued by his government, out of 17,300 Indians who had arrived in Britain in that 3-year period.[12] While it cannot account for the full discrepancy and likely several factors abound, forgery and smuggling was rife, which created 'undocumented' migrants; there is very little information about child migrants coming to Britain in that way, however. The Indian and Pakistani governments had their own strict controls on issuing passports until a 1960 Indian Supreme Court judgement ruled that it was unconstitutional for the Indian government to deny its citizens the freedom to travel and to refuse passports to verifiable nationals. After 1961, from both India and Pakistan, there was a large increase in migration.[13]

While there was no HMT *Empire Windrush* moment for South Asians, only small numbers migrated in the 1950s before increasing in the 1960s. While I have already shown how child migrants have been overlooked in the history of imperial migration, in that immediate post-partition period, migrants to the UK from South Asia were overwhelmingly adult men.[14] When the British government tried to restrict immigration, first with the 1962 Commonwealth Immigration Act, this encouraged male migrants to bring over more women and children to join them and settle permanently in Britain. Partition and its associated migration set a trend for questions of identity, home and belonging as families and homes were torn apart and millions were forced into migration across the subcontinent. During the Second World War, estimates vary on the numbers of South Asians in Britain—it may have been as little as 8,000—but, by 1951, there were 43,000. By 1961, there were roughly 112,000, which does not take into account the people of mixed South Asian heritage who may not have been figured into such numbers.[15]

Partition had been a particularly traumatic and violent experience for all ages. The borders of the new countries not only split the subcontinent but also split interior states. The provinces of Punjab and Bengal were divided between India and Pakistan and people who were once neighbours were now estranged. Millions of families were compelled to cross new borders to the new countries of Pakistan and India at short notice, with no previous planning or warning about the consequences. The uncertainty, fear, loss of home and livelihood and long journeys exacerbated communal tensions and resulted in enormous violence with frequent and open murder, as well as the rape and abduction of women and young girls. Refugee camps were overloaded and makeshift. Clair Wills has written about some of the effects on adult Punjabis who migrated in the 1950s and 1960s to Britain. Many Punjabis were Sikhs and the idea of a Sikh homeland, which was spearheaded by the Khalistan movement, became particularly potent as the narrative of partition concentrated so heavily on Hindus and Muslims.[16] Although partition was a major upheaval for many South Asians, and many families looked to Britain for a new life, refugees from the West Punjab into India generally did not emigrate until their land claims for compensation were settled (although the process was not simple or completed for everyone).[17] And so the picture of post-partition migration to Britain was drawn out, influenced by British immigration policy and the new identities of a postcolonial age.

***

Haroon Ahmed is the father of a good friend and colleague of mine. He was born in Calcutta in 1936. His father, who had trained in Germany in the 1930s, was an Indian civil servant posted there at the time, and his maternal grandfather had been a very successful civil engineer and businessman, involved in the building of Delhi.[18] Haroon had two older sisters and a younger brother and they had ayahs growing up but spoke both Urdu and English at home. At the time of partition, Haroon was about eleven years old and in Delhi with his parents. His father's role in the Indian Civil Service (ICS) involved helping to partition the assets between India and Pakistan but, following an attack, the whole family left for a refugee camp in Delhi with only the clothes on their back. Although Haroon could not remember that time very well, in an interview from 2009 he recalled that they stayed in the refugee camp for months and it was there that he was taught to fire a gun. When the camp became under threat, they luckily got a 'mercy flight' from Delhi to Karachi and in the car journey to the airport their mother hid the children to avoid violence.

At 16, Haroon started a pre-engineering degree course at college in Pakistan but then his father was transferred to England to work in the Pakistan High Commission as a technical inspector in 1954. The family stayed at Regent Palace Hotel for their first few weeks while the High Commission found accommodation. Haroon has remembered that, on his first journey on a bus through central London, he thought the houses looked like the dollhouses they had played with as children. His first impressions of England, as a teenager, were very favourable, but he did think the food was terrible. Haroon attended Chiswick Polytechnic to complete his A-levels, where his maths teacher, Miss Tompkins, encouraged him and pushed him ahead of others. The physics teacher, Mr Kilburn, made Haroon his assistant to help lay out experiments before class for the other children—and, following his A-levels, Haroon was admitted to Imperial College to study Electrical Engineering.[19]

Haroon's younger brother was enrolled at the Latymer School in London. Their parents had to return to Pakistan after two years, so Haroon had to look out for his younger brother. His brother was 14 but looked older and it was difficult to find accommodation. Their parents had found them 'digs' (lodgings) before they left but they were soon after closed down and they had to find an alternative. There were no laws against racial discrimination and doors were slammed in their faces when they were out looking for a shared room. They soon found a place in Shepherds Bush but the brothers nearly got beaten up by Teddy Boys when they had laughed at their clothes. Having lived through the turmoil and atrocity of partition, they had migrated in its aftermath and now faced different forms of tensions and conflict in Britain while still young. Haroon has since said that moving to England as a 17-year-old was more dislocating than the experience of partition.[20] The everyday racism and institutional racism was more acute than he could have imagined as a boy in British India and in the new Pakistan. Despite these dislocations, Haroon regarded himself as British and took British nationality in 1967.

As stories like Haroon's suggest, it is the experiences of children during partition and their subsequent migration that has shaped much of the psychology of both the Indian subcontinent and the global South Asian diaspora of the late twentieth and early twenty-first century. In more recent years in Britain, commentators and academics have been interested in why memories of partition have been buried in families and how younger generations have come to terms with the feelings of trauma that have been passed down. The BBC broadcaster Anita Rani presented some television documentaries on this topic in 2017, the 70th anniversary of partition, and in the same year Kavita Puri, another BBC broadcaster, presented a radio documentary and published a book from her interviews with survivors. Increasingly, within Britain and among a British South Asian cohort, there has been interest in what partition has meant for British South Asian families and this has led to further discussion of migration as part of the story and legacy of partition. Academics have conducted further interviews and put together oral histories of survivors and their descendants in Britain. This includes a group of researchers at Loughborough University on a Leverhulme Trust-funded project 'Migrant Memory and the Postcolonial Imagination (MMPI): British Asian Memory, Identity and Community after Partition'. The Loughborough project, for example, interviewed Bahadur, a British Pakistani whose father, aged 10 in 1947, had been forced to leave India as a child and refused to be called Pakistani, even as an adult, despite acquiring Pakistani citizenship.[21] While nationality was being contested both in South Asia and in Britain, politicians and officials who were making decisions about borders and immigration legislation paid little attention to the lives of children although the machinations of partition and post-war immigration had tremendous effects on children's lives.

Meanwhile, Anindya Raychaudhuri has written extensively about the cultural ramifications of partition and conducted extensive interviews between 2011 and 2013 both in the subcontinent and in Britain. His interviewees have noted the trauma of being separated from friends through partition. K. S., who was 13 or 14, remembers how his Muslim neighbours left at partition for a nearby camp and the tears he and his friend had at their parting.[22] An 8-year-old at the time of partition, Uzair has recalled how vivid his memory of leaving Mainpuri was; even though he was young, he understood exactly that he would never be returning to his childhood home. It was a lonely experience.[23] Raychaudhuri has noted how helpless children felt in the throes of partition, as clearly they had no control over the arbitrary design and operation of the borders. He has also noted that stories of how children were abandoned or survived were stories that many survivors clung on to. For example, Parkash, who was roughly 17 at the time of partition, told Raychaudhuri about how her 6-month-old sister was wrapped up and pushed under a seat for four days without food or drink: 'When they took out my sister from under the seat, she was alive, God protected her, and she survived, and lives in Ilford'.[24] There was a similar story of a baby boy who fell into a ditch on the way to a refugee camp but whose mother was not allowed to return for him: 'in the morning a few of the men got together and just to give her peace of mind, they went looking, but they found the baby, he was there in a ditch. And I mean, he lives in Newcastle now.'²⁵ As Raychaudhuri has noted, not only did these stories highlight the danger to life experienced in the Punjab of 1947 but they also emphasised that successful migration to British towns and cities provided a contrasting safe space, despite the challenges of integration and negotiating new identities.

Of course, partition affected all families who lived in the subcontinent, including white British families. Kavita Puri interviewed Kenneth Miln, born to Scottish parents just outside of Calcutta in 1937. He attended a boarding school, St Paul's School, in Darjeeling from the age of 7 until 1949 when his parents decided to return to Britain and first lived in Beckenham in Kent, before eventually relocating to Dundee. He remembered the violence leading up to partition, including the Great Calcutta Killings of 1946 and how immune he became to the dead bodies even as a child (or perhaps because he was a child). My own father, born in 1943 in Calcutta, was too small to really remember these events but he too has told me how he heard stories of how, like Kenneth, his family became immune to the dead bodies on the street. While partition did not materially affect Kenneth's family at first, he did notice differences in interactions between Hindus and Muslims. For Kenneth, the move to Britain post-partition when he was 12 was heart-wrenching; due to his upbringing there, he regarded himself as Indian, and missed India very much.²⁶

Children were not absolved of violence in partition though. Swaran Singh Rayit was 15 during partition and was chosen in his Sikh village to join a group who sought revenge amidst the violence of partition on a nearby Muslim village. In 1951, his family migrated to Uganda only to then have to migrate to the UK after Idi Amin ordered the expulsion of Asians from Uganda in 1972. Karan Singh Hamdard, another Sikh Punjabi, lost all of his family in the violence of partition when he was just 16 years old. In 1949, he migrated to Tanzania, also in East Africa, having just turned 18, and then in 1970 moved to the UK.²⁷ The double migration of South Asians to East Africa before migrating to Britain was a common feature for many South Asian communities who live in Britain at the time of writing. Their cohort includes Rishi Sunak, the former British prime minister, whose mother, Usha, migrated to Britain in 1968 from Tanzania with her parents. Her father Raghubir Sain Berry had been born in Ludhiana in the Punjab around 1930, a province severely affected by partition, and worked in Tanzania between 1953 and 1968 as a tax collector.

Another East African Asian migrant to Britain was Sewa Singh Mandla, who was born in Nairobi on 4 January 1927. His father had been a civilian in the Indian Army during the First World War and, after the war ended, chose to migrate to Kenya where he worked as a 'turner' on a lathe machine for engineering and car manufacturing firm Harts and Bell. Mandla had one brother and eight sisters; his brother and three of his sisters had been born in India, the other five in Nairobi. They lived in a house with four rooms made from wood and iron. Mandla went to the Government Indian Primary School from 1932 to 1940. He had to walk nearly 5 miles to get to school every day. He then went to the Government Indian High School for boys until 1944. Mandla was heavily involved in extra curricula activities including sports, athletics, scouts, debating society, prefects and issuing cinema passes for pupils. He used to help the headmaster, Mr Maxwell, with extra tasks, who described him as an 'outstanding boy', and he went up to the highest grade with fifteen other boys all keen to gain admission to higher educational institutions in the UK. Immediately after graduating from school, he took up a post as a teacher at the Indian primary school while he waited to hear about university admissions. He stayed a teacher for seven years as he tried to raise the money to afford to study abroad. In 1952, having already enrolled with Lincoln's Inn, Mandla sailed to England to complete his studies for the Bar.[28]

Mandla's childhood and education in Kenya may not be so unusual compared to some of his peers but he is noteworthy for what happened later in his career in the UK and the ongoing legacies of colonialism in Britain after the Second World War. In 1957, Mandla married Mohinder Kaur, also a Punjabi-Kenyan, and they had three children all born in Nairobi. The children all went to school in Nairobi but, in 1974, the family migrated to the UK. They initially stayed in London before moving to Birmingham in 1977 where Mandla set up a solicitor's office. He was the first solicitor of colour to practise at Birmingham Magistrate's Court. The youngest of his children, and only son, Gurinder had enrolled in a comprehensive state school in London. In Birmingham, Mandla tried to gain admission for Gurinder at a private school called Park Grove School, in the Harborne area. However, Gurinder was declined admission by the headmaster, Audley Dowell Lee, who said that the school had uniform rules, requiring pupils to wear a cap: 'Your son must wear a cap while in school. I cannot accept a boy with a turban'.[29] Mandla decided to challenge the decision by taking the school to court. He took the issue to the County Court under the provisions of the Race Relations Act 1976, arguing that this was a case of racial discrimination against Sikhs. Dowell Lee argued that Sikhs could not rely on the provisions of the Race Relations Act as the Act did not apply to Sikhs.[30]

Mandla lost the case in the County Court and in the Court of Appeal but the case had ignited the Sikh community who were eager to prove that Sikhs were a minority group and should be protected by the Race Relations Act. A petition with more than 75,000 signatures was presented to the then-Prime Minister Margaret Thatcher. A public rally took place at Hyde Park on 10 October 1982, attended by more than 40,000 Sikhs. Mandla and the Commission for Racial Equality took the appeal to the House of Lords and, in 1983, they overturned the decision of the appeal court, ruling that Gurinder had been the victim of unlawful racial discrimination.[31] While the focus of this case is often on the role of Gurinder's father, including by the press at the time, this case emphasises the ways in which children's experiences as migrants were shaping political formations and community activism in post-war Britain. South Asian children continued to be marked out for their appearance, religion, race and ethnicity, and their value could be challenged from a young age.[32]

* * *

The independence of India and Pakistan helped form the first part of a domino effect, following the Second World War, of nations gaining independence from the British Empire. These moments of independence were hard-won by anti-colonialists and nationalists but the manner of independence was often dictated by a British imperial power which left distressing economic, social and political legacies for countries across Asia and Africa. As mentioned at the beginning of this book, the British Sri Lankan theorist Sivanandan famously said: 'We are here because you were there' in reference to the post-Windrush generation of migrants from the former empire to Britain. The legacies of decolonisation are not only seen in the Global South but in Britain as well. For Indian and Pakistani children who migrated to Britain in the immediate aftermath of partition, their identities were shaped by the trauma of partition as well as the confusion of new Indian and Pakistani identities—including an East Pakistani entity that would not become independent Bangladesh until 1971. As concepts of language, religion and belonging became heightened within the Indian subcontinent, children were confronted with these issues twice over when navigating their space and place within Britain and their right to Britishness.

I must return to my own mother who migrated to Britain just six years after partition. She was born after partition but her mother's family had lost their homes in East Bengal—then East Pakistan, now Bangladesh—and then her parents gave up their home in West Bengal through the decision to settle permanently in London. My uncle was only a toddler during partition, and 8 years old when he migrated to London, but throughout his life he had a yearning for a life lost in India. He could code switch between holding court on cricket, politics and history with a cut-glass English accent and, amid his desire to fit into a Kolkata middle-class social scene, speaking fluent Bengali, wearing Indian pyjama trousers and expressing his penchant for traditional Bengali cuisine. Both my mother and uncle were the only South Asian children in their school classes but they did get the chance to meet and socialise with Indian children in London through their parents' engagement with other Bengali families, use of specialist grocery stores and attendance at religious festivals. They could not rid themselves of the legacies of empire, though. As children, they stood out because of their skin colour and when walking to school, they were often stopped by white British men who would want to speak Hindi and tell them about their military or civil service careers in India. They were not allowed to be ignorant of the history of empire, even if some of the memories of partition were glossed over.

My mother and uncle were part of a growing population of South Asian children in Britain—one that increased exponentially in the 1960s and 1970s—that staked its claim to Britain and Britishness because of the role Britain had in colonising and then breaking apart their countries of origin. Their citizenship and identity were often contested by people around them as well as government machines and border controls but, as children, they were often innocent victims of international conflict. The child migrants of the 2020s too, the ones who board boats and ships or who are dependent on smugglers, remain victims of the conflicts of war and immigration offices as well. While the children of partition had different experiences, the longstanding effects of trauma, both on them and intergenerationally, should not be overlooked. As Sivanandan has also noted, however, colonialism was not just a one-way street and was something that could be resisted, even as a child.[33] As Britain and its former colonies were tangled together indelibly, the South Asian children who migrated, and increasingly were born in Britain, were rooted in those legacies of empire and, for some, resistance.

EPILOGUE

WHERE ARE YOU FROM?

'Where are you from?' is a question I distinctly remember being asked on numerous occasions as a child, causing me to resent the question and the implication that I was not British. Since childhood I have switched between cultures; I have at least three different pronunciations of my name—an anglicised version, an anglicised Bengali version and a Bengali-Indian version. I learnt to adapt and code-switch but my experiences were not unique. Nikesh Shukla, a contemporary of mine who grew up in Harrow, has written eloquently about this both in his fiction and non-fiction.[1] Riz Ahmed grew up in North-West London and is of a similar age too. His lyrics in the song 'Where You From' (2020) emphasise the refrain of our childhoods and those questions of belonging, both from within and imposed from outside. Crucially, South Asian children have historically 'belonged' to Britain and are 'from' Britain, as well as belonging to diverse parts of South Asia. Modern Britain and India, Pakistan and Bangladesh would not exist if it were not for these children. Child migrants were instrumental in the fashioning of the British Empire project and the downfall of that empire in India but they belong to the histories of Britain as much as the histories of the subcontinent.

The issue of migration and child migration are ongoing political issues, though, and South Asian child migration to Britain beyond the mid-twentieth century has fundamentally shaped the outlook and reality of modern Britain. Many more people of South Asian heritage who migrated as children in the last quarter of the twentieth century have written about these experiences, including many well-known figures within the British media and literary landscape. A member of the groundbreaking and influential BBC comedy series *Goodness Gracious Me* (1996–2001), Meera Syal's book *Anita and Me* (1996) is a semi-autobiographical but fictional account of growing up in a village in the East Midlands in the late 1960s. The heroine of the book, Meena, is nine years old at the start and the only child of South Asian heritage in her village. The book discusses Meena's friendships, school, experiences of facing racism and relationship with her family and Indian culture. The book has since been featured on GCSE English literature syllabi in British schools, made into a film in 2002 and adapted for the stage by Tanika Gupta in 2015; it offers a familiar account of South Asian childhood in modern Britain.

On the other hand, another member of the *Goodness Gracious Me* writing team, Sanjeev Bhaskar, had a very different childhood from Syal's as he grew up in a much more racially diverse city. His home was above a launderette in Ealing, West London, in the 1970s. In an interview with *The Guardian* in 2010, he poignantly pointed out that he felt protective towards his parents as a child: 'Even at four or five, I felt instinctively that I fitted in better here than they did. I understood the colloquialisms, the pop culture. I knew they were far away from home...'[2] Bhasker admitted that he faced difficulties at school as he was always marked out as different from his white classmates but also criticised by Asian schoolmates for talking to white people.

Issues around language and fitting in resonate among the memories of this period. *Greetings from Bury Park* (also titled *Blinded by the Light*)—subsequently made into a film directed by Gurinder Chadha—follows journalist Sarfraz Manzoor's childhood and young adulthood growing up in Luton in the 1970s and '80s. Sarfraz's father, Mohammed, arrived in England in January 1963, having left behind his wife and Sarfraz's older sister and brother (both babies) in Karachi, Pakistan, in pursuit of a better economic life for them. Sarfraz was born in Pakistan in 1971, conceived when his father visited the family in 1970, but it was only in 1974 that the family joined Mohammed in Bury Park, Luton, when Sarfraz was not yet 3. His mother started working as a seamstress at home and, from the age of 4, before he started school, he would start helping her with her bundles. In his memoir, Manzoor talks about the tensions within the Pakistani community in Luton about where their children should be educated and then the tensions he experienced with his father around music and work. He was desperate to leave the family house (and Luton) and the book revolves around different stories from his youth, his relationship with his parents and siblings, with his Pakistani identity and his love for the music of Bruce Springsteen.[3] As he recalled: 'At school I was just another schoolboy collecting Panini football stickers and stealing peeks at the girls doing handsprings in the playground in the hope of seeing a glimpse of their knickers, but at home my parents were constantly reminding me I was Pakistani and different from my friends.'[4] It is important to reiterate here that the identities of 'South Asian' children were never homogenous, whether in the nineteenth century or twenty-first century, as there was so much disparity around religious, cultural, class, caste and linguistic backgrounds. Modern India has twenty-two official languages, but over sixty are spoken, and so considering linguistic diversity in India alone is testament to the difference in experiences South Asian children would have had in Britain.

These tensions over the location of 'home', over religion, culture and language and over 'Britishness' were resonant for many South Asian children in the post-war period where migration journeys meant that there was less likelihood of 'returning' to the subcontinent and a greater cultural shift to a post-war 'multicultural' British identity. Sathnam Sanghera in his book *The Boy with the Topknot* (2008) has written about growing up navigating tensions with religion and culture, as the only one of his four siblings who was required to grow his hair long in the Sikh religious tradition. Language also became a site of contestation; although he only spoke Punjabi as a child pre-attending school, as he grew older, language would form a barrier between him and his parents. Like Manzoor, Sanghera highlights the contrasts between the 'western' television and music he would enjoy with the clothes he would wear at home and life as a Punjabi Sikh family in 1980s Wolverhampton.[5]

In the 1990s, the anthropologist Dhooleka Raj conducted interviews with South Asian families where similar stories about language and code-switching emerge. For example, Karnal Bhandari told Raj about his teenage years in London in the 1970s and the perfect English accents other children with South Asian heritage had at school but how they could also switch to their own form of Punjabi, Bengali, Gujarati or Tamil at home or with other friends who spoke the same language.[6] Raj also talked to families who knew they could never 'go back' to India or Pakistan or Bangladesh. They had 'lost' the language and were used to Britain and, as more generations were born in Britain, it became increasingly unlikely that these families would ever 'return'.[7] Meanwhile, the sociologist Parminder Bhachu interviewed South Asian mothers in Britain in the 1980s who expressed concerns about Western cultural influences such as music, make up and co-educational spaces upon their children.[8] The demands on children to maintain 'South Asian' culture at home, while engaging with their non-South Asian peers at school and outside of the domestic space, were challenges that continued into the 1990s and 2000s. At the start of an era of mass capitalism and globalisation, these pressures became more acute, perhaps, as it became more difficult to shield children from Western influences in their socialisation and preserve an unmediated South Asian culture.[9]

There are many more interesting accounts of childhood in this period. They include broadcaster Anita Rani's book, *The Right Sort of Girl* (2021). Rani grew up in Yorkshire in the 1980s, following her grandfather's migration from the Punjab to Bradford in 1953, and her book offers lessons to her 16-year-old self, reassuring her about her future, and discussing some of the travails of girlhood and being South Asian in Britain.[10] Meanwhile, Babita Sharma was born to Hindu Punjabi parents in Reading in April 1977. Her parents bought a corner shop that year and became entrepreneurs who lived above the shop with their three children. By the 1980s, 50 per cent of independent corner shops were owned by Asian families in Britain.[11] In her book, *The Corner Shop* (2019), Sharma remembers how her childhood was different from her friends; this was mainly because she lived above a shop rather than because of her 'Asian culture'. Margaret Thatcher, the daughter of grocery-shop keepers, championed Asian entrepreneurship during the 1980s but the Sharmas were not immune to racism from customers. In that same decade, there were riots in 1981 in Brixton and elsewhere; Black and Asian youths were targeted by the police and 'Paki' was a common slur. The Southall riots in 1979 had seen violence from fascists, discriminate policing and the death of anti-fascist teacher Blair Peach, despite the peaceful organisation by the Southall Youth Movement in response to the murder of 18-year-old Gurdip Singh Chaggar in Southall in 1976. Accounts like these reveal the varied experiences of South Asian children in post-war Britain alongside similar refrains around belonging and identity.

* * *

What about more contemporary children of South Asian heritage in Britain? An infamous example is Shamima Begum, born in August 1999 in London to Bangladeshi parents. At the age of 15 she left the country, along with two other classmates, to join ISIS in Syria. Within a matter of days of her arrival, she married a 22-year-old Dutch Islamic State recruit. Known in the British media as a 'Jihadi bride', she was immediately condemned by politicians and the press despite her young age. In 2019, when she was still only 19, she was found in a Syrian refugee camp. She had had two children, who died in infancy, and was heavily pregnant with a third child. The UK Home Secretary decided to strip Begum of her British citizenship, leaving her outside of statehood, with the argument that she could technically apply for Bangladeshi citizenship through her parental lineage. Although she left the UK as a child, managing to pass through border controls in the UK, Turkey and Syria as an unaccompanied minor, and then having children below the age of consent, the UK government solely focused on her political threat. Her Britishness was immediately stripped without acknowledgement of her birth and upbringing in Britain or the legacies this could have for other people of colour in Britain if the state could legally suggest—as they did successfully—that they should return to the homelands of their parents.[12] It should not be ignored that the home secretary at the time was Sajid Javid, who had been born in Lancashire in 1969 to Pakistani parents.

Begum's case reveals the contradictions around the perception and role of children in society. Children are denied political rights such as voting, or other social rights such as driving or drinking alcohol, and yet the age which determines legal childhood has constantly changed over history. There is nothing fixed about childhood and nothing that necessarily separates children from 'adults' in terms of their capacity to enact social and political change. As Faisal Devji has argued, when children do engage in political or environmental activism, they are motivated by a need to have a say in their future. However, when 'children' enter the public sphere, they are expected to act like 'adults' and are open to harsh critiques with little consideration of their age or vulnerability.[13]

Beyond Begum, we can see how young children of South Asian heritage have entered the public eye in the twenty-first century and the contradictions inherent in their objectification as well as also how important they are for the ongoing shaping of contemporary society and politics. In 2012, Malala Yousafzai was 15 when she was shot by the Taliban in Pakistan in response to her public demands for girls to be educated. She was taken immediately to Birmingham in the UK for medical attention and established a new life with her family in Britain. She continued to agitate for girls' education and was awarded the Nobel Peace Prize in 2014 at the age of 17. Meanwhile, Mya-Rose Craig, born in 2002, is a British Bangladeshi environmental activist who began writing blogs around climate change under the moniker 'Birdgirl' from a young age. When she was 13 she started organising an annual nature camp for 'inner-city BAME teenagers and naturalists' and was vocal about the need for there to be more people from diverse racial and ethnic backgrounds in the conservation field and on nature TV.[14] She wrote about the barriers she faced as a person of colour in the environmental sector, highlighting the white privilege of causes such as school strikes for climate or Extinction Rebellion Youth and the tokenistic use of BAME (Black, Asian and Minority Ethnic) faces.[15] These examples reveal the risks and challenges that South Asian children continue to

EPILOGUE

take on and face in the ongoing political life of Britain and, beyond it, the world.

* * *

What links Malala or Begum or Craig to Duleep Singh or Rajkumari Amrit Kaur or Albert Mahomet? While a child with brown skin in Britain is much more common now than in the 1800s, do the racialised signifiers of difference—hijabs and topknots—attached to them mark them out more than those associated with nineteenth-century South Asian children in Britain? Were South Asian children in the nineteenth century accepted as part and parcel of the Empire in more benevolent ways than South Asian children in postcolonial Britain? With the examples I have discussed in this book, I have wished to argue that South Asian children were—and are—important parts of British life and that there is a long history of South Asian childhood in Britain. Their experiences varied along class, linguistic, religious and gendered lines—and this affects what records we have of them—but their very presence fundamentally shaped the histories of Britain and the Indian subcontinent. There are some clear continuities across time in the navigation of racial identities whilst young but the period of empire also brought out its own distinct relations. Before 1947, South Asian children in Britain were British subjects and part of the Empire. They were constrained by the hierarchies of empire and the political ideologies that underpinned it. Their education, work and family life in Britain was mediated by the physical distance from the subcontinent and their lives as minorities were tempered by fluid notions of race, Britishness and childhood as the nature of empire and nationalism evolved.

The British Empire was a crucial part of British history and we can bring this history alive through the stories of the migration of colonised children to the imperial heartland. To understand modern British history fully, we need to include histories of race, of empire, of women and of children. These children offer us a new and fuller sense of the breadth of British and South Asian history still to uncover. The nostalgia for empire continues in some places—in tourist companies that exploit stereotypes of imperial history and culture war debates about the benefits of empire—but the legacies and realities for children continue too—dealing with exclusion and racism, debates about identity and distance from imagined 'homelands'. South Asian children have indelibly left their imperial footprints upon the histories of Britain, of empire and of the Indian subcontinent. This book has been an attempt to showcase those hidden lives and connections.

ACKNOWLEDGEMENTS

One of the greatest pleasures in researching and putting this book together has been meeting and corresponding with some wonderful school archivists, whose interest and advice allowed me to follow some fruitful leads and ideas for shaping this book. I have learnt so much from them and wish I could have included more from the photographs and school records that they so kindly shared with me. I am so grateful to: Rachel Hassall, Archivist at Sherborne School; Dr C. S. Knighton, Principal Assistant Keeper of Archives at Clifton College; Calista Lucy, Keeper of the Archive, and Freddie Witts, Archivist, at Dulwich College; Hilary Cummings, Librarian at Kayton Library, St Paul's School; Dr Lucy Inglis, School Archivist at King's College School Wimbledon; Jenny Bartlett, Head of Library and Archive, and Deborah Greatrex, librarian, at North London Collegiate School; Howard Bailes, Archivist at St Paul's Girls' School; Paul Godsland of the Malvernian Society; David Jones, Archivist at Perse School; and Dorothy Goldsack, former Archivist at Sherborne Girls' School. I am also incredibly grateful to all the archivists and institutions who gave permission to reproduce the photographs in this book and I am thankful for funding support from the University of Bristol.

I would not have written this book without the conversations I had with Suresh Ariaratnam (who I was fortunate to first meet in 2017) and I am grateful for his introductions to Shoaib Rokadiya, Mitchell Albert and Fritha Saunders, whose valuable advice helped me to shape the direction of this book early on. Thank you so much to Michael

ACKNOWLEDGEMENTS

Dwyer for taking *Imperial Footprints* on, to Mei Jayne Yew for her editorial support, to Kathleen May and all the team at Hurst, to Becca Hirst for such thoughtful copy-editing, as well as the peer reviewers. I am so grateful for this chance to share this work with a wider audience.

I might have given up thinking of and writing this book several times if not for the support and advice of Rowena Kennedy-Epstein. I would like to thank D-M Withers, Amy Edwards and Vivian Kong too. I am grateful for helpful conversations I have had along the way with Arunima Datta, Antoinette Burton and Andrew Whitehead. Thank you also to steadfast friends and colleagues: Rakesh Ankit, Mark Freeman, Josie Gill, Josie McLellan and Tara Puri. Thank you to Kathryn Gleadle and to Christina de Bellaigue, Sian Pooley and the Oxford History of Childhood Seminar Group. I am grateful for comrades in the History Department at the University of Bristol—too numerous to mention individually—for useful conversations and care; we have been through a lot together and I am thankful for the collegiality. I appreciate working alongside Rehana Ahmed, Hilary Carey, Aleena Din, Maya Parmar, Ellen Smith, Florian Stadtler and Lucy Wray in recent years. Thank you to the wonderful students on my former 'Race, Migration and Diaspora' module, and to my former MA students, for kind ongoing interest in my research and writing.

Some people have asked me if my attention to the history of children was inspired by becoming a mother, perhaps implying a new interest in children that I did not have before. The idea for this book came well before I became a mother and was always, instead, inspired by looking up to my own mother and (perhaps self-indulgently) my own childhood experiences. It has also been inspired by the talks I have given in schools and my desire to consider those who are often excluded from history. Although this is not a family history, this book is clearly inspired by my mother's family and I want to thank Soma Chaudhury for her support. I am sorry that Biman Chaudhury is not alive to read this. I would not be anywhere without my parents, Arabinda and Nita Mukherjee, and my brother Chiron. Words cannot describe what I owe them for their love and encouragement.

This book is for Koni.

কনি

NOTES

INTRODUCTION

1. See Figure 1.
2. From *The Beatles Anthology*, quoted in: https://www.thatericalper.com/2017/09/28/george-harrisons-sitar-1965-going-auction/
3. Violet Stebbings, 'Transcript of Reminiscences'. From North London Collegiate School Archives, March 1972.
4. Rozina Visram, *Ayahs, Lascars and Princes: The Story of Indians in Britain 1700–1947* (London: Pluto Press, 1986); Rozina Visram, *Asians in Britain: 400 Years of History* (London: Pluto Press, 2002); Sathnam Sanghera, *Empireland: How Imperialism Has Shaped Modern Britain* (London: Penguin Books, 2021).
5. See also BBC, 'You're Dead to Me' (Podcast), 'Sake Dean Mahomed', first released 1 October 2021.
6. Norman Moore and Rachel E. Davies, 'Mahomed, Frederick Henry Horatio Akbar (1849–1884), Physician', *Oxford Dictionary of National Biography* (Oxford: Oxford University Press, online 2004).
7. J. Stewart Cameron, Jackie Hicks and Carl Gottschalk, 'Frederick Akbar Mahomed and His Role in the Description of Hypertension at Guy's Hospital', *Kidney International*, 49: 5 (1 May 1996), pp. 1488–1506, https://doi.org/10.1038/ki.1996.209; Arup K. Chatterjee, *Indians in London: From the Birth of the East India Company to Independent India* (New Delhi: Bloomsbury India, 2021), p. 161.
8. Lady Login, *Sir John Login and Duleep Singh* (London: W. H. Allen & Co., 1890).

9. Michael Alexander and Sushila Anand, *Queen Victoria's Maharajah: Duleep Singh 1838–93* (London: Phoenix Press, 1980), p. 61.
10. https://www.sikhnet.com/news/prince-punjab-and-perthshire-scotland-remembering-maharajah-duleep-singh
11. Alexander and Anand, *Queen Victoria's Maharajah*.
12. Christy Campbell, *The Maharajah's Box: An Imperial Story of Conspiracy, Love and a Guru's Prophecy* (London: HarperCollins, 2001), p. 24. See also Anindya Raychaudhuri, *Homemaking: Radical Nostalgia and the Construction of a South Asian Diaspora* (London: Rowman & Littlefield Publishers, 2018), chap. 1.

1. THE WHITE INDIANS

1. BBC television, 'Who Do You Think You Are', Series 15: 2, first aired 9 July 2018.
2. Chatterjee, *Indians in London*, pp. 169–70.
3. *Census of India, 1901. Part II. Tables* (Calcutta: Office of the Superintendent of Government Printing India, 1903), pp. 428–9.
4. See Durba Ghosh, *Sex and the Family in Colonial India: The Making of Empire* (Cambridge: Cambridge University Press, 2006).
5. Lydia Murdoch, '"Suppressed Grief": Mourning the Death of British Children and the Memory of the 1857 Indian Rebellion', *Journal of British Studies*, 51 (2012), 364–92.
6. David Gilmour, *The British in India: Three Centuries of Ambition and Experience* (London: Allen Lane, 2018), pp. 365–6.
7. Robin Bernstein, *Racial Innocence: Performing American Childhood from Slavery to Civil Rights* (New York: New York University Press, 2011), pp. 4–6.
8. Radhika Mohanram, *Imperial White: Race, Diaspora, and the British Empire* (Minneapolis: University of Minnesota Press, 2007), p. 3.
9. Mohanram, *Imperial White*, p. 25.
10. Ellen Filor, '"He Is Hardened to the Climate & a Little Bleached by It's [Sic] Influence": Imperial Childhoods in Scotland and Madras, c. 1800-1830', in *Children, Childhood and Youth in the British World*, ed. Simon Sleight and Shirleene Robinson (Basingstoke: Palgrave Macmillan, 2015), p. 79.
11. Niamh Dillon, *Homeward Bound: Return Migration from Ireland and India at the End of the British Empire* (New York: New York University Press, 2023), chap. 1.
12. Gilmour, *The British in India*, p. 373.
13. Hauke Wiebe and Roger Jeffery, 'Edinburgh Schools: Suppliers of

14. Filor, 'He Is Hardened', p. 82.
15. Filor, 'He is Hardened', p. 83.
16. Suzanne Conway, 'Ayah, Caregiver to Anglo-Indian Children, c. 1750-1947', in *Children, Childhood and Youth in the British World*, ed. Simon Sleight and Shirleene Robinson (Basingstoke: Palgrave Macmillan, 2015), pp. 41–58.
17. Visram, *Asians in Britain*, p. 50.
18. Arunima Datta, *Waiting on Empire: A History of Indian Travelling Ayahs in Britain* (Oxford: Oxford University Press, 2023).
19. Frances Hodgson Burnett, *The Secret Garden* (London: Phillips Publishing Company, 1911), p. 1.
20. Flora Annie Steel and Grace Gardiner, *The Complete Indian Housekeeper and Cook*, 7th edn, p. 3, and 'Chota Mem' (Mrs C. Lang), *The English Bride in India: Hints on Indian Housekeeping* (Madras, 1909), p. 56, quoted in Olivia Robinson, 'Travelling Ayahs of the Nineteenth and Twentieth Centuries: Global Networks and Mobilization of Agency', *History Workshop Journal*, 86 (2018), p.46.
21. Visram, *Asians in Britain*, p. 53.
22. Satyasikha Chakraborty, '"Nurses of Our Ocean Highways": The Precarious Metropolitan Lives of Colonial South Asian Ayahs', *Journal of Women's History*, 32:2 (2020), pps. 44, 51–2.
23. Margery Freda Perham, *Lugard: The Years of Adventure, 1858–1898* (London: Collins, 1956), pp. 3–23.
24. Vyvyen Brendon, *Children of the Raj* (London: Weidenfeld & Nicolson, 2005), pp. 99–103.
25. *Hampshire Chronicle and General Advertiser for the South and West of England*, 11 September 1886, p. 4.
26. *The Morning Post*, 10 July 1900, p. 1.
27. *The Scotsman*, 28 February 1900, p. 9.
28. Brendon, *Children of the Raj*, chap. 4.
29. Reproduced in Rudyard Kipling, *The Man Who Would Be King: And Other Stories* (Oxford: Oxford University Press, 2020).
30. Brendon, *Children of the Raj*, pp. 117–18. For more on Kipling's account of his childhood see Rudyard Kipling, *Something of Myself: For My Friends Known and Unknown* (Harmondsworth: Penguin, 1977).
31. Quoted in Brendon, *Children of the Raj*, p. 194.
32. British Library (BL), Mss Eur T53. Tape Transcript, *The Raj*: Mrs Iris Portal, 31 July 1973.

33. Dillon, *Homeward Bound*, p. 36.
34. John Christie, *Morning Drum* (London: British Association for Cemeteries in South Asia, 1983), pp. 7–8.
35. Gilmour, *The British in India*, p. 371.
36. Wilfred R. Bion, *The Long Week-End 1897–1919: Part of a Life* (Routledge: Abingdon, 1982).
37. Brendon, *Children of the Raj*, p. 197.

2. THE VICTORIAN CURIOSITIES

1. Theoretically outlined in Edward Said's seminal *Orientalism* (New York: Pantheon, 1978).
2. Lydia Murdoch, *Imagined Orphans: Poor Families, Child Welfare, and Contested Citizenship in London* (Ithaca: Rutgers University Press, 2006), chap. 5.
3. Henry Mayhew, *London Labour and the London Poor* (London, 1861), p. 242.
4. Mayhew, *London Labour*, p. 188.
5. A. J. Mahomet, *From Street Arab to Pastor* (Cardiff: J. B. Thomasson, 1901), chap. 1.
6. Mahomet, *From Street Arab*, chap. 2.
7. Mahomet, *From Street Arab*, p. 53.
8. Mahomet, *From Street Arab*, chaps 5–6; Visram, *Asians in Britain*, pp. 69–71.
9. Sumanta Banerjee, 'The Mysterious Alien: Indian Street Jugglers in Victorian London', *Economic and Political Weekly* XLVI: 14 (2 April 2011), pp. 60–1.
10. Joseph Salter, *The Asiatic in England: Sketches of Sixteen Years' Work Among Orientals* (London: Seeley, Jackson and Halliday, 1873), p. 223.
11. Ibid., p. 116.
12. *London Gazette*, 1688; *Morning Chronicle*, 17 February 1795; *Morning Chronicle*, 6 October 1795, as cited in Visram, *Ayahs, Lascars and Princes*, pp. 14–15.
13. *Flying Post; or, The Post Master*, 14 July 1702.
14. *Daily Advertiser*, 5 September 1774.
15. *Edinburgh Advertiser*, 26 May 1775.
16. For more on runaway slaves of African descent in Britain, see the Runaway Slaves in Britain project: https://www.runaways.gla.ac.uk/
17. 'Tiny Traces: African and Asian Children at London's Foundling Hospital', Exhibition Guide 2022-23: https://foundlingmuseum.org.uk/wp-content/uploads/2023/02/TinyTraces-Booklet.pdf

18. *Saunders' News-Letter*, 5 August 1776.
19. *Caledonian Mercury*, 4 October 1766.
20. Visram, *Ayahs, Lascars and Princes*, pp. 11–12.
21. Michael H. Fisher, *Counterflows to Colonialism: Indian Travellers and Settlers in Britain 1600–1857* (Delhi: Permanent Black, 2004), pp. 232–40. See portrait of Hickey and Munnew by William Thomas (1819) in National Portrait Gallery collection: https://www.npg.org.uk/collections/search/portrait/mw03129/William-Munnew-or-Munnoo-William-Hickey
22. Miles Taylor, *Empress: Queen Victoria and India* (New Haven: Yale University Press, 2018), p. 58.
23. Saloni Mathur, 'Living Ethnological Exhibits: The Case of 1886', *Cultural Anthropology*, 15:4 (2000), p. 498.
24. Saloni Mathur, *India by Design: Colonial History and Cultural Display* (Berkeley: University of California Press, 2007), p. 60.
25. Royal Collection Trust, 'Ramlal 1886', Rudolph Swodoba: https://www.rct.uk/collection/403823/ramlal
26. Brendan Edward Gregory, 'The Spectacle Plays and Exhibitions of Imre Kiralfy, 1887–1914' (PhD Thesis, University of Manchester, 1988).
27. *The Illustrated Police News*, 10 October 1896, p. 8.
28. *Lloyds' Weekly Newspaper*, 4 October 1896, p. 9.
29. *The Morning Post*, 1 October 1896, p. 3.
30. 'The Queen and the Black Baby', *South Wales Daily News*, 22 July 1896, p. 3.
31. *The Daily Mail*, 30 March 1910.
32. *The Daily Mail*, 8 April 1910.
33. *Weekly Irish Times*, 16 April 1910.
34. *Pall Mall Gazette*, 22 April 1912.
35. Wikimedia, 'Photo of an Indian woman and child, from the Coronation Exhibition, London 1911': https://commons.wikimedia.org/wiki/File:Photo_of_an_Indian_woman_and_child,_from_the_Coronation_Exibition,_London_1911.jpg
36. B. F. Campbell, *Ancient Wisdom Revived: A History of the Theosophical Movement* (Berkeley: University of California Press, 1980), p. 128.
37. Emily Lutyens to Edwin Lutyens, 10 August 1911, RIBA Archives, London: Lutyens Letters, Book 62, LuE/27/6/32.
38. Annie Besant, 'J. Krishnamurti', *Theosophist*, XLIV: 4 (January 1923), pp. 423–4.
39. Emily Lutyens, *Candles in the Sun* (London: Rupert Hart-Davis, 1957), p. 30.

40. See Krishnamurti correspondence held in Krishnamurti Foundation Trust (KFT) Archive, Brockwood Park.
41. Mary Lutyens, *To Be Young: Some Chapters of Autobiography* (London: Corgi, 1959), pp. 12–13.
42. Krishnamurti to Besant, 29 August 1912, 6 March 1913, passim, KFT archive; Lutyens, *Candles in the Sun*, pps. 30, 33, 38.
43. Emily Lutyens to Edwin Lutyens, 26 April 1911, RIBA, Lutyens Letters, Book 62, LuE/27/6/8.
44. Lutyens, *Candles in the Sun*, p. 69.
45. Krishnamurti to Besant, 15 July 1915; Krishnamurti to Leadbeater, 11 January 1916, KFT archive.
46. Emily Lutyens to Edwin Lutyens, 3 August 1913, RIBA, Lutyens Letters, Book 63, LuE/28/2/19.

3. THE YOUNG BROWN ENGLISHMEN

1. Ashitha Nagesh, 'How woman with coconut placard was tracked down, taken to court—and acquitted', BBC News, 14 September 2024: https://www.bbc.co.uk/news/articles/cvgwew5v4qyo
2. T. B. Macauley, 'Minute on English Education, 2nd February 1835', in H. Sharp (ed.), *Selections from Educational Records Part I, 1781–1839* (Calcutta: Superintendent Government Printing, 1920), pp. 107–117.
3. Elmer H. Cutts, 'The Background of Macaulay's Minute', *The American Historical Review*, 58: 4 (1953), pp. 824–53.
4. *Eton College Chronicle*, 18 May 1882, p. 1384; *The Field: The Country Gentleman's Paper*, 24 June 1882, p. 862.
5. Ralph Nevill, *Floreat Etona: Anecdotes and Memories of Eton College* (London: Macmillan, 1911), ch. X.
6. *Perthshire Advertiser*, 6 March 1882.
7. 'Eton College Jubilee Celebrations', *Eton College Chronicle*, 13 July 1897, p. 391; Sunity Devee, *The Autobiography of an Indian Princess* (London: John Murray, 1921), chap. XI.
8. Copy of contract from June Harben, Ref CD Coles family papers 212, provided by Rachel Hassall, archivist at Sherborne School, December 2022.
9. *The Shirburnian*, June 1890.
10. Information provided by Rachel Hassall, archivist, Sherborne School December 2022 and May 2024. See also *Cheltenham Looker-On*, 10 September 1887; *Englishman's Overland Mail*, 6 November 1895;

Homeward Mail from India, China and the East, 16 June 1902; *The Shirburnian*, March 1903.

11. Laurence Binyon, 'Introductory Memoir' in Manmohan Ghose, *Songs of Love and Death* (Oxford: Basil Blackwell, 1926), p. 10.
12. Peter Heehs, *The Lives of Sri Aurobindo* (New York: Columbia University Press, 2008), pp. 13–14.
13. Rachel Kneale, 'Hoots from the Archive—Spotlight on Old Mancunians: Manmohan Ghose—Celebrated Indian Poet', *MGS Life*, 26 November 2024, https://www.mgs-life.co.uk/article/hoots-from-the-archive-spotlight-on-old-mancunians-manmohan-ghose-celebrated-indian-poet?ref=
14. Heehs, *The Lives of Sri Aurobindo*, p. 15.
15. Ghose to Binyon, March 1882, in Manmohan Ghose, *Collected Poems*, ed. Lotika Ghose (Calcutta: University of Calcutta Press, 1970), p. 196.
16. Laurence Binyon to Arthur Symonds, 19 September 1890, British Library, Manuscript Reading Room Loan 103: Laurence Binyon Collection.
17. Elleke Boehmer, *Indian Arrivals 1870–1915: Networks of British Empire* (Oxford: Oxford University Press, 2015), chap. 3; Mary Ellis Gibson, *Indian Angles: English Verse in Colonial India from Jones to Tagore* (Athens: Ohio University Press, 2011), chap. 6.
18. Janaki Agnes Penelope Majumdar, *Family History*, ed. Antoinette Burton (New Delhi: Oxford University Press, 2013), p. 45.
19. Majumdar, *Family History*, chap. 2.6.
20. 'Kidderpore', as the house was named, later became an orphanage for Army men and is, at the time of writing, the site of a large office building.
21. Majumdar, *Family History*, p. 72.
22. *The Meteor*, 7 February 1888; 6 March 1888.
23. *The Meteor*, 16 February 1899, pp. 6–7.
24. *The Meteor*, 3 December 1901, p. 122; 19 December 1901, p. 136.
25. Majumdar, *Family History*, p. 88.
26. *Little Folks: The Magazine for Boys and Girls*, XV, nd.
27. Majumdar, *Family History*, passim.
28. *Rugby School Register, Volume III, May 1874 to May 1904*, Rev. A. T. Mitchell (Rugby, 1904), p. 312. See numerous issues of *Meteor*, 1 August 1911 to 13 November 1912.
29. 'An Indian Lad at Bisley', *Civil and Military Gazette*, 1 August 1910, p. 3.

30. Parish Register in London, England. Church of England Marriage and Banns, 1754–1940 [via ancestry.com].
31. London, England. Church of England Births and Baptisms, 1813–1924 [via ancestry.com].
32. 'Local Law and Police', *Bayswater Chronicle*, 24 September 1870, p. 2.
33. 'Administration of Police Justice', *Morning Advertiser*, 29 September 1870, p. 6.
34. Information from 1871 and 1881 England, Wales and Scotland Census; England and Wales Deaths 1837–2007, Strand, London.
35. London Bethlehem Hospital Patient Admission Register and Casebook, 1912–13.
36. *London Gazette*, 11 July 1899.
37. 'An Indian Wedding in London', *India*, 15 January 1909, p. 35.
38. 'Indian Marriages in England', *The Indian Magazine and Review*, September 1908, p. 245; 'The Weddings of the Week', *The Gentlewoman*, 22 August 1908, p. 247.
39. 'Death of Mr Newton Dutt', *Hendon and Finchley Times and Guardian*, 18 October 1935, p. 24.
40. 'Trade and Literary Gossip', *The Bookseller*, 6 February 1914, p. 161.
41. Sumita Mukherjee, '"Narrow-majority" and "Bow-and-agree": Public attitudes towards the elections of the first Asian MPs in Britain, Dadabhai Naoroji and Mancherjee Merwanjee Bhownaggree, 1885–1906', *Journal of the Oxford University History Society* (2004), pp. 1–20.
42. Dinyar Patel, *Naoroji: Pioneer of Indian Nationalism* (Cambridge: Harvard University Press, 2020), p. 147.
43. 1901 Census of England and Wales.
44. 'Scotsman called Duleep Singh Fergie', Daily Record, 31 August 2012: https://www.dailyrecord.co.uk/news/local-news/scotsman-called-duleep-singh-fernie-2728502
45. Coralie Younger, *Wicked Women of the Raj* (New Delhi: HarperCollins, 2003), pp. 91–3.
46. See Figure 2.
47. Younger, *Wicked Women of the Raj*, p. 190.
48. 'Jehan Warliker, Prince Seesodia of India', (1930–9), Redpath Chautauqua Collection, University of Iowa, South Asian American Digital Archive.

4. THE NATIONALISTS

1. David Shariatmadari, 'Musa Okwonga: "Boys don't learn shamelessness at Eton, it's where they perfect it"', *The Guardian*, 10

April 2021: https://amp.theguardian.com/books/2021/apr/10/musa-okwonga-boys-dont-learn-shamelessness-at-eton-it-is-where-they-perfect-it
2. 'More Indians applying for UK student visas in 2021', Study International, 12 July 2021: https://www.studyinternational.com/news/uk-student-visa-indian-applications/
3. Sumita Mukherjee, *Nationalism, Education and Migrant Identities: The England-Returned* (Abingdon: Routledge, 2010).
4. Christopher Tyerman, *A History of Harrow School 1324–1991* (Oxford: Oxford University Press, 2000), chap. 14.
5. Jawaharlal Nehru, *An Autobiography* (New Delhi: Penguin Books, 2004), pp. 19–21.
6. Motilal Nehru to Jawaharlal Nehru, 20 October 1905, in R. Kumar and D. N. Parighari, *Selected Works of Motilal Nehru*, vol. 1 (New Delhi: Vikas, 1982), p. 80.
7. Jawaharlal Nehru to Motilal Nehru, 22 October 1905, S. Gopal, ed., *Selected Works of Jawaharlal Nehru*, vol. 1 (New Delhi: Orient Longman, 1972), p. 4.
8. Jawaharlal to Motilal, 11 December 1905, Gopal, *Selected Works*, p. 7.
9. Jawaharlal to Motilal, 5 July 1907, Gopal, *Selected Works*, p. 28.
10. Jawaharlal to Motilal, 3 January 1906, Gopal, *Selected Works*, p. 11.
11. Alfred Gollin, 'The Wright Brothers and the British Authorities, 1902–1909', *The English Historical Review*, XCV: CCCLXXV (1 April 1980), pp. 293–320.
12. Jawaharlal Nehru, *An Autobiography* (New Delhi: Penguin, 2004), pp. 20–1.
13. Jawaharlal to Motilal, 1 February 1907, Gopal, *Selected Works*, p. 18.
14. Jawaharlal to Motilal, 18 January 1907, Gopal, *Selected Works*, p. 16.
15. 'How Harrow made Nehru', *The Times of India*, 16 November 2005: https://timesofindia.indiatimes.com/world/rest-of-world/how-harrow-made-nehru/articleshow/1296553.cms
16. Nehru, *An Autobiography*, p. 31.
17. Renuka Ray, *My Reminiscences: Social Development During Gandhian Era and After* (New Delhi: Allied Publishers, 1982), pp. 9–10.
18. B. R. Nanda, *Jawaharlal Nehru: Rebel and Statesman* (Delhi: Oxford University Press, 1998), p. 256.
19. Nehru, *An Autobiography*, p. 436.
20. Angela Bartie, Linda Fleming, Mark Freeman, Tom Hulme, Alex Hutton, Paul Readman, 'Batley Empire Day Pageant', The Redress of the Past, http://www.historicalpageants.ac.uk/pageants/986/
21. Hertfordshire Local Archives Catalogue.

22. N. B. Bonarjee, *Under Two Masters* (Oxford: Oxford University Press, 1970), p. 54.
23. Sherborne School Archives. See Figure 8.
24. More on Sahebzada in 'The Leftists' chapter.
25. BL, Mss Eur T81/2, Interview with N. B. Bonarjee, 1975/6.
26. Bonarjee, *Under Two Masters*, p. 38.
27. Bonarjee, *Under Two Masters*, p. 40.
28. Bonarjee, *Under Two Masters*, p. 41.
29. Bonarjee, *Under Two Masters*, p. 44.
30. BL, Mss Eur T81/2, N. B. Bonarjee, 1975/6.
31. Mss Eur T81/2.
32. Dulwich College Register Questionnaires and Form and Class Lists, Dulwich College Archives.
33. See Figure 3.
34. K. C. Bakhlé to McC Christison, 7 July 1935, in Dulwich College Archives.
35. Nanda, *Jawaharlal Nehru*, p. 254.
36. See Elizabeth Buettner, *Empire Families: Britons and Late Imperial India* (Oxford: Oxford University Press, 2004).
37. 'The Chamber Music Club', *The Ousel,* 10 June 1938, pp. 247–9; 23 July 1938, pp. 285–7.
38. Nari Rustomji, *Enchanted Frontier: Sikkim, Bhutan and India's North-Eastern Borderland* (Bombay: Oxford University Press, 1971), p. 17.
39. 'Rustomji embraces his faith', *Daily Mirror*, 31 August 1921, p. 2.

5. THE SPORTING STARS

1. Emma John, 'Azeem Rafiq on Racism, Cricket and why he had to leave Britain', *The Guardian*, 11 June 2024: https://www.theguardian.com/sport/article/2024/jun/11/azeem-rafiq-on-racism-cricket-and-why-he-had-to-leave-britain-i-never-started-this-to-be-popular
2. J. A. Mangan, *Athleticism in the Victorian and Edwardian Public School* (Cambridge: Cambridge University Press, 1981), p. 9; Richard Holt, *Sport and the British: A Modern History* (Oxford: Oxford University Press, 1989), pps. 205, 218.
3. Boria Majumdar, 'Tom Brown Goes Global: The "Brown" Ethic in Colonial and Post-Colonial India', *The International Journal of the History of Sport*, 23: 5 (2006), pp. 805–20.
4. C. L. R. James, *Beyond a Boundary* (London: Yellow Jersey Press, 2005 [first pub. 1963], p. 32.

5. Satadru Sen, 'Chameleon Games: Ranjitsinhji's Politics of Race and Gender', *Journal of Colonialism and Colonial History*, 2: 3 (2001).
6. Ramachandra Guha, *A Corner of a Foreign Field: The Indian History of a British Sport* (London: Picador, 2003), pps. xi, 4, 30, 118.
7. Kathryn Castle ed., 'Princes and Paupers: India in Children's Periodicals', in *Britannia's Children: Reading Colonialism through Children's Books and Magazines* (Manchester: Manchester University Press, 2017), pp. 33–4.
8. Holt, *Sport and the British*, p. 220.
9. Suvam Pal, '"Legacies, Halcyon Days and Thereafter": A Brief History of Indian Tennis', *The International Journal of the History of Sport*, 21: 3–4 (2004), pps. 454, 457.
10. His cousin, Pratapsinhji, who was two years younger, may also have studied at Cheltenham College.
11. 'Cricketer of the Year', *Wisden* (1930): http://www.espncricinfo.com/wisdenalmanack/content/story/154691.html
12. From Andy Carter, *A Flash Outside the Off Stump*: https://aflashoutsidetheoffstump.wordpress.com/2018/02/26/chapter-8-a-chip-off-the-old-block-duleepsinhji-and-the-nawabs-of-pataudi/
13. Sen, 'Chameleon Games'.
14. 'Public School Cricket—Part II', *The Illustrated Sporting and Dramatic News*, 21 June 1916, p. 468.
15. *The Bystander*, 10 January 1923, p. 106.
16. 'Ranji's Nephew at Malvern', *The Daily Mirror*, 15 April 1913, p. 14.
17. *The Malvernian*, July 1914, p. 246.
18. *The Malvernian*, July 1944, p. 12.
19. Somerset Playne, *Indian States: A Biographical, Historical, and Administrative Survey* (New Delhi: Asian Educational Services, 2006), p. 716.
20. E. H. D. Sewell, 'Malvern and Shrewsbury Cricket', *The Tatler*, 12 July 1916, p. 38.
21. E. H. D. Sewell, 'Public School Cricket—Part V', *The Illustrated Sporting and Dramatic News*, 15 July 1916, p. 557.
22. *Salopian Magazine*, 1918.
23. 'The Sport Spotlight, *The Daily Express*, 14 August 1925, p. 13.
24. *The Malvernian*, November 1935, pp. 2–3.
25. *The Malvernian*, December 1942, p. 8.
26. M. R. A. Baig, *In Different Saddles* (London: Asia Publishing House, 1967), pp. 26–8.
27. *Madras Weekly Mail*, 22 February 1906, p. 189.
28. Isha'at Habibullah, 'Memories of the British and Feudal India—part

1: Westward Bound—an English Childhood in Lucknow', *Dawn*, 6 September 1991, Sec. Magazine, pp. 1–2; 'The British and Feudal India—part II: We Were Nicknamed "The Hallelujah Chorus"', *Dawn*, Friday 13 September 1991, Sec. Magazine, p. 3.

29. Wajhat Habibullah, 'When Jawaharlal Nehru ordered "Dronacharya" out of NDA', *National Herald*, 14 November 2019, https://www.nationalheraldindia.com/opinion/when-jawaharlal-nehru-ordered-dronacharya-out-of-the-nda; 1921 Census for Monkton Rectory, Dorset.
30. Muneeza Shamsie, 'Kakori kababs, pickles and a Lucknow heritage: Recalling a father's gastronomic adventures', *Scroll.in*, 2 January 2022, https://scroll.in/article/1013280/kakori-kababs-pickles-and-a-lucknow-heritage-recalling-a-fathers-gastronomic-adventures
31. See 1921 Census for 35, Florence Park, Bristol.
32. BL, Mss Eur T77-78, Interview with Mirza Rashid Ali Baig, 1975/6.
33. Extract from Begum Habibullah's 'Impressions of a Journey to Europe' in Siobhan Lambert-Hurley, Daniel Majchrowicz, and Sunil Sharma, eds., *Three Centuries of Travel Writing by Muslim Women* (Bloomington: Indiana University Press, 2022), chap. 28.
34. See Figure 4.
35. Isha'at Habibullah, 'The British and Feudal India—part II: We Were Nicknamed "The Hallelujah Chorus"', *Dawn*, Friday 13 September 1991, Sec. Magazine, p. 3.
36. 'Young Local Artists', *The Western Daily Press*, 1 April 1927, p. 12.
37. Muneeza Shamsie, 'Imperial Shadows: A Tale of Two Childhoods, Colonial and Post-Colonial', *Journal of Commonwealth and Postcolonial Studies*, 16: 1 (2009), pp. 114–30.
38. 'Domestic Situations—Vacant', *Western Daily Press,* 25 September 1924, p. 2; 26 September 1924, p. 2.
39. 'Badminton Championships', *Western Daily Press*, 14 March 1925, p. 5.
40. 'Outward Bound', *The Civil & Military Gazette*, 13 September 1925, p. 10.
41. Bafig, *In Different Saddles*, p. 11.
42. School reports all provided by Dr C. S. Knighton, archivist, Clifton College, Bristol.
43. *The Birmingham Post*, 20 October 1928, p. 10; *Dundee Courier*, 14 July 1932, p. 12; *Tatler*, 18 July 1934, 3 June 1936; *Dundee Evening Telegraph*, 28 January 1938, p. 6.
44. *Rugby School Register, Volume III, May 1874 to May 1904*, Rev. A. T. Mitchell (Rugby, 1904), p. 202.
45. *The Meteor*, 27 June 1896; 10 October 1896.

46. 'Wedding To-day', *Westminster Gazette*, 22 December 1906, p. 7.
47. *Rugby School Register, 1911–1946*, Alan H. Maude and Allan Archer (Rugby: George Over, 1957), p. 220.
48. *The Meteor*, 31 May 1932; 13 February 1934.
49. *The Meteor*, 6 April 1937; 4 April 1938.
50. 1921 Census for Bedale's School; *The Bedale's Record, 1921–1927*; *St John's College Cambridge Register of Twentieth Century Johnians, Volume I 1900–1949* (Cambridge: St Johns, 2004).
51. Cynthia Salvadori, *We Came in Dhows*, vol. II (Nairobi: Paperchase Kenya, 1996), pp. 58–9.
52. Mihir Bose, 'Khan, Muhammad Iftikhar Ali, nawab of Pataudi (1910–1952), cricketer,' *Oxford Dictionary of National Biography* (Oxford: Oxford University Press, online 2004).
53. Boria Majumdar, 'The Golden Years of Indian Hockey: "We Climb the Victory Stand"', *The International Journal of the History of Sport*, 25: 12 (2008), pp. 1592–1611.
54. 'Mansur Ali Khan Pataudi Wisden Obituary', 15 April 2012, https://www.espncricinfo.com/story/mansur-ali-khan-pataudi-wisden-obituary-564480
55. Holt, *Sport and the British*, p. 210.
56. Frank Richards, 'Aliens at Greyfriars', *The Magnet*, 6, 21 March 1908.
57. Castle, 'Princes and Paupers', pp. 43–5.

6. THE SUFFRAGISTS

1. See Carol Dyhouse, *Girl Trouble: Panic and Progress in the History of Young Women* (London: Bloomsbury, 2013), chap. 2.
2. Anita Anand, *Sophia: Princess, Suffragette, Revolutionary* (London: Bloomsbury, 2015), p. 79.
3. Anand, *Sophia*, p. 103.
4. 'Bazaar Season', *Nottingham Daily Express*, 30 November 1912, p. 5; 'An Oriental Fete', *The Standard*, 2 December 1912, p. 12; 'Oriental Fete', *The Standard*, 7 December 1912, p. 13.
5. Anand, *Sophia*, p. 108.
6. See Sumita Mukherjee, *Indian Suffragettes: Female Identities and Transnational Networks* (New Delhi: Oxford University Press, 2018).
7. *Western Gazette*, 8 July 1949.
8. Information from Dorothy Goldsack, Archivist, Sherborne Girls School, 6 December 2016.
9. See Figure 5.
10. *Thanet Advertiser and Echo*, 23 November 1945, p. 4.

11. Bonarjee, *Under Two Masters*, p. 37. Aparna Basu, 'Amrit Kaur [Rajkumari Amrit Kaur] (1889–1964), Politician and Advocate of Women's Rights', *Oxford Dictionary of National Biography* (Oxford: Oxford University Press, online 2004).
12. Rosalind Parr, *Citizens of Everywhere: Indian Women, Nationalism and Cosmopolitanism, 1920–1952* (Cambridge: Cambridge University Press, 2021), p. 47.
13. *Unesco and Public Opinion Today* (Chicago: National Opinion Research Center, 1947), p. 38.
14. Emmeline Tanner, 'Rajkumari Amrit Kaur', *Sherborne School for Girls (1899–1949)* (1949), pp. 105–6.
15. *Rugby School Register, Volume III, May 1874 to May 1904*, Rev. A. T. Mitchell (Rugby, 1904), p. 202.
16. Livia Manera Sambuy, *In Search of Amrit Kaur* (London: Chatto & Windus, 2023).
17. Avabai B. Wadia, *The Light Is Ours: Memoirs and Movements* (London: International Planned Parenthood Federation, 2001), p. 30.
18. Passenger list for the Straithard, 1938. From Passenger Lists Leaving UK 1890–1960 [via findmypast.com].
19. Wadia, *The Light Is Ours*, p. 31.
20. Kishwar Desai, *The Life and Times of Devika Rani: The Longest Kiss* (Chennai: Westland, 2020), p. 42.
21. Chitra Deb, *Women of the Tagore Household* (Delhi: Penguin India, 2010).
22. Desai, *The Life and Times of Devika Rani: The Longest Kiss*, p. 60.
23. Wadia, *The Light Is Ours*, pp. 30–4.
24. Mukherjee, *Indian Suffragettes*, p. 262.
25. *The Gentlewoman*, 30 March 1912, p. 464.
26. *Liverpool Echo*, 2 March 1914.
27. Phyllis, 'In the Looking Glass', *British Australasian*, 1 November 1917, p. 18.
28. Mukherjee, *Indian Suffragettes*, p. 100.
29. Beth R. Jenkins, 'Bonarjee, Dorothy Noel ('Dorf') (1894–1983), poet and lawyer', *Dictionary of Welsh Biography* (2020), https://biography.wales/article/s12-BONA-NOE-1894
30. See Majumdar, *Family History*.
31. Harihar Das, 'The Late Miss Susila Anita Bonnerjee', *Britain and India* (Oct–Dec 1920), p. 360. A photo of Susie Bonnerjee with the CLWS in Brighton in 1913 is available online: https://www.lse.ac.uk/News/Latest-news-from-LSE/2019/g-July-2019/Unearthed-photograph-highlights-important-role-of-Indian-suffragettes;

https://www.newn.cam.ac.uk/newnham-news/newly-discovered-photograph-highlights-the-role-of-indian-suffragists-newnhams-dr-susila-bonnerjee-nc-1891/. Thank you to Clare Wichbold for alerting me to this photo.
32. 'The Women's Procession: Descriptive Programme of the Order of the March', *The Vote*, 17 June 1911, p. 95. For more on the India section at the procession see Mukherjee, *Indian Suffragettes*, pp. 32–6.
33. *The Times*, 21 July 1922, in Dulwich College Archives, Dulwich College, London.
34. 'A Brahmo Somaj Wedding in London', *Indian Magazine and Review* (January 1911), pp. 25–6.
35. Various Lupton prizes were established very early in the school's history (SPGS opened on 19th Jan. 1904) by Dr J.H. Lupton, then Surmaster (deputy head). Information from Howard Bailes, Archivist, St Paul's School for Girls.
36. Diary entries by Atiya Fyzee on 19 April 1907 and 25 July 1907 in Siobhan Lambert-Hurley and Sunil Sharma, eds., *Atiya's Journeys: A Muslim Woman from Colonial Bombay to Edwardian Britain* (New Delhi: Oxford University Press, 2010), pps. 189, 207.
37. Dhanvanthi Rama Rau, *An Inheritance: The Memoirs of Dhanvanthi Rama Rau* (New York: Harper & Row, 1977), p. 168.
38. 'The Women of India To-day', *The Vote*, 17 April 1931.
39. Padmini Sengupta, *Sarojini Naidu: A Biography* (New York, 1966), p. 158.
40. *Norwich Mercury*, 19 August 1899, p. 3; Padmini Sengupta, *The Portrait of an Indian Woman* (Calcutta: YMCA Publishing House, 1956), p. 26.

7. THE CASUALTIES OF WAR

1. Santanu Das, 'Indians at Home, Mesopotamia and France, 1914–1918: Towards an Intimate History', in *Race, Empire and First World War Writing*, ed. Santanu Das (Cambridge: Cambridge University Press, 2011), p. 70.
2. Das, 'Indians at Home', p. 79.
3. Hardit Singh Malik, *A Little Work, A Little Play: The Autobiography of H. S. Malik* (New Delhi: Bookwise, n.d.), pp. 30–2.
4. Malik, *A Little Work*, p. 34.
5. Malik, *A Little Work*, pp. 35–6.
6. H.C.G. Matthew, 'Haldane, Richard Burdon, Viscount Haldane (1856–1928), politician, educationist, and lord chancellor', *Oxford*

Dictionary of National Biography (Oxford: Oxford University Press, online 2004).
7. BL, IOR/Q/10/4/2, Lytton Report: Oxford. Hardit Singh testimony, 3 June 1921.
8. Stephen Barker, *The Flying Sikh* (Barnsley: AirWorld, 2022), various pages.
9. BL, Mss Eur T53. Tape Transcript, *The Raj*: Mrs Iris Portal, 31 July 1973.
10. 'Major Dalpat Singh', *Eastbourne Chronicle*, 14 December 1918, p. 7; Bill Bowden and Michael Partridge, 'Major Thakur Dalpat Singh', *Old Eastbournian*, 2012, pp. 18–19.
11. Barker, *The Flying Sikh*, p. 23.
12. Paul Jordan, 'The Singhs and the Willingdon Connection', *The Old Eastbournian*, 2021, p. 22.
13. Santanu Das, *India, Empire, and First World War Culture: Writings, Images, and Songs* (Cambridge: Cambridge University Press, 2018), p. 298.
14. 'The Late Lieut. I. L. Roy', *India*, 6 September 1918, p. 85.
15. 'The Public Schools, *Sportsman*, 1 October 1918, p. 1.
16. 'Obituary', *The Pauline*, November 1918, p. 134.
17. Das, *India, Empire, and First World War Culture*, p. 22.
18. 'Obituary', *The Pauline*, November 1918, p. 135.
19. 'School Boxing Competition', *The Pauline*, June 1911, pp. 80–1.
20. 'The Roy Brothers: fighting for King and Emperor', Great War London: https://greatwarlondon.wordpress.com/2013/10/09/the-roy-brothers-fighting-for-king-and-emperor/. Thank you to Prabir Roy for details about Roy family names.
21. 'Obituary', *The Pauline*, March 1921, p. 35.
22. 'Novices Boxing Competition', *The Pauline*, February 1914, p. 26.
23. 'School Boxing Competition', *The Pauline*, June 1913, pp. 86–7.
24. Mukherjee, *Nationalism, Education and Migrant Identities*, p. 23.
25. Alan Wren, *The Ambush of SS Persia: Voices from a Lost Liner* (York: Alan Wren, 2020).
26. 'Obituary', *The Pauline*, April 1916, p. 42.
27. See front cover of Ruvani Ranasinha et al., eds., *South Asians and the Shaping of Britain, 1870-1950: A Sourcebook* (Manchester: Manchester University Press, 2012).
28. See Figure 6.
29. *The Graphic*, 29 September 1917, p. 375.
30. 'High Master's Address, 28 September 1914', *The Pauline*, October 1914, p. 187.

31. BL, IOR/L/PJ/6/1454. Mr H. D. Girdwood Cinema Show and Lecture, File 3569/1916. John Slater, 8 November 1917.
32. Samuel Hyson and Alan Lester, '"British India on Trial": Brighton Military Hospitals and the Politics of Empire in World War I', *Journal of Historical Geography*, 38: 1 (2012), pp. 18–34.
33. *Brighton Herald*, 16 January 1915, quoted in Hyson and Lester, p. 27.
34. Pir Zia Inayat Khan, 'Noor Inayat Khan: A British Muslim Hero?', in *Muslim Women in Britain 1850–1950: 100 Years of Hidden History*, ed. Sariya Cheruvallil-Contractor and Jamie Gilham (London: C. Hurst & Co., 2023), pp. 181–197.
35. Shrabani Basu, *Spy Princess: The Life of Noor Inayat Khan* (Stroud: The History Press, 2011), pp. 21–9.
36. *The Malvernian*, December 1946, p. 64.
37. Anuj Tiwari, 'How an Indian Maharaja Helped Save the Lives of Thousands of Polish People During World War II', 11 September 2021, https://www.indiatimes.com/trending/social-relevance/maharaja-jam-saheb-digvijaysinhji-and-world-war-ii-polish-refugees-story-549242.html
38. *The Malvernian*, December 1942, p. 8.
39. Thanks to Paul Godsland of the Old Malvernian Society for information on Pratapsinhji.
40. The sisters attended South Hampstead High School for Girls and North London Collegiate for Girls. They both qualified as lawyers when they grew up: Chaya Ray, 'An Extraordinary Life', *Magazine for the Old North Londoners' Association*, 21 (2016), p. 11.
41. Savitri Chowdhary, *I Made My Home in England* (Laindon: Savitri Chowdhary, 1961), pp. 45–52.
42. Shakun Banfield, 'A Memory of my Mother Savitri Devi Chowdhary 1919–1996', 8 July 2012, https://www.laindonhistory.org.uk/content/people/noteworthy_people/a-memory-of-my-mother-savitri-devi-chowdhary-1919-1996
43. Chowdhary, *I Made My Home in England*, p. 65.
44. *Daily Mirror*, 13 March 1946, p. 2.

8. THE LASCARS' CHILDREN

1. Enoch Powell, Birmingham Conservative Association, 20 April 1968: https://www.channel4.com/news/articles/dispatches/rivers%2Bof%2Bblood%2Bspeech/1934152.html
2. G. S. Aurora, *The New Frontiersmen: A Sociological Study of Indian*

Immigrants in the United Kingdom (Bombay: Popular Prakashan, 1967), pps. 5, 22.
3. Chamion Caballero, 'Interraciality in Early Twentieth Century Britain: Challenging Traditional Conceptualisations through Accounts of "Ordinariness"', *Genealogy*, 3: 21 (2019).
4. William Dalrymple, *White Mughals* (London: HarperCollins, 2002).
5. 'Queen Victoria and the British Maharajah', dir. Maninderpal Sahota, first aired Channel Four, August 2022.
6. M. Page Baldwin, 'Subject to Empire: Married Women and the British Nationality and Status of Aliens Act', *Journal of British Studies*, 40: 4 (2001), pp. 522–56.
7. Shompa Lahiri, *Indians in Britain: Anglo-Indian Encounters, Race and Identity 1880–1930* (London: Frank Cass, 2000), p. 122. 'White Wives of Brown Men', *The Daily Mail*, 1 May 1913, p. 7.
8. See Visram, *Ayahs, Lascars and Princes*.
9. 1921 Census of England and Wales.
10. Laura Tabili, *Global Migrants, Local Culture: Natives and Newcomers in Provincial England, 1841–1939* (London: Palgrave Macmillan, 2011), p. 115.
11. Derek G. Law, 'From Goa to Greenock: The Sinking of the SS City of Benares', in *Scotland's Lascar Heritage*, ed. Emily Malcolm, Isobel McDonald, and Susan Pacitti (Glasgow: Glasgow Museums Publishing, 2023).
12. Laura Tabili, 'The Construction of Racial Difference in Twentieth-Century Britain: The Special Restriction (Coloured Alien Seamen) Order, 1925', *Journal of British Studies*, 33: 1 (1994), pp. 54–98.
13. BL, IOR/L/PJ/6/613. File 2011/02. Ankaram, of Madras, a destitute young native.
14. David Holland, 'The Social Networks of South Asian Migrants in the Sheffield Area During the Early Twentieth Century', *Past & Present*, 236: 1 (2017), pp. 243–45.
15. Diane Robinson-Dunn, *The Harem, Slavery and British Imperial Culture: Anglo-Muslim Relations in the Late Nineteenth Century* (Manchester: Manchester University Press, 2006), p. 159.
16. Salter, *Asiatic*, p. 27.
17. Robinson-Dunn, *The Harem*, p. 159. See also Mahummad Mashuq Alley, 'The Growth and Organization of the Muslim Community in Britain', *Centre for the Study of Islam and Christian Muslim Relations Research Papers*, 1 (March 1979), p. 6.
18. Sydney F. Collins, 'The Social Position of White and "Half-Caste" Women in Colored Groupings in Britain', *American Sociological Review*,

16: 6 (1951), pp. 796–802; Sydney F. Collins, 'The British-Born Coloured', *Sociological Review*, 3:1 (1955), pp. 77–92.
19. Howard Spring, *Heaven Lies About Us: A Fragment of Infancy* (London: Readers' Union Limited, 1940), p. 29.
20. Howard Bloch, *Canning Town Voices* (Chalford: Chalford Publishing Company, 1998), p. 29.
21. Joseph Salter, *The Asiatic in England* (London: Seeley, Jackson and Halliday, 1873), p. 203.
22. 'The Street of Hopeless Children', *Daily Express*, 18 March 1930.
23. Bloch, *Canning Town Voices*, p. 13.
24. Chamion Caballero and Peter J. Aspinall, *Mixed Race Britain in the Twentieth Century* (London: Palgrave Macmillan, 2018), pp. 69–72.
25. Caballero and Aspinall, *Mixed Race Britain*, p. 76.
26. Ranasinha et al., *South Asians and the Shaping of Britain*, pp. 75–6.
27. David Holland, *Imperial Heartland: Immigration, Working-Class Culture and Everyday Tolerance, 1917–1947* (Cambridge: Cambridge University Press, 2023), pps. 106, 114.
28. Holland, *Imperial Heartland*, pp. 264–5.
29. 'Children's Corner', *Sheffield Daily Telegraph*, 14 November 1939, p. 8.
30. Robinson-Dunn, *The Harem*, p. 155.
31. Gwilym Beckerlegge, 'Followers of "Mohammed, Kalee and Dada Nanuk": The Presence of Islam and South Asian Religions in Victorian Britain', in *Religion in Victorian Britain. Volume V: Culture and Empire*, ed. John Wolffe (Manchester: Manchester University Press, 1997), p. 248.
32. Rehana Ahmed, *Writing British Muslims: Religion, Class and Multiculturalism* (Manchester: Manchester University Press, 2015), p. 35.
33. *National School Admission Register*, Surrey 1914.
34. Rozina Visram, 'Kamal A. Chunchie of the Coloured Men's Institute: The Man and the Legend', *Immigrants & Minorities*, 18: 1 (1999), p. 33.
35. 'Photos of Kamal Chunchie, his family and his work with the Coloured Men's Institute', Eastside Community Heritage archive, https://catalogue.eastsidecommunityheritage.org/catalogue_item/kamal-chunchie-and-the-coloured-mens-institute/a-selection-of-photographs-associated-with-kamal-chunchie-his-family-and-the-work-with-the-coloured-mens-institute/photos-of-kamal-chunchie-his-family-and-his-work-with-the-coloured-mens-institute: see Figure 7.
36. 'Kamal Chunchie's Grandson: The Coloured Men's Institute of

Canning Town', oral history audio clip: https://soundcloud.com/hiddenheroesuk/kamal-chunchies-grandson-the-coloured-mens-institute-of-canning-town

37. The Mixed Museum: https://mixedmuseum.org.uk/
38. 'The George Green Schools', *East London Observer*, 4 August 1888, p. 6; 'The George Green Schools', *The East End News*, 19 July 1889; 'George Green Schools', *East London Observer*, 26 July 1890, p. 6; 'George Green Schools', *The Eastern Post and City Chronicle*, 16 July 1892, p. 5; 'The George Green Schools', *East London Observer*, 29 July 1893, p. 5.
39. 'The George Green Girls Entertain', *The East End News*, 13 February 1895.
40. Sehri Saklatvala, *The Fifth Commandment: A Biography of Shapurji Saklatvala and Memoir by His Daughter* (Miranda Press, 1991), pp. 57, 80–1.
41. Saklatvala, *The Fifth Commandment*, p. 342.
42. Saklatvala, *The Fifth Commandment*, pp. 471–2.
43. Saklatvala, *The Fifth Commandment*, pp. 376–7, 450–1; Visram, *Asians in Britain*, p. 319.
44. 'Ruxton Execution', *Daily Mirror*, 13 May 1936, p. 4; 'Buck Ruxton', *The Scotsman*, 4 May 1936, p. 11; 'Fund for Dr Ruxton's Children', *Aberdeen Press and Journal*, 29 July 1936, p. 7; 'Tragic Children of Accused Doctor', *Daily Mirror*, 2 March 1936, p. 7; 'Sixth Day of Ruxton Trial', *The Sunday Times*, 8 March 1936, p. 28; 'Fund for Ruxton Children', *Dundee Courier*, 16 March 1936, p. 7; '8 children pining for parents', *Daily Mirror*, 28 April 1936, p. 6; 'The Ruxton Children', *The Daily Mirror*, 30 June 1936, p. 6; 'Guardian Memories', *Lancaster Guardian*, 21 March 1986, p. 11.
45. Caroline Adams, *Across Seven Seas and Thirteen Rivers: Life Stories of Pioneer Sylheti Settlers in Britain* (London: THAP Books, 1987), pp. 62–5.
46. See Lucy Bland, 'Interracial Relationships and the "Brown Baby Question": Black GIs, White British Women, and Their Mixed-Race Offspring in World War II', *Journal of the History of Sexuality*, 26: 3 (2017), pp. 424–53. Also, Hazel Carby, *Imperial Intimacies: A Tale of Two Islands* (London: Verso, 2019).

9. THE LEFTISTS

1. See John Callaghan, *Rajani Palme Dutt: A Study in British Socialism* (London: Lawrence and Wishart, 1993).

2. For more on Indian involvement in the LAI and parallel groups in Britain, see Mark Reeves, 'Two Leagues, One Front? The India League and the League Against Imperialism in the British Left, 1927–1937', in *The League Against Imperialism: Lives and Afterlives*, ed. Carolien Stolte et al. (Leiden: Leiden University Press, 2020), pp. 283–308.
3. 'Perse Boys' School', *Cambridge Independent Press*, 13 July 1906, p. 4.
4. 'A British School which teaches', *The Pioneer*, 9 May 1910.
5. S. J. D. Mitchell, *Perse: A History of the Perse School 1615–1976* (Cambridge: The Oleander Press, 1976), pp. 94–95.
6. Information from David Jones, Perse School Archivist.
7. 'The Perse School', *Cambridge Independent Press*, 8 November 1907, p. 8; 'Perse Boys' School', *Cambridge Independent Press*, 6 November 1908, p. 8; *Cambridge Independent Press*, 26 June 1914, p. 5; 'Future of the Perse School', *Cambridge Independent Press*, 7 November 1913, p. 9.
8. 'Perse School Swimming Sports', *Cambridge Independent Press*, 8 July 1910, p. 5.
9. Information from David Jones, Perse School Archivist.
10. 'Perse Morris Men', *Cambridge Independent Press*, 2 May 1913, p. 12; 'Perse Morris Dancers', *Cambridge Independent Press*, 30 May 1913, p. 12.
11. John Callaghan, 'Rajani Palme Dutt, British Communism, and the Communist Party of India', *Journal of Communist Studies*, 6: 1 (1990), p. 258.
12. Dilip Bose, 'Rajani Palme Dutt—Great Son of the Indian People', *Labour Monthly*, 57:3 (March 1975), Marxists Internet Archive.
13. Callaghan, *Rajani Palme Dutt*, pp. 9, 13.
14. *Cambridge Independent Press*, 12 August 1910, p. 4.
15. 'Town and County News', *Cambridge Independent Press*, 21 December 1906, p. 8.
16. Eric Warmington, 'Society and Education in Cambridge 1902–1922', *New Universities Quarterly*, 30:1 (1975), pp. 28–29.
17. Callaghan, *Rajani Palme Dutt*, p. 13.
18. Callaghan, 'Rajani Palme Dutt, British Communism'. TNA, KV 2/1807, surveillance files on Rajani Palme Dutt; BL, IOR/L/PJ/12/30, India Office files on Rajani Palme Dutt.
19. TNA, KV 2/2504, Clemens Palme Dutt.
20. H. R. King's diary, 6 March 1927, from Sherborne School archivist.
21. Sherborne School Archives, Dorset. See Figure 8.
22. Isha'at Habibullah, The British and Feudal India—part II: We Were Nicknamed 'The Hallelujah Chorus', *Dawn*, Friday 13 September 1991, Sec. Magazine, p. 3; 'British and Feudal India - 'Indianisation' at Oxford', *Dawn*, 20 September 1991, Sec. Magazine, p. 6.

23. Marcus F. Franda, 'India's Third Communist Party', *Asian Survey*, 9:11 (1969), p. 798.
24. Hamida Saiduzzafar, 'JSAL Interviews Dr. Hamida Saiduzzafar: A Conversation with Rashid Jahan's Sister-in-Law, Aligarh, 1973', *Journal of South Asian Literature*, 22:1 (1987), pp. 158–65. Rakhshanda Jalil, 'A Comrade and a Gentleman, on the life and times of Mahmuduzzaffar Khan, a founding member of the Progressive Writers' Movement', *The Friday Times*, Lahore, Pakistan, 11–17 March 2011.
25. Michael P. Ortiz, 'Spain! Why? Jawaharlal Nehru, Non-Intervention, and the Spanish Civil War', *European History Quarterly*, 49:3 (2019), pp. 445–66.
26. BL, IOR/L/PJ/12/631.
27. BL, IOR/L/I/1/1295, Confidential Note from C. E. N., 17 January 1940.
28. BL, IOR/L/PJ/12/452, Scotland Yard Report, no. 185, 22 January 1941.
29. BL, IOR/L/PJ/12/452, Secret Memo to Mr Silver, 4 December 1941.
30. Michele L. Louro, '"Where National Revolutionary Ends and Communist Begins": The League against Imperialism and the Meerut Conspiracy Case', *Comparative Studies of South Asia, Africa and the Middle East*, 33:3 (2013), pp. 331–44.
31. England & Wales Birth records for Jayawant G. Subbarayan, 1915, and Surendra Mohan Subbarayan, 1916, and Passenger Lists 1918.
32. 'The Talk of London', *The Daily Express*, 2 December 1930, p. 19.
33. 'Speech Day at St Hugh's', *Bromley Mercury*, 2 August 1929, p. 4; *Eton College Chronicle*, 29 June 1933, p. 1490.
34. H. S. Ferns, *Reading from Left to Right: One Man's Political History* (Toronto: University of Toronto Press, 1983), pp. 79, 105.
35. Michael Barratt Brown, 'An African Road for Development: Are We All Romantics?', *Leeds African Studies Bulletin* 62 (1997), pp. 13–40.
36. V. G. Kiernan, 'Mohan Kumaramangalam in England', *Socialist India*, 23 February 1974, pp. 5–7; 13–17.
37. *News Chronicle*, 24 October 1930.
38. 'Gifted Indian Lady has Three Sons at Eton', *Belfast Telegraph*, 23 December 1930, p. 7; Ferns, *Reading from Left to Right*, p. 80.
39. *Nottingham Journal*, 7 May 1938, p. 9; 'St Andrews', *The Citizen*, 11 February 1939, p. 8.
40. Eric Hobsbawm, 'War, Peace and Hegemony at the Beginning of the 21st Century', *Book Review India*, n.d., https://thebookreviewindia.org/wp-content/uploads/2017/02/war-peace.pdf.

41. V. G. Kiernan, 'The Communist Party of India and the Second World War: Some Reminiscences', *South Asia*, 10:2 (1987), p. 68.
42. Ibid.
43. Santha Rama Rau, *Gifts of Passage* (New York: Harper and Brothers, 1961), pp. 5–6.
44. Rama Rau, *An Inheritance*, pp. 167–8.
45. Ibid, p. 180.
46. S. K. Desai, *Santha Rama Rau* (New Delhi: Arnold Heinemann, 1976), pp. 13–14.
47. Rama Rau, *Gifts of Passage*, pp. 23–4.
48. Rama Rau, *An Inheritance*, pp. 183–4, 192.
49. Santha Rama Rau, *Home to India* (London: Victor Gollancz, 1945), p. 23.
50. Irene Ng, *The Singapore Lion: A Biography of S. Rajaratnam* (Singapore: Institute of Southeast Asian Studies, 2010), chaps 1–2.

10. PARTITION

1. Majumdar, 'The Golden Years of Indian Hockey'.
2. Nandini Sundar, '"We Will Teach India Democracy": Indigenous Voices in Constitution Making', *Journal of Imperial and Commonwealth History*, 52:1 (2023), pp. 181–213.
3. *Parliament of India. Who's Who 1950* (New Delhi: Government of India Press, 1950).
4. Shefali Jha, 'Secularism in the Constituent Assembly Debates, 1946–1950', *Economic and Political Weekly*, 30 (2002), p. 3176.
5. *King's College School Magazine*, July 1912.
6. *King's College School Magazine*, December 1914.
7. For more on the history of partition, see Yasmin Khan, *The Great Partition: The Making of India and Pakistan* (New Haven: Yale University Press, 2007).
8. Clair Wills, *Lovers and Strangers: An Immigrant History of Post-War Britain* (London: Allen Lane, 2017), p. 33.
9. Sarah Ansari, 'Subjects or Citizens? India, Pakistan and the 1948 British Nationality Act', *The Journal of Imperial and Commonwealth History*, 41:2 (2013), pp. 285–312.
10. Ansari, 'Subjects or Citizens?', p. 292.
11. Rashmi Desai, *Indian Immigrants in Britain* (London: Oxford University Press, 1963), p. 6.
12. Wills, *Lovers and Strangers*, p. 57.
13. Dilip Hiro, *Black British, White British: A History of Race Relations in Britain* (London: Paladin, 1992), p. 114.

14. James Walvin, *Passage to Britain: Immigration in British History and Politics* (Harmondsworth: Penguin Books, 1984), p. 110.
15. Kavita Puri, *Partition Voices: Untold British Voices* (London: Bloomsbury, 2019), pp. 201–3.
16. Wills, *Lovers and Strangers*, p. 57.
17. Arthur Wesley Helweg, *Sikhs in England* (Delhi: Oxford University Press, 1986), p. 24.
18. Alan McFarlane interview with Haroon Ahmed, 8 December 2009: https://www.sms.cam.ac.uk/media/1106114
19. Lives Retold, https://livesretold.co.uk/haroon-ahmed
20. Puri, *Partition Voices*, p. 153.
21. Clelia Clini et al., 'Partition at 75: Reflections on Migrant Memories in the British South Asian Diaspora', *South Asian Diaspora* 16.1 (2023), pp. 167–85.
22. K.S. (born 1933, east Punjab, interview with AR, 27 August 2013). Anindya Raychaudhuri, *Narrating South Asian Partition: Oral History, Literature, Cinema* (Oxford: Oxford University Press, 2019), p. 61.
23. Uzair, interview with AR, 16 October 2011. Raychaudhuri, *Narrating South Asian Partition*, pp. 73-4.
24. Parkash (born 1930, west Punjab) interview with AR, 2 Feb. 2012. Raychaudhuri, *Narrating South Asian Partition*, pp. 65–6.
25. Sukhwant Kaur Pall (born 1949, Glasgow), interview with AR, 3 Dec 2012. Raychaudhuri, *Narrating South Asian Partition*, pp. 65–6.
26. Puri, *Partition Voices*, pp. 60–7.
27. Puri, *Partition Voices*, chaps 10–11.
28. Darshan Singh Tatla, 'Sewa Singh Mandla: A Biographical Interview', *Sikh Formations*, 14: 2 (2018), pp. 190, 192–6.
29. Tatla, 'Sewa Singh Mandla', p. 205.
30. Lucy Hodges, 'Father sues school over son's turban', *The Times*, 22 July 1982, p. 4.
31. Tatla, 'Sewa Singh Mandla', pp. 205–8.
32. Kanwaljit Kaur-Singh, 'Orthodoxy and Openness: The Experience of Sikh Children', in *Freedom and Authority in Religions and Religious Education*, ed. Brian Gates (London: Bloomsbury, 1996), pp. 165–173.
33. A. Sivanandan, 'The Heart Is Where the Battle Is: An Interview with A. Sivanandan', *Race & Class*, 59:4 (2018), p. 5.

EPILOGUE

1. See Nikesh Shukla, *Coconut Unlimited* (London: Quartet, 2010) and Nikesh Shukla (ed.), *The Good Immigrant* (London: Unbound, 2017).

2. Tina Jackson, 'Sanjeev Bhaskar: Goodness, I'm home!', *The Guardian*, 4 December 2010, https://www.theguardian.com/lifeandstyle/2010/dec/04/sanjeev-bhaskar-childhood-channel-4
3. Sarfraz Manzoor, *Greetings from Bury Park: Race. Religion. Rock 'N' Roll*. (London: Bloomsbury, 2007).
4. Manzoor, *Greetings from Bury Park*, p. 241.
5. Sathnam Sanghera, *The Boy with the Topknot* (London: Penguin, 2020), passim, esp. pp. 32–7.
6. Dhooleka Sarhadi Raj, *Where Are You From?: Middle-Class Migrants in the Modern World* (Berkeley: University of California Press, 2003), pp. 70–1.
7. Raj, *Where Are You From?*, pp. 172–4.
8. Parminder Bhachu, 'Ethnicity Constructed and Reconstructed: The Role of Sikh Women in Cultural Elaboration and Educational Decision-Making in Britain', *Gender and Education*, 3:1 (1991), pp. 55–6.
9. Kaveri Qureshi, 'Sending Children to School "Back Home": Multiple Moralities of Punjabi Sikh Parents in Britain', *Journal of Moral Education*, 43:2 (2014), pp. 213–26; Caroline Osella and Filippo Osella, 'Nuancing the "Migrant Experience": Perspectives from Kerala, South India', in *Transnational South Asians: The Making of a Neo-Diaspora*, ed. S. Koshy and R. Radhakrishnan (New Delhi: Oxford University Press, 2008), pp. 146–80.
10. Anita Rani, *The Right Sort of Girl* (London: Bonnier Books, 2021).
11. Babita Sharma, *The Corner Shop: Shopkeepers, the Sharmas and the Making of Modern Britain* (London: Two Roads, 2019), p. 107.
12. Devyani Prabhat, 'The Begum Case: Why Ministerial Discretion Precludes Human Rights Issues', *Verfassungs Blog*, 16 March 2023, https://verfassungsblog.de/the-begum-case-why-ministerial-discretion-precludes-human-rights-issues/ See also Milly Williamson and Gholam Khiabany, 'The British State, Citizenship Rights and Gendered Folk Devils: The Case of Shahmima Begum', *European Journal of Cultural Studies* (2024), pp. 1–16.
13. Faisal Devji, 'The Childhood of Politics', *Public Culture*, 33:2 (2021), pp. 222–4.
14. Simon Harold, 'Q&A: Young Voices', *Nature Ecology & Evolution*, 23 May 2017, pp. 1–2.
15. Mya-Rose Craig, 'Race, Environment, Young People and Mental Health', *BMJ Paediatrics Open*, 5:1 (2021).

BIBLIOGRAPHY

School Archives

Clifton College, Bristol
Dulwich College, London
King's College School, London
Malvern College, Malvern
North London Collegiate School, London
Sherborne School, Dorset
St Paul's School, London

Other Archives

India Office Records and Manuscript Collections, British Library, London
Krishnamurti Foundation Trust Archives, Hampshire
Modern Manuscript Collections, British Library, London
RIBA Archives, London
The National Archives, Kew, London

School Newspapers and Magazines

The Alleynian
The Eton College Chronicle
King's College School Magazine
The Malvernian
The Meteor
The Ousel: The Journal of Bedford School
The Pauline

BIBLIOGRAPHY

Periodicals

Britain and India
Daily Express
Daily Mail
Daily Mirror
The Guardian
India
Indian Magazine and Review
The Old Eastbournian
Magazine for the Old North Londoners' Association
The Times
The Vote
Western Daily Press

Online Resources

Baptism Records, Birth, Marriage and Death Registers; National School Admission Register via Ancestry.com and Findmypast.com
British Newspaper Archives
Censuses of England and Wales, 1841–1921
Marxists Internet Archive
Oxford Dictionary of National Biography
South Asian American Digital Archive

Books and Articles

Adams, Caroline, *Across Seven Seas and Thirteen Rivers: Life Stories of Pioneer Sylheti Settlers in Britain* (London: THAP Books, 1987).

Ahmed, Rehana, *Writing British Muslims: Religion, Class and Multiculturalism* (Manchester: Manchester University Press, 2015).

Alexander, Michael and Sushila Anand, *Queen Victoria's Maharajah: Duleep Singh 1838–93* (London: Phoenix Press, 1980).

Alley, Mahummad Mashuq, 'The Growth and Organization of the Muslim Community in Britain', *Centre for the Study of Islam and Christian Muslim Relations Research Papers*, 1 (March 1979).

Anand, Anita, *Sophia: Princess, Suffragette, Revolutionary* (London: Bloomsbury, 2015).

Ansari, Sarah, 'Subjects or Citizens? India, Pakistan and the 1948 British Nationality Act', *The Journal of Imperial and Commonwealth History*, 41:2 (2013), pp. 285–312.

BIBLIOGRAPHY

Aurora, G. S., *The New Frontiersmen: A Sociological Study of Indian Immigrants in the United Kingdom* (Bombay: Popular Prakashan, 1967).

Baig, M. R. A, *In Different Saddles* (London: Asia Publishing House, 1967).

Baldwin, M. Page, 'Subject to Empire: Married Women and the British Nationality and Status of Aliens Act', *Journal of British Studies*, 40:4 (2001), pp. 522–56.

Banerjee, Sumanta, 'The Mysterious Alien: Indian Street Jugglers in Victorian London', *Economic and Political Weekly*, XLVI:14 (2 April 2011), pp. 59–65.

Banfield, Shakun, 'A Memory of my Mother Savitri Devi Chowdhary 1919–1996', 8 July 2012: https://www.laindonhistory.org.uk/content/people/noteworthy_people/a-memory-of-my-mother-savitri-devi-chowdhary-1919-1996

Barker, Stephen, *The Flying Sikh* (Barnsley: AirWorld, 2022).

Barratt Brown, Michael, 'An African Road for Development: Are We All Romantics?', *Leeds African Studies Bulletin*, 62 (1997), pp. 13–40.

Bartie, Angela, Linda Fleming, Mark Freeman, Tom Hulme, Alex Hutton and Paul Readman, 'Batley Empire Day Pageant', *The Redress of the Past*: http://www.historicalpageants.ac.uk/pageants/986/

Basu, Shrabani, *Spy Princess: The Life of Noor Inayat Khan* (Stroud: The History Press, 2011).

Beckerlegge, Gwilym, 'Followers of "Mohammed, Kalee and Dada Nanuk": The Presence of Islam and South Asian Religions in Victorian Britain', in John Wolffe ed., *Religion in Victorian Britain. Volume V: Culture and Empire* (Manchester: Manchester University Press, 1997), pp. 221–67.

Bernstein, Robin, *Racial Innocence: Performing American Childhood from Slavery to Civil Rights* (New York: New York University Press, 2011).

Bhachu, Parminder, 'Ethnicity Constructed and Reconstructed: The Role of Sikh Women in Cultural Elaboration and Educational Decision-Making in Britain', *Gender and Education*, 3:1 (1991), pp. 45–60.

Bion, Wilfred R., *The Long Week-End 1897–1919* (Routledge: Abingdon, 1982).

Bland, Lucy, 'Interracial Relationships and the "Brown Baby Question": Black GIs, White British Women, and Their Mixed-Race Offspring in World War II', *Journal of the History of Sexuality*, 26:3 (2017), pp. 424–53.

Bloch, Howard, *Canning Town Voices* (Chalford: Chalford Publishing Company, 1998).

Boehmer, Elleke, *Indian Arrivals 1870–1915: Networks of British Empire* (Oxford: Oxford University Press, 2015).

BIBLIOGRAPHY

Bonarjee, N. B., *Under Two Masters* (Oxford: Oxford University Press, 1970).

Brendon, Vyvyen, *Children of the Raj* (London: Weidenfeld & Nicolson, 2005).

Buettner, Elizabeth, *Empire Families: Britons and Late Imperial India* (Oxford: Oxford University Press, 2004).

Burnett, Frances Hodgson, *The Secret Garden* (London: Phillips Publishing Company, 1911).

Caballero, Chamion, 'Interraciality in Early Twentieth Century Britain: Challenging Traditional Conceptualisations through Accounts of "Ordinariness"', *Genealogy*, 3:21 (2019).

Caballero, Chamion, and Peter J. Aspinall, *Mixed Race Britain in the Twentieth Century* (London: Palgrave Macmillan, 2018).

Callaghan, John, *Rajani Palme Dutt: A Study in British Socialism* (London: Lawrence and Wishart, 1993).

———, 'Rajani Palme Dutt, British Communism, and the Communist Party of India', *Journal of Communist Studies*, 6:1 (1990), pp. 49–70.

Cameron, J. Stewart, Jackie Hicks, and Carl Gottschalk, 'Frederick Akbar Mahomed and His Role in the Description of Hypertension at Guy's Hospital', *Kidney International*, 49:5 (1 May 1996), pp. 1488–1506.

Campbell, B. F., *Ancient Wisdom Revived: A History of the Theosophical Movement* (Berkeley: University of California Press, 1980).

Campbell, Christy, *The Maharajah's Box: An Imperial Story of Conspiracy, Love and a Guru's Prophecy* (London: HarperCollins, 2001).

Carby, Hazel, *Imperial Intimacies: A Tale of Two Islands* (London: Verso, 2019).

Carter, Andy, *A Flash Outside the Off Stump*: https://aflashoutsidetheoffstump.wordpress.com/2018/02/26/chapter-8-a-chip-off-the-old-block-duleepsinhji-and-the-nawabs-of-pataudi/

Castle, Kathryn, 'Princes and Paupers: India in Children's Periodicals', in Kathryn Castle ed., *Britannia's Children: Reading Colonialism through Children's Books and Magazines* (Manchester: Manchester University Press, 2017), pp. 31–62.

Census of India, 1901. Part II. Tables (Calcutta: Office of the Superintendent of Government Printing India, 1903).

Chakraborty, Satyasikha, '"Nurses of Our Ocean Highways": The Precarious Metropolitan Lives of Colonial South Asian Ayahs', *Journal of Women's History*, 32:2 (2020), pp. 37–64.

Chatterjee, Arup K., *Indians in London: From the Birth of the East India Company to Independent India* (New Delhi: Bloomsbury India, 2021).

Chowdhary, Savitri, *I Made My Home in England* (Laindon: Savitri Chowdhary, 1961).

Christie, John, *Morning Drum* (London: British Association for Cemeteries in South Asia, 1983).

Clini, Clelia, Jasmine Hornabrook, Paul Nataraj and Emily Keightley, 'Partition at 75: Reflections on Migrant Memories in the British South Asian Diaspora', *South Asian Diaspora*, 16:1 (2023), pp. 167–185.

Collins, Sydney F., 'The British-Born Coloured', *Sociological Review*, 3:1 (1955), pp. 77–92.

———, 'The Social Position of White and "Half-Caste" Women in Colored Groupings in Britain'. *American Sociological Review*, 16:6 (1951), pp. 796–802.

Conway, Suzanne, 'Ayah, Caregiver to Anglo-Indian Children, c. 1750–1947', in Simon Sleight and Shirleene Robinson eds., *Children, Childhood and Youth in the British World* (Basingstoke: Palgrave Macmillan, 2015), pp. 41–58.

Craig, Mya-Rose, 'Race, Environment, Young People and Mental Health', *BMJ Paediatrics Open*, 5:1 (2021).

Cutts, Elmer H., 'The Background of Macaulay's Minute', *The American Historical Review*, 58:4 (1953), pp. 824–53.

Dalrymple, William, *White Mughals* (London: HarperCollins, 2002).

Das, Harihar, 'The Late Miss Susila Anita Bonnerjee', *Britain and India* (Oct–Dec 1920).

Das, Santanu, *India, Empire, and First World War Culture: Writings, Images, and Songs* (Cambridge: Cambridge University Press, 2018).

———, 'Indians at Home, Mesopotamia and France, 1914–1918: Towards an Intimate History', in Santanu Das ed., *Race, Empire and First World War Writing* (Cambridge: Cambridge University Press, 2011), pp. 70–89.

Datta, Arunima, *Waiting on Empire: A History of Indian Travelling Ayahs in Britain* (Oxford: Oxford University Press, 2023).

Deb, Chitra, *Women of the Tagore Household* (Delhi: Penguin India, 2010).

Desai, Kishwar, *The Life and Times of Devika Rani: The Longest Kiss* (Chennai: Westland, 2020).

Desai, Rashmi, *Indian Immigrants in Britain* (London: Oxford University Press, 1963).

Desai, S. K., *Santha Rama Rau* (New Delhi: Arnold Heinemann, 1976).

Devee, Sunity, *The Autobiography of an Indian Princess* (London: John Murray, 1921).

Devji, Faisal, 'The Childhood of Politics', *Public Culture* 33:2 (2021), pp. 221–37.

Dillon, Niamh, *Homeward Bound: Return Migration from Ireland and India at the End of the British Empire* (New York: New York University Press, 2023).

BIBLIOGRAPHY

Dyhouse, Carol, *Girl Trouble: Panic and Progress in the History of Young Women* (London: Bloomsbury, 2013).

Ferns, H. S., *Reading from Left to Right: One Man's Political History* (Toronto: University of Toronto Press, 1983).

Filor, Ellen, '"He Is Hardened to the Climate & a Little Bleached by It's [Sic] Influence": Imperial Childhoods in Scotland and Madras, c. 1800–1830', in Simon Sleight and Shirleene Robinson eds., *Children, Childhood and Youth in the British World* (Basingstoke: Palgrave Macmillan, 2015), pp. 77–91.

Fisher, Michael H., *Counterflows to Colonialism: Indian Travellers and Settlers in Britain 1600–1857* (Delhi: Permanent Black, 2004).

Franda, Marcus F., 'India's Third Communist Party', *Asian Survey* 9:11 (1969), pp. 797–817.

Ghose, Manmohan in Lotika Ghose ed., *Collected Poems. Volume I: Early Poems and Letters* (Calcutta: Calcutta University Press, 1970).

———, *Songs of Love and Death* (Oxford: Basil Blackwell, 1926).

Ghosh, Durba, *Sex and the Family in Colonial India: The Making of Empire* (Cambridge: Cambridge University Press, 2006).

Gibson, Mary Ellis, *Indian Angles: English Verse in Colonial India from Jones to Tagore* (Athens: Ohio University Press, 2011).

Gilmour, David, *The British in India: Three Centuries of Ambition and Experience* (London: Allen Lane, 2018).

Gollin, Alfred, 'The Wright Brothers and the British Authorities, 1902–1909', *The English Historical Review*, XCV:CCCLXXV (1 April 1980), pp. 293–320.

Gopal, S., ed., *Selected Works of Jawaharlal Nehru*, Vol. 1 (New Delhi: Orient Longman, 1972).

Gregory, Brendan Edward, 'The Spectacle Plays and Exhibitions of Imre Kiralfy, 1887–1914', PhD Thesis, University of Manchester, 1988.

Guha, Ramachandra, *A Corner of a Foreign Field: The Indian History of a British Sport* (London: Picador, 2003).

Habibullah, Isha'at, 'Memories of the British and Feudal India—part 1: Westward Bound—an English Childhood in Lucknow', *Dawn*, 6 September 1991, Sec. Magazine, pp. 1–2; 'The British and Feudal India—part II: We Were Nicknamed "The Hallelujah Chorus"', *Dawn*, Friday 13 September 1991, Sec. Magazine, p. 3; 'British and Feudal India—"Indianisation" at Oxford', *Dawn*, 20 September 1991, Sec. Magazine, p. 6.

Harold, Simon, 'Q&A: Young Voices', *Nature Ecology & Evolution* (23 May 2017), pp 1–2.

Heehs, Peter, *The Lives of Sri Aurobindo* (New York: Columbia University Press, 2008).

Helweg, Arthur Wesley, *Sikhs in England* (Delhi: Oxford University Press, 1986).

Hiro, Dilip, *Black British White British: A History of Race Relations in Britain* (London: Paladin, 1992).

Hobsbawm, Eric, 'War, Peace and Hegemony at the Beginning of the 21st Century', *Book Review India*, n.d.: https://thebookreviewindia.org/wp-content/uploads/2017/02/war-peace.pdf.

Holland, David, *Imperial Heartland: Immigration, Working-Class Culture and Everyday Tolerance, 1917–1947* (Cambridge: Cambridge University Press, 2023).

———, 'The Social Networks of South Asian Migrants in the Sheffield Area During the Early Twentieth Century', *Past & Present*, 236:1 (2017), pp. 243–79.

Holt, Richard, *Sport and the British: A Modern History* (Oxford: Oxford University Press, 1989).

Hyson, Samuel and Alan Lester, '"British India on Trial": Brighton Military Hospitals and the Politics of Empire in World War I', *Journal of Historical Geography*, 38:1 (2012), pp. 18–34.

Jenkins, Beth R., 'Bonarjee, Dorothy Noel ('Dorf') (1894–1983), poet and lawyer', *Dictionary of Welsh Biography* (2020): https://biography.wales/article/s12-BONA-NOE-1894

Jha, Shefali, 'Secularism in the Constituent Assembly Debates, 1946–1950', *Economic and Political Weekly*, 30 (2002), pp. 3175–80.

Kaur-Singh, Kanwaljit, 'Orthodoxy and Openness: The Experience of Sikh Children', in Brian Gates ed., *Freedom and Authority in Religions and Religious Education* (London: Bloomsbury, 1996), pp. 165–173.

Khan, Pir Zia Inayat, 'Noor Inayat Khan: A British Muslim Hero?', in Sariya Cheruvallil-Contractor and Jamie Gilham eds., *Muslim Women in Britain 1850–1950: 100 Years of Hidden History* (London: C. Hurst & Co., 2023), pp. 181–197.

Khan, Yasmin, *The Great Partition: The Making of India and Pakistan* (New Haven: Yale University Press, 2007).

Kiernan, V. G., 'Mohan Kumaramangalam in England', *Socialist India* (23 February 1974), pps. 5–7; 13–17.

———, 'The Communist Party of India and the Second World War: Some Reminiscences', *South Asia*, 10:2 (1987), pp. 61–73.

Kipling, Rudyard, *Something of Myself: For My Friends Known and Unknown* (Harmondsworth: Penguin, 1977).

———, *The Man Who Would Be King: And Other Stories* (Oxford: Oxford University Press, 2020).

Kneale, Rachel, 'Hoots from the Archive—Spotlight on Old Mancunians: Manmohan Ghose—Celebrated Indian Poet', *MGS Life*, 26 November 2024: https://www.mgs-life.co.uk/article/hoots-from-the-archive-spotlight-on-old-mancunians-manmohan-ghose-celebrated-indian-poet?ref=

Kumar, R. and D. N. Parighari, *Selected Works of Motilal Nehru*, vol. 1 (New Delhi: Vikas, 1982).

Lahiri, Shompa, *Indians in Britain: Anglo-Indian Encounters, Race and Identity 1880–1930* (London: Frank Cass, 2000).

Lambert-Hurley, Siobhan, Daniel Majchrowicz and Sunil Sharma, eds., *Three Centuries of Travel Writing by Muslim Women* (Bloomington: Indiana University Press, 2022).

Lambert-Hurley, Siobhan and Sunil Sharma, eds., *Atiya's Journeys: A Muslim Woman from Colonial Bombay to Edwardian Britain* (New Delhi: Oxford University Press, 2010).

Law, Derek G., 'From Goa to Greenock: The Sinking of the SS City of Benares', in Emily Malcolm, Isobel McDonald and Susan Pacitti eds., *Scotland's Lascar Heritage* (Glasgow: Glasgow Museums Publishing, 2023).

Login, Lady, *Sir John Login and Duleep Singh* (London: W. H. Allen & Co., 1890).

Louro, Michele L., '"Where National Revolutionary Ends and Communist Begins": The League against Imperialism and the Meerut Conspiracy Case', *Comparative Studies of South Asia, Africa and the Middle East*, 33:3 (2013), pp. 331–44.

Lutyens, Emily, *Candles in the Sun* (London: Rupert Hart-Davis, 1957).

Lutyens, Mary, *To Be Young: Some Chapters of Autobiography* (London: Corgi, 1959).

Mahomet, A. J., *From Street Arab to Pastor* (Cardiff: J. B. Thomasson, 1901).

Majumdar, Boria, 'The Golden Years of Indian Hockey: "We Climb the Victory Stand"', *The International Journal of the History of Sport*, 25:12 (2008), pp. 1592–1611.

———, 'Tom Brown Goes Global: The "Brown" Ethic in Colonial and Post-Colonial India', *The International Journal of the History of Sport*, 23:5 (2006), pp. 805–20.

Majumdar, Janaki Agnes Penelope in Antoinette Burton ed., *Family History* (New Delhi: Oxford University Press, 2013).

Malik, Hardit Singh, *A Little Work, A Little Play: The Autobiography of H. S. Malik* (New Delhi: Bookwise, n.d.).

BIBLIOGRAPHY

Manera Sambuy, Livia, *In Search of Amrit Kaur* (London: Chatto & Windus, 2023).

Mangan, J. A., *Athleticism in the Victorian and Edwardian Public School* (Cambridge: Cambridge University Press, 1981).

Manzoor, Sarfraz, *Greetings from Bury Park: Race. Religion. Rock 'N' Roll* (London: Bloomsbury, 2007).

Mathur, Saloni, *India by Design: Colonial History and Cultural Display* (Berkeley: University of California Press, 2007).

———, 'Living Ethnological Exhibits: The Case of 1886', *Cultural Anthropology*, 15:4 (2000), pp. 492–524.

Mayhew, Henry, *London Labour and the London Poor* (London, 1861).

Mitchell, S. J. D., *Perse: A History of the Perse School 1615–1976* (Cambridge: The Oleander Press, 1976).

Mohanram, Radhika, *Imperial White: Race, Diaspora, and the British Empire* (Minneapolis: University of Minnesota Press, 2007).

Mukherjee, Sumita, *Indian Suffragettes: Female Identities and Transnational Networks* (New Delhi: Oxford University Press, 2018).

———, '"Narrow-majority" and "Bow-and-agree": Public attitudes towards the elections of the first Asian MPs in Britain, Dadabhai Naoroji and Mancherjee Merwanjee Bhownaggree, 1885–1906', *Journal of the Oxford University History Society* (2004), pp. 1–20.

———, *Nationalism, Education and Migrant Identities: The England-Returned* (Abingdon: Routledge, 2010).

Murdoch, Lydia, *Imagined Orphans: Poor Families, Child Welfare, and Contested Citizenship in London* (Ithaca: Rutgers University Press, 2006).

———, '"Suppressed Grief": Mourning the Death of British Children and the Memory of the 1857 Indian Rebellion', *Journal of British Studies*, 51 (2012), pp. 364–92.

Nanda, B. R., *Jawarhalal Nehru: Rebel and Statesman* (Delhi: Oxford University Press, 1998).

Nehru, Jawaharlal, *An Autobiography* (New Delhi: Penguin, 2004).

Ng, Irene, *The Singapore Lion: A Biography of S. Rajaratnam* (Singapore: Institute of Southeast Asian Studies, 2010).

Ortiz, Michael P., 'Spain! Why? Jawaharlal Nehru, Non-Intervention, and the Spanish Civil War', *European History Quarterly*, 49:3 (2019), pp. 445–66.

Osella, Caroline and Filippo Osella, 'Nuancing the "Migrant Experience": Perspectives from Kerala, South India', in S. Koshy and R. Radhakrishnan eds., *Transnational South Asians: The Making of a Neo-Diaspora* (New Delhi: Oxford University Press, 2008), pp. 146–80.

Pal, Suvam, '"Legacies, Halcyon Days and Thereafter": A Brief History of

Indian Tennis', *The International Journal of the History of Sport*, 21:3–4 (2004), pp. 452–66.

Parliament of India. Who's Who 1950 (New Delhi: Government of India Press, 1950).

Parr, Rosalind, *Citizens of Everywhere: Indian Women, Nationalism and Cosmopolitanism, 1920–1952* (Cambridge: Cambridge University Press, 2021).

Patel, Dinyar, *Naoroji: Pioneer of Indian Nationalism* (Cambridge: Harvard University Press, 2020).

Perham, Margery Freda, *Lugard: The Years of Adventure, 1858–1898* (London: Collins, 1956).

Playne, Somerset, *Indian States: A Biographical, Historical, and Administrative Survey* (New Delhi: Asian Educational Services, 2006).

Prabhat, Devyani, 'The Begum Case: Why Ministerial Discretion Precludes Human Rights Issues', *Verfassungs Blog*, 16 March 2023: https://verfassungsblog.de/the-begum-case-why-ministerial-discretion-precludes-human-rights-issues/

Puri, Kavita, *Partition Voices: Untold British Voices* (London: Bloomsbury, 2019).

Qureshi, Kaveri, 'Sending Children to School "Back Home": Multiple Moralities of Punjabi Sikh Parents in Britain', *Journal of Moral Education*, 43:2 (2014), pp. 213–26.

Raj, Dhooleka Sarhadi, *Where Are You From?: Middle-Class Migrants in the Modern World* (Berkeley: University of California Press, 2003).

Rama Rau, Dhanvanthi, *An Inheritance: The Memoirs of Dhanvanthi Rama Rau* (New York: Harper & Row, 1977).

Rama Rau, Santha, *Gifts of Passage* (New York: Harper and Brothers, 1961).

———, *Home to India* (London: Victor Gollancz, 1945).

Ranasinha, Ruvani, Rehana Ahmed, Sumita Mukherjee and Florian Stadtler, eds., *South Asians and the Shaping of Britain, 1870–1950: A Sourcebook* (Manchester: Manchester University Press, 2012).

Rani, Anita, *The Right Sort of Girl* (London: Bonnier Books, 2021).

Ray, Renuka, *My Reminiscences: Social Development During Gandhian Era and After* (New Delhi: Allied Publishers, 1982).

Raychaudhuri, Anindya, *Homemaking: Radical Nostalgia and the Construction of a South Asian Diaspora* (London: Rowman & Littlefield Publishers, 2018).

———, *Narrating South Asian Partition: Oral History, Literature, Cinema* (Oxford: Oxford University Press, 2019).

Reeves, Mark, 'Two Leagues, One Front? The India League and the League Against Imperialism in the British Left, 1927–1937', in Carolien

Stolte, Heather Streets-Salter, Sana Tannoury-Karam and Michele Louro eds., *The League Against Imperialism: Lives and Afterlives* (Leiden: Leiden University Press, 2020), pp. 283–308.

Robinson, Olivia, 'Travelling Ayahs of the Nineteenth and Twentieth Centuries: Global Networks and Mobilization of Agency', *History Workshop Journal* 86 (2018), pp. 44–66.

Robinson-Dunn, Diane, *The Harem, Slavery and British Imperial Culture:Anglo-Muslim Relations in the Late Nineteenth Century* (Manchester: Manchester University Press, 2006).

Rugby School Register, Volume III, May 1874 to May 1904, Rev. A. T. Mitchell (Rugby, 1904).

Rugby School Register, 1911–1946, Alan H. Maude and Allan Archer (Rugby: George Over, 1957).

Rustomji, Nari, *Enchanted Frontier: Sikkim, Bhutan and India's North-Eastern Borderland* (Bombay: Oxford University Press, 1971).

Saiduzzafar, Hamida, 'JSAL Interviews Dr Hamida Saiduzzafar: A Conversation with Rashid Jahan's Sister-in-Law, Aligarh, 1973', *Journal of South Asian Literature*, 22:1 (1987), pp. 158–65.

Saklatvala, Sehri, *The Fifth Commandment: A Biography of Shapurji Saklatvala and Memoir by His Daughter* (Salford: Miranda Press, 1991).

Salter, Joseph, *The Asiatic in England: Sketches of Sixteen Years' Work Among Orientals* (London: Seeley, Jackson and Halliday, 1873).

Salvadori, Cynthia, *We Came in Dhows*, Vol. II (Nairobi: Paperchase Kenya, 1996).

Sanghera, Sathnam, *Empireland: How Imperialism Has Shaped Modern Britain* (London: Penguin Books, 2021).

———, *The Boy with the Topknot* (London: Penguin, 2020).

Sen, Satadru, 'Chameleon Games: Ranjitsinhji's Politics of Race and Gender', *Journal of Colonialism and Colonial History*, 2:3 (2001).

Sengupta, Padmini. *Sarojini Naidu: A Biography* (New York: Asia Publishing House, 1966).

———, *The Portrait of an Indian Woman* (Calcutta: YMCA Publishing House, 1956).

Shamsie, Muneeza, 'Imperial Shadows: A Tale of Two Childhoods, Colonial and Post-Colonial'. *Journal of Commonwealth and Postcolonial Studies*, 16:1 (2009), pp. 114–30.

Sharma, Babita, *The Corner Shop: Shopkeepers, the Sharmas and the Making of Modern Britain* (London: Two Roads, 2019).

Shukla, Nikesh, *Coconut Unlimited* (London: Quartet, 2010).

———, (ed.), *The Good Immigrant* (London: Unbound, 2017).

Sivanandan, A., 'The Heart Is Where the Battle Is: An Interview with A. Sivanandan', *Race & Class*, 59:4 (2018), pp. 3–14.

Spring, Howard, *Heaven Lies About Us: A Fragment of Infancy* (London: Readers' Union Limited, 1940).

Sundar, Nandini, '"We Will Teach India Democracy": Indigenous Voices in Constitution Making', *Journal of Imperial and Commonwealth History*, 52:1 (2023), pp. 181–213.

St John's College Cambridge Register of Twentieth Century Johnians, Volume I 1900–1949 (Cambridge: St Johns, 2004).

Tabili, Laura, *Global Migrants, Local Culture: Natives and Newcomers in Provincial England, 1841–1939* (London: Palgrave Macmillan, 2011).

———, 'The Construction of Racial Difference in Twentieth-Century Britain: The Special Restriction (Coloured Alien Seamen) Order, 1925', *Journal of British Studies*, 33:1 (1994), pp. 54–98.

Tatla, Darshan Singh, 'Sewa Singh Mandla: A Biographical Interview', *Sikh Formations*, 14:2 (2018), pp. 188–211.

Taylor, Miles, *Empress: Queen Victoria and India* (New Haven: Yale University Press, 2018).

Tyerman, Christopher, *A History of Harrow School 1324–1991* (Oxford: Oxford University Press, 2000).

Visram, Rozina, *Asians in Britain: 400 Years of History* (London: Pluto Press, 2002).

———, *Ayahs, Lascars and Princes: The Story of Indians in Britain 1700–1947* (London: Pluto Press, 1986).

———, 'Kamal A. Chunchie of the Coloured Men's Institute: The Man and the Legend', *Immigrants & Minorities*, 18:1 (1999), pp. 29–48.

Wadia, Avabai B., *The Light Is Ours: Memoirs and Movements* (London: International Planned Parenthood Federation, 2001).

Walvin, James, *Passage to Britain: Immigration in British History and Politics* (Harmondsworth: Penguin Books, 1984).

Warmington, Eric, 'Society and Education in Cambridge 1902–1922', *New Universities Quarterly* 30:1 (1975), pp. 28–35.

Wiebe, Hauke and Roger Jeffery, 'Edinburgh Schools: Suppliers of Men for Imperial India in the Long 19th Century', in Roger Jeffery ed., *India in Britain: 1750s to the Present* (Abingdon: Routledge, 2020), pp. 134–61.

Williamson, Milly and Gholam Khiabany, 'The British State, Citizenship Rights and Gendered Folk Devils: The Case of Shamima Begum', *European Journal of Cultural Studies* (2024), pp. 1–16.

Wills, Clair, *Lovers and Strangers: An Immigrant History of Post-War Britain* (London: Allen Lane, 2017).

BIBLIOGRAPHY

Wren, Alan, *The Ambush of SS Persia: Voices from a Lost Liner* (York: Alan Wren, 2020).

Younger, Coralie, *Wicked Women of the Raj* (New Delhi: HarperCollins, 2003).

INDEX

accents 2, 17, 62, 95, 163, 168, 170, 186, 192
adverts 24–5, 35–6, 40–1, 61, 97, 158
Agra 38, 162
Ahmed, Haroon 180–1
Ahmed, Riz 189
alcohol 10, 50, 55, 85, 194
Alexander, Ivy 145
Allahabad 24, 67, 95, 159
All-Asian Women's Conference 111, 114
Ambedkar, B. R. 173
Amidulla, Gisalic 143
Amritsar massacre 70, 132
army 23–4, 78–9, 123, 127, 134; *see also* Indian Army
asylum (mental health institution) 57–8
Ayah's Home 21–2
ayahs 21–3, 25, 41, 97–8, 180

badminton (sport) 97, 102
Badminton School 167
Bahadurjee, Rustomjee 77
Bahadursinhji, K. S. 91–2
Baig, Enver Ali 93, 98

Baig, Mirza Osman Ali 93, 98
Baig, Mirza Rashid Ali 93, 96, 98
Baig, Sikander 93, 95, 98
Bakhlé, Nalinaksha Chintaman 77
Bar (Inns of Courts) 3, 53, 56, 69, 79, 95, 115; *see also* barrister
Baroda 59, 68, 133, 164
barrister 3, 22, 53, 55, 59, 62, 69, 79, 83, 97, 115, 164; *see also* Bar (Inns of Courts)
Batley Pageant 73
Batlivala, Bhicoo 99, 164
Batlivala, Homi Sorabji 99
Bedford 20, 79–83
Bedford Girls High School 79–80, 82–3
Bedford School 79–83
Begum, Shamima 193–5
Bengal famine 136–7
Benthall, Clement 24
Besant, Annie 42–4, 112
Bhandari, Karnal 192
Bhaskar, Sanjeev 10, 190
Bhola Nauth, Bhagwati 116
Bhola Nauth, Veshasher 116
Bhose, Cyril 151
Bhose, Ebenezer Bholanath 150–1

INDEX

Bhose, Emma Florence 151
Bhose, Mabel 151
Bhose, Mary 151
Binyon, Laurence 51, 53
Bion, Wilfred 27
Birmingham 56, 69, 184–5, 194
blacking up 73, 162
Blavatsky, Madam 42
boarding schools 15–16, 20, 25–7, 29, 49, 59, 65, 93–4, 100, 110–11, 148, 158, 174, 183; see also Clifton College, Dulwich College, Eton College, Rugby School, Sherborne School, Sherborne School for Girls et al.
Bombay 3, 19, 50, 60, 93, 97–8, 108, 112, 122, 130, 151
Bonarjee, Dorothy (Dorf) 115–116, 118
Bonarjee, Neil Bruniat 73–7, 79, 82–4, 110, 115–16
Bonetta, Sarah Forbes 38
Bonnerjee, Fanny 54
Bonnerjee, Hemangini 53–7
Bonnerjee, Janaki 54–7, 174
Bonnerjee, Kalikrishna Wood (Kali) 54–5
Bonnerjee, Kamalkrishna (Shelley) 53–6
Bonnerjee, Kew Edwin 56–7
Bonnerjee, Kitty 54, 56
Bonnerjee, Nalini (Nellie) 53–4
Bonnerjee, Pramila (Millie) 54–5
Bonnerjee, Ratnakrishna Curran (Teenie) 54–5
Bonnerjee, Susila (Susie) 53–4, 56, 116
Bonnerjee, Womesh Chunder 53–6, 59, 116
Bournemouth 101, 131

boxing 10, 75, 79, 81, 101, 126–30, 166
Boy Scouts 18, 184
Braverman, Suella 47, 171
Brighton 10, 26, 95, 99, 107, 125, 131–2, 158
Bristol 15–16, 29, 93, 96–7, 167, 175
British Commonwealth League (BCL) 110, 114
British Dominions Woman Suffrage Union (BDWSU) 115–16, 118
British Nationality Act (1948) 177–8
Brown, Leila 27
Buddhism 40, 42, 148
Burlington House School 175
Burnet-Smith, Wallace 26
Burnett, Frances Hodgson 21
Butler, Iris 26–7, 125

Calcutta 2–4, 15, 19, 22, 26, 31, 36, 50, 53, 55, 57, 59, 126, 129, 150, 157–8, 180, 183
Cambridge 61, 78, 157–61
Cambridge University 42, 65–6, 69, 71, 88–9, 112, 114, 116, 160, 167
admission to 52, 62, 81, 97, 100, 112, 114, 158, 170, 175
Castle Menzies 12, 61
Chaggar, Gurdip Singh 193
Charing Cross 43, 122
Charterhouse School 61, 90
Cheltenham College 89–90
Cheltenham Ladies College 99, 105, 164
chess 55, 102–3
Chiswick Polytechnic 180
Chowdhary, Savitri 135–6
Chowdhary, Shakuntala 135–6

INDEX

Chowdhary, Vijay 135–6
Christianity 12, 18, 23, 53, 56, 62, 74, 96, 171, 173
  conversion to 11, 37, 53, 109, 149
Christie, John 26
Christmas 2, 73, 152, 161
Chunchie, Kamal 149–50
Chunchie, Muriel 149
church 12, 19, 33, 37, 52, 55–7, 94, 96, 111, 150
Church League for Women's Suffrage (CLWS) 116
Churchill, Winston 66
Classics 51–2, 77–8, 80–1, 159
Clifton College 93–9, 122, 130, 163
coconut (as slur) 47–9
Coles, Reverend John Jefferies Bartlett 50–1
Collins, Sydney 144
Colman, Olivia 15, 20
Colonial and Indian Exhibition (1886) 38–9
Coloured Men's Institute 150
Commonwealth Immigration Act (1962) 179
communism 157–8, 160–3, 165–8, 170
Communist Party of Great Britain (CPGB) 151–2, 157, 172
Communist Party of India (CPI) 73, 100, 163, 167, 192
Conservative Party 37, 60, 86, 139, 161, 171, 193–4
Cooch Behar 49, 52
Cornwall 136, 141
Coronation of Edward VII (1902) 37, 51, 109
Coronation of King George V (1911) 51, 116–17, 126

Craig, Mya-Rose 7, 194–5
cricket 68, 85–6, 88–92, 94–7, 99–103, 109, 123–5, 134, 166, 186
Cromwell Road 70, 118
Croydon 54, 56
Croydon High School for Girls 54, 116

Darlington Grammar School 101, 173–4
David Copperfield 29, 31, 45
debating 55–6, 80, 83, 159, 174, 184
Delhi 17, 25, 101, 111, 178, 180
Delhi Durbar (1903) 51
Delhi Durbar (1911) 75, 91
Desikacharya, Rajagopal 42
Devi, Sunity 49
Dickens, Charles 29–30, 32, 45
Digvijaysinhji 90–2, 134
doctor 10–11, 33, 52, 58, 61, 111, 121, 124, 127–8, 135, 157, 160, 162
domestic servants 21–3, 31, 33–7, 44, 56, 58, 61, 97–8, 107, 117, 128
Doveton College 50
Doyle, Arthur Conan 69, 123
Drewett, William H. 52
Dublin 26
Duleep Singh, Bamba 106
Duleep Singh, Catherine 106–108
Duleep Singh, Frederick 49–50
Duleep Singh, Maharajah 9, 11–13, 34, 37, 49, 61, 106, 140
Duleep Singh, Sophia 106–109, 115, 117–18, 120
Duleep Singh, Victor 49–50, 140
Duleepsinhji (Duleep) 89–90, 101
Dulwich, south London 115

241

INDEX

Dulwich College 73, 76–7, 116, 162
Dulwich Preparatory School 73–6, 162
Dutt, Anna Palme 157, 160–2
Dutt, Clemens Palme 158–61
Dutt, Ellen Anne Joy 57–8
Dutt, Elna Palme 158, 160–1
Dutt, Ida Shakuntala 57–60
Dutt, Khetter Mohun 57–8
Dutt, Khetterina Marion 57–60
Dutt, Leila Juanita 57–8, 60
Dutt, Mabel Rani 57–60
Dutt, Muriel Edith 57–60
Dutt, Newton Mohun 57–9
Dutt, Rajani Palme 157–161, 163, 171
Dutt, Upendra Krishna 157, 160–1

Ealing 81, 116, 128, 190
East End of London 21, 30–1, 142, 145–52, 154
East India Company 11, 15–17, 37, 51
East London Mosque 148
Eastbourne (town) 26, 111
Eastbourne College 123–6
Edalji, George 68–9
Edinburgh 16, 20, 25, 35–6, 162
Elveden 12
Empire Day 67, 72
Empire of India Exhibition (1895) 39–40
Eton College 19, 49–50, 65, 90, 106, 124, 165–6
evacuees 134–6, 142, 157

fagging 67, 94
Festival of Empire (1911) 41
Finchley 58, 98

First World War 43, 67, 70, 77, 99, 111, 121–2, 124–32, 137, 149, 159, 174, 184
fives (hand tennis) 77, 91, 94, 96, 100, 159
Fletcher, Muriel 146
football 40, 67–8, 86, 90, 100–1, 129, 166, 191
Foundling Hospital 36
France 12, 111, 115, 121, 125–6, 131, 133–4, 152, 161, 169

gambling 55, 69
Gandhi, Indira (née Nehru) 166–7
Gandhi, Mohandas 66, 71, 77, 84, 110, 114, 119, 127, 132–3, 165
George Green School 151
Ghose, Aurobindo 52–3
Ghose, Benoybhusan 52
Ghose, Joy Manny Mohun 59–60
Ghose, Manmohan 51–3
Gordon, Jane Cumming 16
Gouramma, Princess 37–8
Great Exhibition (1851) 37
Gupta, Sailendra Chandra 99
Gupta, Sita Ram 130
Guy's Hospital 10–11
gymnastics 10, 32–3, 77, 80, 114

Habibullah, Ali Bahadur (Sonny) 95–7
Habibullah, Enaith 95–7
Habibullah, Isha'at 95–7, 163
Habibullah, Tazeen 96
Haileybury 20, 78
Hamatsinhji 90–2
Hamdard, Karan Singh 183
Hami, London 40
Hammersmith 77, 128
Hampstead 35, 59, 70, 83, 100, 113, 120

INDEX

Harrow School 19, 62, 65–9, 71, 79, 87, 93, 111, 135
Hastings, Warren 36
Hickey, William 36–7
Highgate Cemetery 11
Himatsinhji, Major General 173
Hindus (Hinduism) 5, 30, 34, 42, 53, 62, 148, 171, 176, 179, 183, 192
Hither Green 130
hockey 100–1, 109, 123, 159, 174
Holkar of Indore, Yeshwant Rao 61
Husain, Tajamul 175
Hussain, Mohammad Ahsanuddin 82
Hyderabad 50, 68, 83, 176

Ideal Home Exhibition 41
India League 136, 164
India Office 21–3, 125, 140–2, 161
Indian Army 15, 94, 111, 116, 121, 132, 173, 184
Indian Civil Service (ICS) 17, 20, 23, 26, 52, 59, 76–8, 82–3, 94, 99, 117, 130, 180
Indian High Commission in London 70, 100
Indian National Congress (INC) 55–6, 59, 66–8, 72, 83–4, 93, 132, 160, 165, 167, 174
Indian Uprising (1857) 17–18, 24, 37
Indian Women's Education Association (IWEA) 116–17
Islam 95–6, 141, 143–4, 147–9, 151, 175–6, 179, 182–3

James, C. L. R. 88–9
Jareja, Kumar Shri 50
Jinarajadasa, Curuppumullage 42

Jinnah, Mohammad Ali 66
Johnson, Jack 75
juggling 33

Kapurthala 68, 100, 109, 111
Kashmir 67–8, 71, 176
Kaur, Amrit (Rani of Mandi) 111
Kaur, Rajkumari Amrit 108–11, 120, 173, 175, 194
Kensington High School 70
Kent 15, 101, 110–11, 165, 174, 183
Kenya 100, 184
Khan of Rampur, Prince Nasir Ali 61
Khan Pataudi, Iftikhar Ali 101–2
Khan Pataudi, Mansur Ali 102
Khan, Doreen 135, 147–8
Khan, Muhammad Ismail 174
Khan, Noor Inayat 133–4, 137
Kidwai, M. H., 94–5
King's College School 175
Kipling, Rudyard 25–6, 55, 95
Kiralfy, Imre 39–40
Koh-i-noor diamond 11, 37
Krishnamma, Noble 119
Krishnamurti, Jiddu 42–4
Krishnamurti, Nitya 43
Krishnan, Parvati (née Kumaramangalam) 164–8
Kumaramangalam, Jayawant Gopal 165, 167
Kumaramangalam, Paramasiva Prabhakar 165–6
Kumaramangalam, Surendra Mohan 165–8, 171

Labour Party 114, 136, 151, 160–1
Lancaster 153–4
lascars 33–4, 141–8, 151–2, 154
Latifi, Danial 100

INDEX

Latymer School 77, 181
Lawrence, Alick 25
Lawrence, Harry 25
Leadbeater, Charles Webster 42–3
League Against Imperialism (LAI) 158, 172
League of Nations 114, 167, 169
Leys School, Cambridge 61
Liverpool Muslim Institute 148
Lucknow 17, 95, 109
Lugard, Frederick 23
Luton 190–1
Lutyens, Emily 43–4
Lutyens, Mary 43

Macaulay, Thomas Babington 48, 53, 58
Madras 4, 19, 23, 43, 59, 94, 108, 119, 142, 168
Madras Communist Conspiracy Trial 165
Mahomed, Frederick Akbar 10–11
Mahomed, Sake Dean 9–10, 13, 37, 140
Mahomet, Albert 31–3, 194
Majlis society 66, 124, 160
Majumdar, Prio Kumar 56–7
Malik, Hardit Singh 122–4, 127, 137
Malvern College 90–3, 134–5, 173
Manchester 22, 34, 52, 151
Manchester Grammar School 52
Mandla, Gurinder 185
Mandla, Sewa Singh 184–5
Manzoor, Sarfraz 190–1
Marlborough College 20, 100
Mary Poppins 23
Mayhew, Henry 30–1
Medhavi, Manoramabai 6
Mehta, Avabai 112–15, 119–20

Mehta, Pherozeshah 56
Mehta, Priojbai 112
Menon, Krishna 136, 164
Merchant Taylors' School 119
Metcalfe, Theophilus 25
Miln, Kenneth 183
Mirza, Hamid Ali 77
Mirza, Moosa Ali 77
Mirza, Prince Nasir Ali 50–1
Mirza, Prince Wasif Ali 50–1
missionaries 17, 21, 23–4, 27, 33, 40, 73, 96, 142, 145, 151, 171
Mitra, Satyendra Nath 100
Mitter, Mona 82
Mitter, Pran Kumar 82
Mitter, Raj Kumar 82
Mitter, Shushila 82
Montagu, Edwin 94
Mukerjea, Leilavati (née Roy) 117
Mukherjee, Subroto 70
Müller, Bamba 12, 107
Munnoo 36–7
Murshidabad 50–1, 77
music 31, 49, 80, 96, 113, 115, 117, 126, 133, 151, 161, 169, 191–2
Muslim Leage 84, 100, 174
Muslims, *see* Islam

Nabob 36–7
Naidu, Leelamani 119
Naidu, Sarojini 114, 119, 133
nannies 23, 33, 41, 153; *see also* ayahs
Naoroji, Ardeshir 60
Naoroji, Dadabhai 60–1
Naoroji, Maki 60–1
Naoroji, Shirin 60
National Indian Association 112, 175
Navjote ceremony 82, 152

INDEX

Nawanagar 88, 92, 124
Nehru, Jawaharlal 66–71, 79, 81, 84, 95, 158, 160, 163–5, 173–4, 178
Nehru, Motilal 67–8, 79
North London Collegiate School 5–6, 105, 109
novels 18, 21, 26, 29, 42, 122, 135, 137
nursery 41

Officer Training Corps (OTC) 123–4, 127–8, 163
Orphan Asylum 58
orphans 148, 153, 155
Oxford University 65–6, 78, 100, 124–5, 161, 163, 166, 174
  admission to 43, 50–2, 54, 59, 76–7, 79, 83, 101, 106, 110, 127, 165, 168

Parnell, Betty 61
Parnell, Dolly 61
Parsees 60, 79, 82, 88, 151–2
Partition of India and Pakistan 3, 6, 9, 13, 84, 176–84, 186–7
Patel, Dev 29, 45
Patuck, Sorab Pestonjee 100
Perse School 158–9, 161
photographer 33
Pirrie, Jane 16
poetry 51–3, 77, 95, 99, 113–15, 169
Pomare, Albert Victor 38
Powell, Enoch 139
Pratapsinhji 135
Pringle, Alexander 20
prison 34, 69, 71, 152, 153, 164
Punjab 11–13, 37, 51, 100, 106, 122, 141, 147, 179, 183–4, 191–2

Quakers 118, 166–7, 169
Queen Victoria's jubilees 37, 50

racket (sports) 90–2, 94
Rafiq, Azeem 85
Rahmat Ali, Choudhry 66
Rahmatullah, Abdullah 149
Raisinhji 90–1
Rajaratnam, Sinnathamby 170–1
Rajendra, Raj 49–50
Rajendrasinhji 90–2, 134
Rama Rau, Benegal 168–9
Rama Rau, Dhanvanthi 118–19, 169
Rama Rau, Premila 118–19, 168–71
Rama Rau, Santha 118–19, 169–71
Ramabai, Pandita 6
Ramlal 38–9
Ramphal 38
Ramulu, Bomdi Sri 94
Rani, Anita 181, 192
Rani, Devika 113
Ranjitsinhji, Kumar Shri (Ranji) 88–92, 101, 124, 131, 134
Rathbone, Eleanor 70
Ray, Chaya (née Bhattacharyya) 6, 135
Ray, Maya (née Bhattacharyya) 6, 135
Ray, Renuka 70–1, 167
Ray, Swaran Singh 183
Reading (town) 192
refugees 134, 169–70, 177, 179, 180, 182, 193
Richards, Frank 103
Roedean School, Brighton 158
Rottingdean 95, 163
Round Table Conferences (1930–2) 166–9

INDEX

Roy, Hirabai 117
Roy, Indra Lal 126–8, 130, 137
Roy, Lolit Kumar 129, 137
Roy, Lolita 117, 126
Roy, Mirabai 117
Roy, Paresh Lal 126, 128–9
Royal Air Force 70
rugby (sport) 77, 82, 116, 123, 127, 163
Rugby School 18, 20, 55–6, 65, 100, 111
Rugely Grammar School 69
running 50, 90, 94, 100
Rustomji, Homi 79
Rustomji, Minoo 79, 81
Rustomji, Nari 79–84
Rustomji, Saros 79
Rustomji, Thritti 79, 81
Ruxton, Buck 153
Ruxton, Diana 153–4
Ruxton, Elizabeth 153–4
Ruxton, William (Billie) 153–4

Sahebzada, Mahmuduzzafar Khan 73, 162–4, 168, 171
Saklatvala, Sehri 151–3
Saklatvala, Shapurji 151–2
Salter, Joseph 33–4, 142, 145
Samee, Ramo 33
Sandhurst 78, 129, 137
Sanghera, Sathnam 9, 191
sari 1–2, 5, 114, 117, 130
Satthianadhan, Kamala 6, 119
Satthianadhan, Padmini 6, 119–120
Schäffer, Lina 107–8
school uniform 2, 26, 67, 185
Second World War 79, 92–3, 116, 132–7, 147–8, 154, 158, 161–2, 170, 176, 179, 184–5
Sen, Anjali 118
Sen, Arati 118

Sen, Mrinalini 99, 118
Sen, Nirmalaya Chunder (George) 99
Sen, Srilata 118
Sharma, Babita 192–3
Sheffield 143, 147–8
Sherborne School 50, 73, 162–3
Sherborne School for Girls 109–110
shooting 12, 49, 56–7, 77, 123–4
Shrewsbury 91–2
Shukla, Nikesh 189
Sikh empire 11–13
Sikhs (Sikhism) 12–13, 109, 123, 136, 176, 179, 183, 185, 191
Simla 19, 26
Singapore 171
Singh, Bawa Mangal 130
Singh, Bawa Pratab 130
Singh, Beryl 110–11
Singh, Dalpat 123, 125, 137
Singh, Jaipal 101, 173–5
Singh, Narpat 123, 125
Singh, Pertab 123, 125
Singh, Hector William Shumshere 100, 111
Singh, Sir Harnam 100, 109
Sinha, Jaswant 94
Sivanandan, Ambalavaner 9, 186–7
Slessor, Harriot 15–16
South Africa 7, 106, 115, 117, 169–70
South Hampstead High School 113
Southall 193
Spanish Civil War 158, 164, 167, 169
SS *City of Benares* 142
SS *Persia* 129–30
St Paul's Girls' School 117–19, 169–70
St Paul's School 51–2, 65, 126–30

INDEX

Staines 34, 124, 131
Strangers' Home for Asiatics, Africans and South Sea Islanders 33–4, 142–3
Subbarayan, Radhabai 124, 165–7
suffrage (female) 70, 105–12, 114–20, 126, 128, 161, 167
Sufism 133
Sunak, Rishi 8, 47, 65, 183
Swamee, Ringa 34
swimming 127, 159, 175
Swodoba, Rudolf 39
Syal, Meera 190

Talyarkhan, Frene 97
Talyarkhan, Lulu 97
Talyarkhan, Rustom (Russie) Fardoonji Sorabji 97
Tanzania 8, 183–4
Tebbit, Norman 86
tennis 83, 89, 99–100, 110
Thatcher, Margaret 185, 193
The Brondesbury and Kilburn High School for Girls 112–14
The Secret Garden 21–2
Theosophical Society 42–4, 112, 114
Tonbridge School, Kent 174
turban 36, 39, 123, 136, 185, 191
Tyabji, Badruddin 56, 59
Tyabji, Nasima 59

Uganda 24, 183
United Services College 20
University College London 60, 66, 115, 122, 134

VE Day 136–7
Verjee, Hassanali 100
Victoria, Queen 11–13, 37–41, 44, 49–50, 72, 106, 140
violin 80, 117

Wales 59, 115, 149
Warlier, Jehan 61–2
Wellington College 20, 90
Weston-super-Mare 100
Weybridge 118, 168
Winchester College 102
Windrush 9, 177, 179, 186
Windsor Castle 38, 40, 49
Woking Mosque 148–9
Women's Auxiliary Air Force (WAAF) 134
Women's Indian Association 114
Women's Social and Political Union (WSPU) 107, 120
Women's Tax Resistance League (WTRL) 107, 120
Woods, Marianne 16
workhouse 22, 31–4

York 23
Yorkshire 22, 85, 124, 192
Yousafzai, Malala 7, 194–5
Yusuf, Zain Maurice 99

Zoroastrians, *see* Parsees